Tea Party Catholic

Tea Party Catholic

The Catholic Case for Limited Government, a Free Economy, and Human Flourishing

by

Samuel Gregg

A Crossroad Book
The Crossroad Publishing Company
New York

The Crossroad Publishing Company
www.CrossroadPublishing.com

Printed in the United States of America in 2013.
Library of Congress Cataloging-in-Publication Data available from the Library of
Congress.

Gregg, Samuel.
    Tea party Catholic: the Catholic case for limited government, a free economy, and
human flourishing / Samuel Gregg.
        pages CCLXIV

ISBN 978-0-8245-4981-7 (pbk.)
1. Catholic Church--Political Activity--United States. 2. Christian conservatism--
United States. 3. Tea Party Patriots. 4. Church and social problems--Catholic Church.
5. Church and social problems--United States. 6. Catholic Church--Doctrines.
7. Christianity and politics--United States. 8. Christianity and politics--Catholic
Church. 1. Title

BX1407.P63G74 2013
261.8088'282--dc23

Cover design by Ray Lundgren

Books published by The Crossroad Publishing Company may be purchased at special
quantity discount rates for classes and institutional use. For information, please email
sales@crossroadpublishing.com.

I hope ever to see America among the foremost nations in examples of justice and liberality. And I presume that your fellow-citizens will not forget the patriotic part which you took in the accomplishment of their Revolution, and the establishment of their government; or the important assistance which they received from a nation in which the Roman Catholic faith is professed. . . . And may the members of your society in America, animated alone by the pure spirit of Christianity, and still conducting themselves as the faithful subjects of our free government, enjoy every temporal and spiritual felicity.

President George Washington
Letter to the Roman Catholics
March 15, 1790[1]

For myself, as a citizen of the United States, and without closing my eyes to our shortcomings as a nation, I say with a deep sense of pride and gratitude, that I belong to a country where the civil government holds over us the aegis of its protection, without interfering with us in the legitimate exercise of our sublime mission as ministers of the Gospel of Christ. Our country has liberty without license, and authority without despotism.

Cardinal James Gibbons
Archbishop of Baltimore
Rome, 1887[2]

Table of Contents

Itaque, fratres, non sumus ancillae filii, sed liberae: qua libertate Christus nos liberavits.

State, et nolite iterum jugo servitutis contineri.[3]

Foreword

Samuel Gregg is the intellectual leader of the second generation of Catholic proponents of limited government, economic freedom, and religious liberty. With all his companions from many quarters of the world, he carries the colors for strong minds and stout hearts indeed. Originally hailing from Australia, with his doctorate won at Oxford under the supervision of perhaps one of the contemporary world's most significant natural law philosophers, John Finnis, Gregg arrived in the United States in 2001, and steadily established his leadership with a series of impressive books, including, most recently, the highly acclaimed *Becoming Europe*.

When I first read the title of the present book, I was worried that Gregg had taken up a partisan theme of today's American politics. It turned out, however, that the book has very little to do with the merely partisan contentions of today and even less to do with the Tea Party movement more specifically. In fact, Gregg's book has things to say to *all* Catholic Americans—regardless of party allegiance or view of the role of government—but also to Catholics living outside America. As I read through his six chapters with growing admiration, I saw that he was aiming at a prey swimming down much deeper—in fact, down in the depths of the ocean that has pushed up the key intellectual energies of the last 300 years. Gregg means to foster three world-transformative ideas: limited government, religious liberty, and economic liberty. And he does so with a strong grasp of the natural law and the long Catholic intellectual tradition, and for profoundly Catholic reasons.

Moreover, Gregg draws upon particular intellectual resources that few American thinkers have applied to contemporary circumstances, most notably the writings

1

and life of the wealthiest supporter of the American War of Independence: Charles Carroll of Carrollton. Carroll experienced the repression of religious freedom and economic liberty and the lash of unlimited government in a very personal way.

As a Catholic, Charles Carroll was formally excluded from holding public office in Britain's Maryland colony, despite the fact that the colony had been established by English Catholics who blessed it with a charter of religious toleration for all Christians. His forebears had seen that liberty and others taken by legislative force from all Catholics in Maryland. Those same restrictions meant that Catholics were denied opportunities for learning in the colony they had first established. Hence Charles Carroll's father was obliged to send him to France and eventually England for his education. This turned out to be a blessing, as it permitted Carroll to breathe in the air of some of the most balanced Enlightenment minds such as Montesquieu, the perennial thought of the natural law tradition associated with Catholic scholars like Francisco Suárez, S.J., and the wisdom contained in the English common law. Such erudition would stand Carroll in good stead in his work as a political commentator and legislator—activities that he combined with being a formidably successful entrepreneur.

Gregg opens his second chapter with the public motto of the Carroll family: "Anywhere so long as There Be Freedom." Prior to 1776, that liberty did not dwell in its fullness in Maryland and in other places in the United States—not, at least, for Catholics. When George Washington reluctantly took up the leadership of the Continental Army (he had really wanted only to serve in it), he said he entered this war, more than for anything else, for religious liberty. When Washington conversed at dinner with Carroll, in the process of persuading him to join the Patriots' Committee to negotiate with the French Catholic colonists and settlers living under British rule in Canada, he probed Carroll's motives for supporting the Revolution. Carroll replied: "So there are no more religious tests for public office." That was his number one request of the new American polity.

Carroll's substantial financial expertise, his service on the Continental Congress's Board of War, and his unwavering moral support of his friend General Washington were among many contributions to the final success of the American Revolution. Today we often forget the risks that generation took in embarking upon their "rebellion," as the British called it. The use of this word was deliberate. Britain meant to accuse men like Washington and Carroll of high treason for flagrantly violating their frequently restated pledges to be loyal to the King—their public oaths—and hang them. The revolutionary generation understood what was at stake in their rebellion. It was freedom itself. In this book, especially chapters three and four, Gregg shows how the "system of natural liberty" serves (and depends upon) the concrete practices of solidarity, subsidiarity, and the limited state—and, along with those practices, religious liberty, the first freedom.

What I especially admire about Gregg's work is that he begins from very different premises than I do. Like myself, he is influenced by Alexis de Tocqueville. But he is well schooled in the "new natural law theory" developed by John Finnis, Robert P. George, Joseph Boyle, and Germain Grisez. Thus he is able to respond to many difficulties and challenges that were beyond my powers. It is not as if I would willingly surrender my own grounding in Reinhold Niebuhr, Jacques Maritain, Alexis de Tocqueville, and John Courtney Murray, S.J., along with Henri de Lubac, S.J., and other teachers and models from that earlier generation. But it is moving to see, on the huge strategic board of particular arguments in history, a fresh army moving up to the front, at one's side, with new energies and capabilities.

In this regard, I especially appreciate the novel ways whereby Gregg interweaves religious liberty and economic liberty. Ironically, though he is Australian by birth and Oxford-educated, he does so in a way more deeply rooted in the American patriotic tradition than the vast majority of American Catholic theologians and philosophers.

Allow me to close by bringing forward three of the *pensées* of Charles Carroll, closely linked to similar well-known convictions expressed by George Washington, John Adams, Thomas Jefferson, and Benjamin Rush of Philadelphia. But note how Carroll speaks with a conspicuously Catholic voice—that is, a distinctly Catholic and *American* voice:

> Without morals a republic cannot subsist any length of time; they therefore who are decrying the Christian religion, whose morality is so sublime & pure, which denounces against the wicked eternal misery, and insures to the good eternal happiness, are undermining the solid foundation of morals, the best security for the duration of free governments.

> The Americans are jealous of their privileges and resolved to maintain them. . . . [They] are not yet corrupt enough to undervalue Liberty, they are truly sensible of its blessings, and not only talk of them as they do somewhere else, but really wish their continuance.

> Liberty will maintain her empire, till a dissoluteness of morals, luxury and venality shall have prepared the degenerate sons of some future age, to prefer their own mean lucre, the bribes, and the smiles of corruption and arbitrary ministers, to patriotism, to glory, and to the public weal.

The American voice, heard so clearly here, is not boastful, arrogant, or nationalistic. It expresses the knowledge that liberty depends upon a culture of virtue, a special quiver full of virtues, and that without these it cannot long survive. In any one age, we may come to see the end of the American experiment, the crash of what more than a few people regard as the last best hope among polities on earth. That time may be closer than we think.

That is why Gregg's call for a new birth of liberty in America—and explanation of how Catholics can contribute to it—is so timely now, and in fact ever timely. To lose freedom requires no more than a generation. Liberty is such a fragile plant. It must be watched over with an eagle's eye, and defended with a lion's courage.

Michael Novak
George Frederick Jewett Scholar Emeritus in Religion,
Philosophy, and Public Policy
The American Enterprise Institute

Introduction

America is changing, and it has been changing for a long time. The forces of globalization are changing our economy and forcing us to rethink the scope and purpose of our government. . . . America is changing on the inside, too. Our culture is changing. . . . We have an elite culture—in government, the media and academia—that is openly hostile to religious faith.

Archbishop José Gomez of Los Angeles
July 28, 2011[4]

Without morals a republic cannot subsist any length of time; they therefore who are decrying the Christian religion, whose morality is so sublime & pure, [and] which denounces against the wicked eternal misery, and [which] insured to the good eternal happiness, are undermining the solid foundation of morals, the best security for the duration of free governments.

Charles Carroll of Carrollton
Letter to Secretary of War James McHenry
November 4, 1800[5]

To say that the past thirteen years have been especially challenging for the Catholic Church in America is surely an understatement. The visible rise in antagonism toward any number of the Church's teachings, well-publicized clashes with the federal government over religious liberty questions, and the clergy sex scandals that exploded into public view in 2002 have lead many Catholic Americans to see the wisdom contained in the adage that you should think twice before wanting to live in interesting times.

Some of these developments reflect broader changes in American life. The Church has proved in no way immune to what Cardinal Donald Wuerl of Washington, DC, described in October 2012 as the "tsunami of secular influence" that has affected every single cultural, legal, economic and political institution since the 1960s, impacting what Wuerl denoted as "such societal markers as marriage, family, the concept of the common good and objective right and wrong."[6]

Other changes specific to the life of the Church in America have also became evident. Demographically, for instance, it is hard not to notice the increasing percentage of Catholics from Spanish-speaking backgrounds in the pews at Sunday Mass. With this trend likely to accelerate in the immediate future, it is bound to produce gradual changes in Catholicism throughout the United States.

For the American Church, such transformations are not unprecedented. During the seventeenth and eighteenth centuries, Catholicism in the territories encompassed by today's America was primarily influenced, on the one hand, by French Catholicism in the Northeast and Midwest (not to mention the Louisiana territories) as well as Spanish Catholicism in the South and West. This terrain was dramatically altered by subsequent waves of Catholic immigration from other European countries from the mid-nineteenth century onward.

As significant as these changes have been, they have arguably distracted attention away from an ongoing *generational* shift among American Catholics over the past forty years. It is always risky to try to summarize any cultural shift in the lives of particular individuals. But one major transformation among the Catholic American laity which has been well underway for some time was in many respects personified by the two vice presidential candidates in the 2012 elections.

On the Democratic ticket was Vice President Joe Biden, a man in many ways reflective of an older, fading generation of American Catholics. Often from Irish Catholic backgrounds, these Catholics grew up with almost tribal expectations concerning where you lived, the organizations you joined, and how you voted. Until the late 1960s this meant the Democratic Party, with Catholics featuring prominently in the politics prevalent in heavily Catholic, Democratic-dominated cities such as Boston, Chicago, and Philadelphia. Though fiercely anti-Communist, many such Catholics tended to favor widespread government economic intervention, having generally aligned themselves with Roosevelt's New Deal following the Great Depression.

As Catholics began exiting the Democratic party from the late 1960s, those who remained such as the late Senator Ted Kennedy and former Speaker Nancy Pelosi were increasingly disinclined to give effect to the Church's non-negotiable teachings on moral issues such as abortion and same-sex marriage. This, however, did not stop them from invoking Catholic language when discussing prudential economic questions. In this regard, Catholics such as Biden and Pelosi seemed to view extensive government involvement in the economy and large welfare states as the logical—if not the only possible—way to give effect to Catholic social teaching in public policy.

In the 2012 election, Biden found himself pitted against the Republican vice presidential candidate, Congressman Paul Ryan. In some ways emblematic of a rather different type of Catholic American, Ryan belonged to that cohort of post-Vatican II Catholics who grew up during the pontificate of Blessed John Paul II.

For those Catholics of this and successive generations who regularly practiced their faith, their embrace of Catholicism seemed much more a matter of choice rather than simply conforming to preexisting cultural expectations. In one sense such a development was miraculous, given the effects upon post-Vatican II Catholics of what Cardinal Wuerl has described as the "manifest poor catechesis or miscatechesis," the "hermeneutic of discontinuity that permeated so much of the milieu of centers of higher education," and the "aberrational liturgical practice" so pronounced throughout North America and Western Europe throughout the 1970s and 1980s.[7]

In general terms, this situation tended to produce two trends. One was the emergence of large numbers of essentially nominal Catholics in America with little to no involvement in the Church's life, and whose children were even less statistically likely to have anything whatsoever to do with Catholicism. By contrast, the other group consisted of many Catholics who sought to live and practice the Catholic Faith in its fullness as a result of their *own* search for truth, their *own* reading, and their *own* subsequent conclusion that the fullness of religious truth was to be found in Catholicism.

In discussing Church dogmas and doctrines, this latter group of Catholic Americans was often surprisingly well-informed. They were also very inclined to defend the Church's teaching on hot-button "cultural" questions such as human life, marriage, and religious liberty. But perhaps most strikingly, a good number of them articulated far more positive assessments of free enterprise and free markets than the Biden-Pelosi generation. Without being instinctively "anti-government" or even "libertarian," they were often more skeptical of the efficaciousness of government intervention than their parents and grandparents. With regard to economic questions, their reference points were likely to be figures such as the theologian Michael Novak, a scholar who began his intellectual career on the political left but who became the first Catholic American to produce a powerful theological defense of the market economy.

Quantifying the numbers of such Catholics in America, let alone their influence, would be a perilous undertaking. What is not in doubt is that this is a new type of Catholic American. It's a profile that has upturned many long-redundant assumptions about the nature of Catholic participation in American life. Yet it is also more deeply rooted in the culture and teaching of a two-thousand-year-old Church than many people realize.

A Vibrant Church, a Divided Public Square

When I first came to live and work in the United States in 2001, it was hard not to be impressed by the vitality of Catholic life in America. Obviously there were many divisions among Catholics on issues ranging from essential Church dogmas to the Church's role in politics. The Catholicism that I experienced growing up in my native Australia had all the same disagreements. Yet Catholicism in Australia—or at least the post-Vatican II wave of experimentation—seemed, for want of a better word, "tired." The quiet and gradual renewal of Australian Catholicism led by the Archbishop of Sydney, Cardinal George Pell, had only just started to acquire momentum. Likewise, Catholicism in the other country in which I lived for several years—England—was visibly marred by complacency on the part of some English bishops and priests, an emphasis on institutional preservation at the cost of moral witness, and timidity, even diffidence, in the face of Britain's accelerating transition to a post-Christian culture.

By contrast, the American Catholicism I encountered in 2001 had, even amidst the turmoil of the sex abuse scandals, begun the long process of escaping the malaise that characterized much of the Church throughout the West during the late 1960s, and into the 70s and 80s. This owed much to the leadership of bishops such as the late Cardinal John O'Connor of New York, a dynamic sense of orthodoxy among what has been called the "John Paul II—Benedict XVI" generation of bishops and priests, the emergence of articulate lay Catholic intellectuals (many of them converts) unencumbered by the old ethnic ties and tribal loyalties (and even tending to view them as obstacles to evangelization), and the rapid growth of new religious orders within the Church such as the Dominican Sisters of Mary Mother of the Eucharist and the Sisters of Life whose sense of joy about living the way of the Gospel without qualification was palpable.

At the same time, these Catholics were proudly and unambiguously *American*, though not in a narrow parochial way. They were Catholic *and* American, and American *and* Catholic. Not only did they believe that Catholicism, as the fullest expression of religious truth, had an indispensable contribution to make to the shaping and uplifting of American life and culture; they also believed American Catholicism had gifts to offer global Catholicism that went far beyond the financial resources which Catholic Americans continue to generously disperse throughout the universal Church. And for many such Catholics, part of their "Americanness" involved affirmation of what John Paul II called in his third social encyclical *Centesimus Annus* "the 'business economy,' 'market economy' or simply 'free economy.'"[8]

It's no secret that American political and economic culture has long taken a somewhat more skeptical view of the efficacy of government intervention in the economy compared to the social democratic consensus prevailing in much of contemporary Europe. Nor, however, is it any news that these assumptions in favor of free enterprise and limited government have long been under challenge by some Americans, the primary intellectual roots of which may be traced to the Progressivist movement of the early 1900s. The practical manifestations of such thought range from Franklin Roosevelt's New Deal and Lyndon Johnson's Great Society, to Barack Obama's efforts to expand government intervention in the economy from 2008 onward.

Throughout the twentieth century, many Catholic Americans featured prominently among supporters of such programs. Politically speaking, this owed much to the alliance between urban Northern Catholics and white overwhelmingly Protestant Southerners that was a staple of Democratic Party politics from the 1920s until the late 1960s. It also flowed from the Tammany Hall style of (and often, to be frank, deeply corrupt) politics adopted by some Catholic Americans:

one which linked voting and holding political office with dispensing favors through government. There were also prominent Catholic intellectual defenders of the economic path pursued by Roosevelt, most notably the Catholic priest popularly known as the "Right Reverend New Dealer," Father John A. Ryan.

Principle and Prudence

For these Catholics to lend their support to expansions of government activity into the economy was in no sense illegitimate. Many of them were—and are—in good faith voting and acting in ways that reflect their prudential application of the principles of Catholic social teaching in the public square. This is appropriate because the *principles* of Catholic social teaching are principles. While they provide an orientation about how to think about social and economic questions, taken together they do not amount to any one specific political program.

Working out the applicability of these principles in the complicated world of politics and economic policy is, for the most part, the role of *lay* Catholics. The Second Vatican Council could not have been clearer about this:

> The laity must take on the renewal of the temporal order as *their own mission*; led by the light of the gospel and the mind of the Church, and motivated by Christian charity, they must act in that order directly and in a distinct way, cooperating as citizens with other citizens, using their own expertise, and acting on their own responsibility, everywhere and in everything seeking the justice of God's kingdom.[9]

As George Weigel points out, Vatican II's conception of the laity is not reducible to those lay Catholics who happen to be employed by the Church, including those engaged by the public policy agencies of bishops' conferences.[10] Rather it embraces *all* lay Catholics. And these same lay Catholics enjoy considerable latitude, subject to the demands of Catholic faith and morals, in "acting upon their own responsibility."

Catholic bishops certainly have a duty to point out where a policy or law involves direct violation of non-negotiable Church teaching or the natural law. Support for laws that legalize or expand access to direct abortion or that seriously impinge upon religious liberty are some examples of such policies. On such subjects—which, it must be reiterated, are relatively few in number—bishops have a responsibility to call Catholic voters and politicians to account and highlight any discrepancy between what they profess as Catholics and their political choices.

Generally speaking, however, it is not part of a bishop's job description to advocate specific economic policies. These are areas in which Catholics are largely free to argue among themselves. The American Catholic moral theologian Germain Grisez explains it this way:

> On some matters, only one position is acceptable for faithful Catholics. For example, abortion and the use of embryonic humans as experimental material should never be permitted by law. In such cases, someone who calls fellow Catholics to cooperate in a course of political action and admonishes any who fail to do so, acts rightly in pointing out the Church's relevant teaching.
>
> On many matters, however, faithful Catholics can legitimately disagree. In some situations, those exercising political power are open only to options incompatible with the Church's teaching, and the question is which of those options should be considered worse and so opposed in order to mitigate the evil. In other situations, there are two or more positions, incompatible with one another but compatible with the Church's teaching. In both kinds of cases, even though someone has arrived at

a position by applying the Church's teaching to the facts of the problem as carefully as possible, he or she should not propose that opinion as the Church's teaching.[11]

There is no Catholic teaching which tells us that, for example, the government's share of GDP *has to* be 23 or 27 or 50 percent, or that the upper tax rate *cannot be anything other than* 50 or 10 or 79 percent of gross annual income, or that fiat money must always be preferred to the gold standard. In many cases, when a good quality of life posture is identified— such as universal health coverage—the precise discernment of *how* a society attains that end may depend upon empirical and prudential judgments reasonably in dispute among people equally well-informed by principles of Catholic teaching.[12] In any event, one would expect any Catholic examining such questions to acknowledge that there are many policies that Catholics can advocate in order to realize such a goal, while remaining in good standing with the Church.

Unfortunately there is often great reluctance to concede some of these very basic distinctions among some of those who might be called, for want of a better expression, "social justice Catholics." For many of them, it seems, the Catholic understanding of human dignity cannot translate into anything but generous welfare states, weak conceptions of property rights, heavy regulation, and more or less social democratic policies. For a Catholic to be an advocate of free markets—let alone to use the word "capitalism" in a positive way—is, for many social justice Catholics, deeply suspect.

The Rise of the Free Market Catholics

Thirty-one years ago the American theologian Michael Novak began the courageous and lonely work of providing Catholic Americans uneasy with economically-expansionist government with the theological resources to begin articulating their own prudential defense of the workings of American capitalism. In his 1982 book, *The Spirit of Democratic Capitalism*, Novak challenged the consensus then prevailing among many Catholics—especially those clergy and laity formed in the Second Vatican Council's immediate aftermath—that capitalism was, at best, a necessary evil, and at worst, largely irreconcilable with Catholic faith.

Upon publication, Novak's book generated fiercely negative reactions from across the American Catholic world. And the negativity did not spring simply from old-fashioned New Deal Catholics. It also came from those Catholic Americans (especially in those religious orders that had prioritized political activism after Vatican II) enchanted by one or more of those forms of often Marxist-influenced liberation theology that had emerged in Latin America. Equally loud were criticisms from the "right" of the Church: from self-described traditionalists and adherents of distributism who tended to associate modern capitalism with Protestantism or nineteenth-century liberalism.

Throughout this same period, the American Catholic bishops conference was issuing an apparently endless stream of commentaries on economic subjects. Few would dispute that these statements generally reflected the mildly left/ liberal economic positions that many bishops of the time had absorbed in the cultural and political milieu of youths spent growing up in large, usually Democratic cities of the 1940s, 50s, and 60s. The pinnacle of these interventions occurred in 1986, when the bishops conference published *Economic Justice for All*, a document whose twenty-fifth anniversary passed almost unnoticed in 2011, and which bore all the hallmarks of the influence of people who thought the "two Johns" (the liberal philosopher John Rawls and the economist John Maynard Keynes) had said all that ever needed to be said about justice and the economy respectively.

Yet in a sign of things to come, a group of prominent lay American Catholics, marshaled together by Novak, decided that the time had come to publish their *own* letter on the economy. Entitled *Towards the Future: Catholic Social Thought and the U.S. Economy* (1984) this lay-authored text presented a vision of economic life which, while condemning collectivism and radical individualism, also celebrated free enterprise, extolled the benefits of competition, and underscored market capitalism's poverty-reducing power in far more explicit terms than anything ever written by America's bishops.

In subsequent years, Novak authored several books outlining a more specifically Catholic case for the free economy. As time passed, his efforts began to be complemented and expanded upon by other Catholic Americans such as the late Father Richard John Neuhaus and Father Robert Sirico. In certain respects much of Novak's work was eventually vindicated in 1991, when John Paul II promulgated *Centesimus Annus*. This articulated a carefully qualified but nevertheless clear approval of what the Pope preferred to call "the free economy."

By the 1990s, debates among Catholic Americans about economic questions were also being shaped by a new breed of priests and bishops coming of age throughout the Church. Apart from reacting against the disorder which had permeated much of the Church in the West in the immediate post-Vatican II era, this clergy seemed (1) more detached from politics *per se*, (2) distrustful of the endless political activism (invariably of a left-wing nature) that had engulfed so many Catholic religious orders whose position on a number of core Catholic dogmas and doctrines was disturbingly ambiguous, (3) quite unsentimental about the fast-disappearing links between practicing Catholics and a Democratic Party that had all but embraced lifestyle-liberalism as its core creed, and (4) not especially inclined to hitch their wagon to the Republican Party either.

To the extent they discussed economic issues, most such bishops and priests affirmed that the details of economic policy are largely a matter of prudential judgment for Catholic laity.

Instead they were generally more concerned with evangelizing their flocks in the actual teachings articulated in the documents of Vatican II, not least so that they could begin the difficult work of correcting the results of the previous thirty years of catechetical neglect.

Much can change, however, in a relatively short period of time. The onset of a severe global recession in late 2007 and the financial sector's subsequent meltdown in 2008 gave new impetus to those Catholics attached to the rhetoric of extensive government economic intervention and anxious to see the Church publically support commensurate policies. The result was a marked uptick of sharp arguments among Catholic Americans concerning matters such as the merits or otherwise of interventionist policies and the economics and morality of socialized medicine.

An Economic Civil War

Catholic Americans are hardly alone in being divided about these issues. The emergence of what came to be known as the "Tea Party" movement was not simply a reaction against Obamacare. It was also a direct response by Americans from a surprising variety of backgrounds against a general sense that government had become too big, too interventionist, and too dismissive of many Americans' concerns about the economic and moral effects of an economically-expansionist state.

Since that time, the sharp divisions of opinion in American society concerning government's economic role has well and truly manifested itself in the American Catholic community. In 2012, this new reality was brought home to Catholic Americans by two factors.

The first was a very public spat between Congressman Paul Ryan and the United States Catholic Bishops Conference's (USCCB) Committee on Domestic Justice and Human Development. When Ryan produced a much-discussed 2012 budget plan to begin addressing America's debt issues, this committee criticized Ryan's proposal on the basis that it reduced funds for a number of anti-poverty initiatives. Rather than back down, Ryan insisted that his proposals were informed by his Catholic faith and, at a minimum, were not contrary to his Catholicism. Ryan—who possessed a sterling pro-life, pro-religious liberty record—even went on pilgrimage to Georgetown University to defend his position as a prudential application of the principles of Catholic social teaching to the technically-complex issue of how we continue assisting the poor while simultaneously seeking to rein in public finances without significantly undermining the American economy's wealth-creating powers.

Even more interesting, however, was the fact that several Catholic bishops politely but forcibly criticized the bishops' justice committee at an open session of a full meeting of America's Catholic bishops in June 2012. Among other things, they claimed the justice committee's intervention had been judged by many as excessively partisan, involved the bishops in an area that was primarily a field for the laity, and ignored widespread evidence of the welfare state's failure to substantially reduce poverty in America.[13]

Several months later in November 2012, the differences among America's bishops on such matters become even more evident. Gathered together in the wake of Barack Obama's reelection as President, the bishops could not agree upon the content of a document on the economy drafted by a designated group of bishops. The draft text itself focused on the moral and spiritual dimensions of America's economic problems rather than technical policy details.[14] And as more than one person noted at the time, the document made no reference whatsoever to the 1986 pastoral letter *Economic Justice for All.*

Some bishops argued the text should have emphasized redistribution. Others, however, responded by saying it was not the bishops' place to enter into the details of economic policy. Interestingly, a number of commentators noticed that these differences reflected a division between retired and close-to-retirement bishops who wanted to see the Church lend its public support to more or less center-left economic policies, and younger bishops who thought the times (and the Church's teaching) called for a greater focus upon ensuring that lay Catholics understood the principles of Catholic social teaching rather than advocating specific policies.[15]

Lost in the commentary, however, was attention to one vital fact. While the document did not receive the required two-thirds majority vote for formal approval—134 bishops voted *in favor* of the text, eighty-five against, and nine abstained—these numbers underscored just how much the thinking of America's Catholic bishops had moved away from promoting the specific economic agenda and policies associated with *Economic Justice for All*—or, for that matter, a desire to lobby for *any* specific set of economic policies.

The second and far more troubling factor that forced many Catholic Americans to reflect upon the wider impact of increasing state economic intervention was an announcement by the Department of Health and Human Services on January 20, 2012 that most Catholic institutions would be required to provide employees with insurance coverage for abortion-inducing drugs, sterilization, and contraceptives: products, procedures, and chemicals used to facilitate acts which the Catholic Church—and plenty of others—considers intrinsically evil. Though the Administration produced revised guidelines a week later to placate Catholic concerns, all of America's Catholic bishops rejected the revised mandate as mere window dressing.

Belatedly it began to dawn on many Catholics that the federal government's effort to take more control of healthcare, and the inevitable diminution of economic freedom associated with this move, was now undermining the Church's liberty to live in accordance with some of its core moral teachings. Economic liberty and religious liberty, many Catholics started realizing, were in many respects indivisible. Just as freedom in one sphere redounded to the well-being of another, so too did an attack on one diminish the other.

Why a Catholic Case for Freedom?

This background, coupled with many Catholic Americans' evident willingness to align themselves with their fellow citizens equally concerned about the growth of government and the diminution of economic and religious liberty, speaks to a need to spell out in an accessible manner the ideas, concerns, and, above all, vision of those who might be called "Tea Party," "free enterprise," or "limited government" Catholics. There are, however, two other reasons to do so.

The first might be called a negative reason. This book is not about the Tea Party movement or any particular group that claims this name. But the millions of Americans who are in some way involved or associated with various "Tea Party" ideas and more broadly limited government initiatives have been derided by many commentators as extremists, anti-government cranks, and even, in some cases, as racists.

All political movements, however noble their origins and aspirations, will attract some undesirables. But to describe the Tea Party movement in such terms, let alone the millions of Americans who favor limited government, is patently unfair, not to mention empirically questionable.

In his 2012 book *Teavangelicals*, the journalist David Brody illustrated that the profile of self-described Tea Party supporters provided clear evidence that it was *not* a movement of government-hating zealots. Tea Party activists, it turned out, were disproportionately religious, tended to be socially conservative, and favored constitutionally-limited government, fiscal responsibility, and free markets.[16]

The point, of course, is that to be in favor of *limited* government and dubious about the prudence of extensive government economic intervention does not mean that one is necessarily opposed to government *per se*. It simply involves arguing on grounds of principle and prudence that government should normally have a small number of clearly-defined functions limited in their scope and impact, including with regard to the economy. Such an ideal has been core to the entire American experiment from its very beginning. It also stands in the very center of the Western tradition.

This has not stopped some critics of limited government or free enterprise Catholics from claiming they sup at the table of people like the pro-capitalist but militantly-atheistic philosopher Ayn Rand. Such assertions are unjust and require comprehensive rebuttal. The Catholic case for limited government, the free economy, and religious liberty is *very* different from that of many self-described libertarians, let alone Randians.

The key difference in play is that Catholics can bring something to the political and economic agenda of America's limited government movement often considered marginal by many libertarians and viewed as metaphysical day-dreaming by others. This is the rich conception of *human flourishing*. This idea is at the very core of the Catholic Church's robust commitment to religious liberty, as spelled out in the Second Vatican Council's 1965 Declaration on Religious Freedom, *Dignitatis Humanae*. But it is quite applicable to the development of a morally "thick"[17] case for the free economy and limiting the government's economic role.

And herein lies the second reason for outlining an explicitly Catholic case for the realization of these ends. Many people who favor free enterprise and limited government tend to argue in terms of freedom being preferable to servitude, or that the free economy, with all its weakness, is "less bad" than social democracy. At the beginning of the twentieth century, for instance, one of economic freedom's most prominent academic advocates in the English-speaking world, the British economist Edwin Cannan, couched almost the entirety of his argument for free markets in terms of skepticism about the alternatives.[18]

These arguments are important. Nevertheless they have their limits, not least among which are rhetorical. Many free marketers often turn out to be better at arguing what they are against rather than what they are for. One major criticism of those free marketers who took issue with John Maynard Keynes in the 1930s is that they focused primarily on discrediting his economic ideas for finding a way out of the Great Depression instead of trying to combine this critique with positive proposals for genuine change.[19]

Catholics who favor limited government and the free economy need to avoid this error. Catholic critiques of interventionist policies are important, but by themselves are not enough. Catholics should also recall that their positive case goes far beyond simply creating more space to allow us to do whatever we just happen to "feel like" doing. In fact, the Catholic argument for freedom is *not* autonomy for the sake of autonomy, or "liberty for liberty's sake." Rather the end is the *excellence* that every person is capable of realizing through the reasonable use of their freedom— an excellence rooted in our very nature as the *imago Dei*: a being called to freely embrace all those goods that make us flourish precisely as human beings rather than embrace mediocrity.

Until recently the involvement of Catholics *as Catholics* on the "non-left" of contemporary American political life has been most commonly associated with their centrality (especially, as many Evangelicals and others happily acknowledge, the formidable intellectual clout brought by Catholics) to the pro-life and traditional marriage movements. But the central thesis of this book is that Catholics who underscore the cause of economic liberty can—nay, *must*—invest the cause for limited government with the same moral depth that Catholics have brought to other issues.

This book consequently seeks to spell out the Catholic case for liberty on the foundation of the Catholic vision of human flourishing. It seeks to outline an *integrated* Catholic argument for economic freedom, for a government with clear but constrained economic functions, for a "thick" conception of religious liberty, and to explain how these ideas fit together.

This focus means that, for the most part, what Americans often call "social issues" (abortion, same-sex marriage, euthanasia, embryonic stem cell research, etc.) are not addressed in detail here. There is no shortage of sound and accessible Catholic writing explaining why, for example, the Church is relentless in its defense of the unborn, and why such advocacy doesn't represent some type of creeping theocratization of America. The specifically *Catholic* case (as opposed to more general Judeo-Christian arguments) for economic liberty and a limited state, however, requires further development.

And this is not just for the sake of Catholic Americans. Over the past forty years, it is hard to dispute that the incomprehension with which many Catholics in Europe, Latin America, Africa, and Asia view many American Catholics' attachment to the causes of economic liberty and limited government has remained and, in some cases, grown. Despite what might be called some of the "American" insights of encyclicals like *Centesimus Annus* (or even parts of Pope Benedict XVI's first encyclical *Deus Caritas Est*) many Catholic Americans' more skeptical views of extensive government intervention, as well as their strong affirmation of economic freedom and business, continue to be considered odd, even suspect, by many Catholics outside the United States—particularly in Western Europe, and including by many who are quite orthodox on matters of faith and morals. This book thus seeks to help such audiences understand the roots and character of many Catholic Americans' views on these matters, and how they represent a legitimate prudential application of Catholic thinking about liberty, the role of government, human flourishing, and the economy.

Things Old and New

Throughout the 1980s and 1990s theologians such as Michael Novak performed yeoman's work in articulating Catholic defenses of the market economy. They did so at a time when writing such works was to risk permanently alienating oneself from many of those who belonged to the immediate post-Vatican II generation of Catholics that was trending leftwards on economic, social, and political questions.

Since that time, there have been several developments which indicate that many of the arguments advanced by Novak and others require elaboration and sharpening. The first is that the dangers to economic freedom have mutated. While old threats in the form of an excessively interventionist government remain, they have been accompanied by new problems upon which there has been relatively little Catholic reflection in recent decades. One example is the manner in which the welfare state has increasingly become a means for disseminating distinctly secularist and materialistic views of the human person.

A second issue concerns the connection now being made by many Catholics between economically-expansionist government and the often negative implications for religious freedom. Such questions were initially brought sharply into focus by the Obama Administration's HHS (Health and Human Services) mandate. But, as explained by the distinguished Catholic historian James Hitchcock, "Less obvious is the fact that such infringements, and many that will be far worse, are endemic to the modern welfare state and were bound to emerge sooner or later."[20] Unpacking precisely how this situation has emerged, and how it can be resolved, should be a pressing concern for all Catholics.

A third—and happy—development has been the considerable growth in Catholic reflection on the nature of freedom and human flourishing since the 1980s. In terms of magisterial teaching, these were perhaps most powerfully outlined in John Paul II's great 1993 encyclical on Catholic moral teaching, *Veritatis Splendor*. Surprisingly little of such reflections, however, have been applied to thinking about the economic realm. This is especially odd, given the sheer number of lay Catholics in America and elsewhere working in the world of commerce.

Fourth, the pontificate of Benedict XVI took Catholic social teaching in new directions. In all his encyclicals Benedict articulated insights grounded in Scripture, the Church Fathers, and his own theological studies that had significant implications for matters ranging from how we understand questions of the government's economic role, to the hows and whys of loving and helping our neighbor in the conditions of a market economy. These and other observations made by Benedict have much to say to Catholics concerned about the growth of government, not least because they elucidate and explain the deeper reasons for their concerns and strengthen their vision of what an America grounded in freedom and virtue might look like.

Lastly, on March 13, 2013, the world witnessed the election of the first pope from *the Americas*. The elevation of Argentina's Jorge Bergoglio to Peter's Chair reflects many things, including the fact that a plurality of the world's Roman Catholics now live in the New World. The history of Latin America is of course intimately tied to that of the United States. Today this is especially reflected in the large number of Roman Catholics who have migrated from Latin America to reside in the United States—many of whom have come to America because they have endured severe poverty and lacked economic opportunity and freedom more generally in the lands of their birth.

From the beginning of Pope Francis's ministry, it was clear that the Argentine intended to use his office to remind Catholics of the concrete obligations they have to their brothers and sisters who live in poverty. This concern for the poor has always been central to the Church's message and mission, and emphasized by all popes from time immemorial, including Francis's immediate two predecessors as pope. But Pope Francis's particular attention to this subject and the fact that he comes from a region of the globe in which poverty is in some places endemic means that all Catholics— including those who favor economic freedom and limited government—are obliged to think even more creatively about how their prudential application of the principles of Catholic social teaching can help alleviate the needs of the materially least among us in the context of the Church's commitment to promoting integral human flourishing.

A More-Than-Academic Discussion

One striking feature of intra-Catholic debates about economic issues in America is the way in which they have long ceased to be a concern primarily of scholars and public policy advocates. Much of the contemporary argument about the stance of Catholic Americans vis-à-vis the wider movement for liberty and limited government has been conducted at a popular level, ranging from the opinion pages of newspapers such as the *New York Times*, the *Wall Street Journal*, the *Los Angeles Times*, and the *Washington Post*, and specifically Catholic outlets such as the *National Catholic Register* and *Our Sunday Visitor*, to a host of Catholic, Christian, and secular blogs.

This should not surprise us. Like millions of their fellow Americans, Catholics are deeply worried about their country and its long-term economic future. Some insist that the government must increase its intervention into the economy in the name of justice. Other Catholic Americans are equally concerned about their country and the well-being of the economic least among us but don't believe that the long-term solution is to adopt essentially social democratic policies. Many of these matters, they maintain, can be substantially addressed if Americans are allowed to embrace and live out the freedoms which were secured for all Americans by the generation that led the thirteen colonies to independence: liberties which, for Catholics and many others, are ultimately a gift of our Creator.

Explaining the nature and scope of these freedoms to Catholics—indeed anyone interested in understanding distinctly Catholic as well as particular natural law arguments for economic liberty and limited government—is this book's purpose. It subsequently avoids entering into details of particular policy issues, save when such discussion helps to illustrate a wider point. These conversations are important. But there is no shortage of policy discussions of matters ranging from regulation and free trade, to whether unions are the most optimal way of advancing employees' interests.

Moreover, clarity at the level of ideas and principles matters for two other reasons. First, it helps diminish confusion at the policy level. Reference to principles soon illustrates whether a policy is advancing or retarding the advance of certain ideas.

Second, and perhaps more important, while conservatives and free marketers are usually very good at developing and articulating sophisticated policies, they often struggle to place these ideas in a broader context of an overall vision of the good that goes beyond efficiency and effectiveness. On some occasions, such policies are described as "distinctly American," but with minimal explanation of why this is the case. American progressivists, especially through their appeal to particular conceptions of social justice (that usually have very little in common with the Catholic understanding of this phrase), are often much better at articulating a vision of where they want to go, regardless of the coherence or otherwise of their specific policy prescriptions.

Beginning therefore with an outline of the Catholic view of human freedom and human flourishing, this book applies this vision to the case for the free economy and the principles that inform the state's economic role, before turning to the question of religious liberty and how it impacts debates about the government's economic responsibilities. These are complicated issues, and this book makes no effort to address every possible nuance. For that reason, extended reading for those wanting to learn more about these subjects is provided at the end of each chapter.

It also goes without saying that these are *controversial* matters, not least among Catholic Americans. The briefest of glances at Catholic publications and the ever-expanding Catholic blogosphere makes it clear that Catholics articulating arguments that criticize, for instance, Obamacare, or who suggest that the Catholic view of trade unions is far more nuanced than most people suppose, quickly encounter (often quite uncivil) criticism. One chapter of this book subsequently seeks to answer the most pertinent of these critiques. How, for example, should Catholics think about something like self-interest? And what about questions of social justice? These are fair and important questions and they deserve a response.

As a final preliminary note, readers should recognize this book does not claim to be articulating the only possible Catholic stance regarding these matters. Plainly neither socialism nor anarcho-capitalism[21] is compatible with Catholic teaching. Socialism has been explicitly and repeatedly condemned by the Church in the most direct terms.[22] Likewise the Church has never regarded government as a "necessary evil." Yet within these parameters, there is plenty of room for Catholics to argue among themselves about economic issues and remain in good standing with the Church. I simply ask those Catholics inclined to center-left economic positions, or attracted to movements such as distributism,[23] to remember this basic point as they engage the positions outlined in these pages.

A Catholic Revolutionary

One reason for the Tea Party's success in quickly attracting support from millions of Americans was surely its name. This resonates with Americans because it harks back to the American Founding and the Revolution that gave birth to a bold and (thus far) lasting experiment in human liberty.

The Tea Party's emergence is also living proof, as the Jesuit theologian John Courtney Murray claimed in his book *We Hold These Truths*, that the United States is a propositional nation. By that, Murray meant America has the capacity to renew itself by going back to its moral, cultural, and political founding, much as the Catholic Church renews its doctrine by returning to the sources of its teaching—Sacred Scripture, the teaching of the Fathers and Doctors of the Church, and the magisterial teachings of popes and councils—and brings these truths to bear upon contemporary problems.

One construal of the American Founding that remains extremely influential is that the American Revolution and subsequent political settlement were primarily shaped and driven by the various intellectual impulses associated with eighteenth-century Enlightenment thinking.

Unquestionably there is some truth to this particular narrative. Influential figures such as Benjamin Franklin and Thomas Jefferson took many of their cues from those seventeenth and eighteenth century commentators who emphasized the importance of the natural sciences and natural philosophy, and stressed the necessity of applying the tools associated with scientific rationality to as many spheres of life as possible. Other Enlightenment intellectual trends included an accent upon utility—understood as enhancing the usefulness or otherwise of particular habits and procedures—and exploring its applicability to all arenas of human endeavor. This included the economy but also religion and religious belief itself.

Some Enlightenment thinkers were neither hostile to Christianity in general nor Catholicism in particular. Others were skeptical of religious claims, and many did not disguise their hostility. Yet above all else, the various Enlightenments[24] insisted upon reason's supremacy—or, at least, a certain form of reason—and the need to liberate people from oppression. As a document issued by the Catholic Church's highest doctrinal office, the Congregation for the Doctrine of the Faith (CDF), affirmed in 1986: "it was above all in the Age of the Enlightenment and at the French Revolution that the call to freedom rang out with full force. Since that time, many have regarded future history as an irresistible process of liberation inevitably leading to an age in which man, totally free at last, will enjoy happiness on this earth."[25]

Twenty years later, the head of that doctrinal office who later succeeded John Paul II in the Chair of Peter pointed out that the culture associated with the Enlightenment was "substantially defined by the rights to liberty" and "its starting point" which regarded liberty as "a fundamental value and the criterion of everything else."[26] This had practical consequences, such as limiting government power, some of which, Joseph Ratzinger noted, Christians would not wish to do without.[27]

But for all the significant Enlightenment influences upon the American Revolution, there was also a religious dimension to the American Founding. Among the Declaration of Independence's signatories were to be found convinced Christians, such as the sixth president of Princeton University the Reverend John Witherspoon (accused by the British of turning Princeton into a "seminary of sedition"), his fellow Presbyterian Richard Stockton, and the Congregationalist Samuel Adams. Yet another of the Signers present at America's creation, however, was a man who enjoys perhaps the strongest claim to being the first "Tea Party Catholic"—the layman, political thinker, legislator, entrepreneur, and American Revolutionary: Charles Carroll of Carrollton.

Chapter 1

Catholic and Free

We consider the establishment of our nation's independence, the shaping of its liberties and laws as a work of special Providence, its framers "building better than they knew, the Almighty's hand guiding them." And if ever the glorious fabric is subverted or impaired, it will be by men forgetful of the sacrifices of the heroes that reared it, the virtues that cemented it, and the principles on which it rests.

The Catholic bishops of the United States,
Third Plenary Council of Baltimore, 1893[1]

On October 15, 1774, the ship *Peggy Stewart* owned by the Annapolis mercantile company of Dick and Stewart sailed into the harbor of Annapolis in the colony of Maryland, carrying with it a cargo of tea. On arriving, the ship's owner paid the tax then applied by Britain to importations of tea to its American colonies in accordance with the Tea Act of May 1773.

This law was intended to avert bankruptcy of the East India Company which had lobbied the British Parliament to exempt it from the tea import duties which its colonial competitors were required to pay. As if this was not enough, the Company was also granted the privilege of being allowed to ship its tea directly to agents in America instead of placing its tea on open auction in Britain. The Company was thus able to undercut American merchants who were required to purchase tea by the regular process of passing through the higher-taxed British controls.

Leaving aside the inherent injustice of using state power to privilege one commercial enterprise over others, the political point of this exercise was to elicit the American colonists' implicit agreement to the British Parliament's right to tax the

American colonies. This at least was how it was understood by those American colonists who were increasingly incensed at what they regarded as a pattern of repression against His Majesty's subjects in British North America.

Opposition to what many Americans viewed as the British government's latest arbitrary act was especially fierce in Maryland. Few were more outspoken in their opposition than one of its leading public figures, Charles Carroll of Carrollton. "It will not do," Carroll insisted, "to export the tea to Europe or the West Indies. Its importation is an offense for which the people will not be so easily satisfied."

Carroll was no man of violence. He was disconcerted by some of the Boston Tea Party's radical undertones and subsequently worried about the potential for anarchy and disorder that is part of any revolution.[2] Such qualms did not, however, prevent Carroll from proposing that the owner of the *Peggy Stewart*, Anthony Stewart, make amends—and save his own skin—by burning not just the tea but also his ship![3]

Even some of Carroll's equally angry contemporaries were taken aback by the strength of Carroll's convictions on this matter. They would have been less surprised had they known that after Britain's imposition of the Stamp Act seven years earlier, Carroll had warned his English friends that "The Americans are jealous of their privileges and resolved to maintain them." And as if seeking to provoke his correspondents in the mother country, Carroll added that the Americans "are not yet corrupt enough to undervalue Liberty, they are truly sensible of its blessings, and not only talk of them as they do somewhere else, but really wish their continuance."[4]

A Signer Unlike the Others

Though most often remembered as the last Signer of the Declaration of Independence to depart this world, Charles Carroll was also distinguished by the fact that he was its sole Roman Catholic signatory. But long before most of the other Signers and

Founders, Carroll had concluded America should be free. "In time," he said in 1763, "it will and must be independent."[5]

In signing the Declaration, Carroll arguably put more at risk, at least materially, than any other member of the Revolutionary generation. At the time, he was probably the richest man in America. As well as inheriting considerable wealth from his equally-entrepreneurial father, Carroll proved to be an extremely able businessman in his own right, increasing the family fortune several times over. A defeat of the Revolution may well have resulted in the government's confiscation of the fruits of his family's business acumen.

Nevertheless the cause of liberty meant so much to Carroll that he was willing to back what must have seemed to be a forlorn endeavor to many at the time. But Carroll had always embraced the deeper meaning of his family's motto: *Ubicumque cum libertate:* "Anywhere so long as There Be Freedom." This devotion to freedom—and what he was willing to put at stake—was noticed by many of Carroll's fellow revolutionaries. Speaking of Carroll, the man who would be America's second president, John Adams, remarked: "In the cause of American liberty, his zeal, fortitude and perseverance have been so conspicuous that he is said to be marked out for particular vengeance by the friends of Administration; but he continues to hazard his all, his immense fortune, the largest in America, and his life."[6]

Unlike the other Signers, however, Carroll and his family knew in a particular way what it meant to have one's liberty violated. Until the 1770s, Carroll was formally barred from voting or holding public office in Maryland because of his Catholic faith. Carroll also knew that, unlike the other revolutionary leaders, his Catholicism made him especially suspect to the British government (and more than a few of his fellow revolutionaries). In their minds, Catholicism was still associated with papist disloyalty to a Protestant crown in an overwhelmingly Protestant British Empire.

Another feature distinguishing Carroll from his fellow patriots was his reasons for making his stand for freedom. All of Carroll's biographers affirm that his political and economic thought was influenced by his Catholicism, by what the Catholic Church's greatest minds had said about the nature and limits of government, and by the Church's long history of resisting the incursions of temporal power into its affairs. Carroll was quite aware that the Catholic Church had always insisted that the state had certain legitimate functions. Yet the same Church also maintained—and continues to do so—that there were bounds beyond which governments cannot go.

The limits of state power vis-à-vis the rights of individuals and communities were central to the events leading to and following the American Revolution. The sources to which America's Founders turned in explaining their choice to embark upon a new experiment in ordered liberty were diverse. They ranged from classical figures associated with the Roman Republic, to philosophers such as John Locke who had helped shape England's revolution of 1688. The language and ideas employed by many of these figures when discussing questions of liberty, property, and the nature of government was not, however, completely dissimilar from that of the Catholic tradition. All belong, after all, to what is often called the Western canon of ideas.

Notwithstanding these similarities, the Catholic position in favor of limited government and the free economy does differ in important ways from pre-Christian and post-Enlightenment schools of thought. These disparities owe much to Catholicism's specific understanding of the nature of human freedom. For Catholics, human freedom is grounded in what man is—an individual, sinful, and social being graced with reason and free will—and directed to what Benedict XVI called in his 2009 encyclical *Caritas in Veritate*, "integral human development," or what some Catholic moral theologians and philosophers describe as "integral human flourishing."

This is the distinct contribution that Catholics can bring to the much needed renewal of the movement for economic freedom and limited government throughout America: a deeper and coherent understanding of *why* freedom really matters, including in the economy. More specifically, they can demonstrate that:

- Entrepreneurship, economic liberty, and the market economy are not simply more efficient than the alternatives; they also create tremendous opportunities for human flourishing.
- A highly economically-activist state is not just economically ineffective but also tends to damage the moral culture and undermines human flourishing.
- There are better ways for Americans to realize their concrete obligations to those in need than large welfare states (not least through churches and other intermediate associations), and in a manner which contributes to the integral development of those being assisted.
- A robust conception of religious liberty is essential for human flourishing and limiting government power—including in economic life.
- The market economy and the ideal of limited government are more reliant on a strong civil society, intact families, and a robust moral culture than many people realize.

These are just some of the specifically Catholic and sometimes corrective glosses that limited-government Catholics can help to integrate into the broad movement for freedom in America. It cannot, however, be repeated enough: the *coherence* of these positions stands or falls upon the Catholic conception of human flourishing, and its subsequent meaning for the free choices and actions of individuals and communities as well as what Catholics call the common good.

Human Liberty, Human Flourishing

The idea of human flourishing is as old as Aristotle. It also finds resonance in the aspirations contained in the immortal phrase, "Life, Liberty, and the Pursuit of Happiness." But what is the Catholic conception of human flourishing? And how does it relate to human freedom?

The beginnings of an answer are to be found in the Church's specific understanding of the nature of liberty. Right from the beginning of Christ's ministry, freedom was seen in terms of man's liberation *from* sin and his free submission to the one who sets us free: Jesus Christ. The New Testament attests to this over and over again. "For freedom," Saint Paul proclaims, "Christ set us free; so stand firm and do not submit again to the yoke of slavery" (Gal 5:1).[7]

The same conception of liberty is at the heart of Saint Augustine's great work *The City of God*: "the good man, although he is a slave, is free; but the bad man, even if he reigns, is a slave, and that not of one man, but, what is far more grievous, of as many masters as he has vices."[8] Of all the Roman pontiffs, the medieval pope Gregory VII perhaps did more than any other to help secure the Church's freedom (*libertas ecclesiae*) from the princes of this world. Nevertheless Gregory affirmed that full freedom in the Christian sense can only be realized through the freedom of life in the Lord in eternity.[9]

This understanding of freedom differed from the idea of liberty articulated by particular pagan writers whose influence is still felt today. The Roman philosopher Cicero, for instance, understood freedom as being able to live as one wishes.[10] Yet the difference between his position and that of Catholicism should not be exaggerated. Cicero also viewed the attachment to freedom as something that distinguished people like his fellow Romans from barbarians.[11] In that sense, Cicero also associated freedom with *civilized* people: the implication being that civilized people *don't* do whatever they want whenever they want to. Instead they seek to offer *reasons* for their choices that go beyond the "because I just felt like it" argument of adolescents seeking to justify themselves to disapproving parents.

Pope Leo XIII is perhaps most famous for inaugurating the modern tradition of Catholic social teaching with his 1891 encyclical *Rerum Novarum*. Rather fewer people know that the same pope devoted an entire encyclical to the subject of freedom. Published in 1888, *Libertas Praestantissimum* (On the Nature of Liberty) stressed the Church's recognition that the widespread yearning for freedom that seemed so characteristic of modernity was something that the Church had always affirmed. God had made man *free*. This meant that the Church did not see freedom as a feature of life to be simply tolerated. The very first sentences of *Libertas* begin by insisting that liberty is the "highest of natural endowments."[12]

Such an explicit affirmation of freedom by a pope living in the modern world was important for two reasons. First, it represented an effort by the Church to demonstrate that a concern for freedom was not somehow the exclusive property of the French Revolution, its Enlightenment progenitors, and their nineteenth-century liberal (and usually anti-Catholic) offspring. The Church, Leo wanted to make clear, was not an enemy of freedom. Second, it allowed the Church to enter into contemporary debates about the *nature* of liberty: an engagement that involved affirming particular modern insights but also offering necessary amplifications, correctives, and, when necessary, rebuttals.

Libertas particularly stressed that liberty was in no way to be equated with license: that is, a freedom detached from man's natural capacity for reason. Through reason, Leo affirmed, humans could know the *truth* about themselves, the natural world, and good and evil. With the aid of grace, human reason was thus able to free human beings from error and ignorance as they sought to freely orient their will, know these truths and integrate them into their lives through their free choices and free actions.

Over the past fifty years, these and related matters have been particularly explored by many Catholic minds, especially popes John Paul II and Benedict XVI. One reason for this attention has been the very real threat to liberty emanating from sources such as Marxism-Leninism and radical jihadism. But many Catholics have also engaged these questions because they believe that most modern conceptions of liberty which prevail today—including those present throughout much of America—are inadequate because they don't do justice to the human person and his or her potential for excellence or the intimate connection between freedom and truth.

Called to Willfulness?

Strong conceptions of human flourishing are rarely invoked by many self-described modern people when they celebrate autonomy and individuality. Instead the idea of liberty is often subsumed into a juxtaposition of two visions of man.

One is the notion of the sovereign individual whose identity is largely to be found in his exercise of the will. The ends he chooses are not so important, provided they bring him pleasure rather than pain. More significant is the fact that this individual embodies *rights to choose*. This entails his liberation from as many constraints as possible in order to pursue whatever he finds pleasurable. The supposed contrast with this rather hedonistic conception of human beings is a vision of people as creatures essentially bound by obligations to others to whom they must simply submit: their families, civil associations, religious communities, and the state, among others.

These understandings of freedom are often traced back to early and late Enlightenment thinkers such as Locke, Hume, and Rousseau, not to mention nineteenth-century figures such as Hegel and Nietzsche. In truth, they enjoy a far longer pedigree; one that was present in the world of the ancient Greeks but which manifested itself with particular force in the writings of certain medieval theologians, most notably the Oxford Franciscan William of Ockham.

Much ink has been spilled, most notably by the Dominican moral theologian, the late Servais-Théodore Pinckaers, on the manner in which Ockham reshaped the world of ideas in the West. Ockham died in 1347. But it is difficult to downplay the influence of Ockham's conception of freedom as simply the neutral factor of choice that comes about when I exercise my will. Ockham's vision of freedom is not one of a will guided by reason toward the good. To Ockham's mind, freedom is simply liberty to choose. *What* I choose—what Catholic thinkers call the "object" of one's choice—is more or less irrelevant. What really matters is *that* I choose.[13]

Ockham's fully articulated position is more complicated than this. It is hard to deny, however, that his conception of freedom is what you find at the heart of most modern visions of liberty. It is not a view of freedom associated with truth. Nor does it have anything to do with the pursuit of "thick" conceptions of human happiness. Instead we are left with thoroughly self-absorbed human beings who simply make choices, and for whom happiness is a merely subjective state of mind that cannot be substantially distinguished from subjective states of unhappiness. Life subsequently becomes a matter of a contest of competing wills: my will against everyone else's wills, and everyone's wills against God's will.

The paradox is that such radical conceptions of autonomy (which plainly imply that nothing is intrinsically good or intrinsically evil) have actually provided fertile ground for the *expansion* of government power and the *diminishment* of freedom. Without any way of distinguishing which choices are rational and ought to be encouraged from those that are thoroughly irrational and to be discouraged, and absent any sense that certain things may never be done, the way is open for individuals (the Leader) or groups (the Party) to impose order through the state once they gain control.

Lacking, however, is any objective criteria to define the extent of this government-imposed order. The result is an inability to limit the growth of state power. This in turn facilitates arbitrary raw power—that, which by its nature, destroys human liberty, human dignity, and, all too often, human life itself.

Freedom as Flourishing

Central to Catholic efforts to lay out conceptions of human freedom that counter the Ockhamite visions of liberty that dominate large swaths of Western culture (including, alas, the outlook of many Americans and Catholics) has been the development and articulation of:

- a vision of man which explains *who* he is, how he becomes happy, and the content of that happiness;
- a conception of practical reason which enables moral principles to be naturally known (hence, the phrase "natural law") and applied in the realm of practical judgment; and
- an understanding of the virtues that shape and integrate human dispositions, and which subsequently give life to the possibility of living in a free society.

Many of the Catholic thinkers seeking to develop this understanding of freedom and human flourishing after the Second Vatican Council have been found in the Anglo-American world. Theologians and philosophers such as the American Catholic scholars Germain Grisez, Joseph Boyle, Robert George, and their Oxford-based Anglo-Australian collaborator John Finnis have sought to identify the content of human happiness in terms of what they call "reasons for action" or "basic human goods." These include goods such as life and health, friendship, marriage (one man and one woman for life and open to new life), knowledge, integrity, beauty, work, religion (understood as our ordering of our choices and actions in accordance with the truth about the transcendent), and the exercise of what Benedict XVI called "creative reason."[14]

The *basicness* of these goods arises from the fact that they are all intrinsically and fundamentally good. This being the case, human flourishing consists in reverencing, actively choosing, and never intentionally violating any of these goods. These goods and our participation in them are the very stuff of human happiness. They point to the ultimate contentment which is found in contemplation of God in the fellowship of the saints.

So how does a human being flourish?[15] The argument of Grisez, Boyle, George, and Finnis—echoing age-old Catholic teaching—is that he does so *in the process of free choice*. When we freely choose one or more of these goods, we integrate them into our identity through our deliberation, choices, and actions. These choices about ourselves *last* until they are negated by a contrary choice. In this sense, humans are truly *self*-determining and *self*-determined beings. For better and for worse, we *become* the content of our free choices. Centuries ago, Saint Thomas Aquinas described this process in the following manner:

> Action is of two sorts: one sort—action [*actio*] in a strict sense—issues from the agent into something external to change it . . . the other sort—properly called activity [*operatio*]—does not issue into something external but remains within the agent itself perfecting it.[16]

The more we freely choose to act in a virtuous way, the more virtuous we become. Thus we achieve a type of *self-mastery* over our actions and therefore ourselves. As the French Dominican theologian Réginald Garrigou-Lagrange wrote, virtue "grows thus into a second nature which these acts make easy and connatural."[17] We endeavor to live according to what is most excellent in ourselves precisely as human beings. This makes us fully human and fully alive.

This Catholic understanding of free choice and human flourishing contrasts sharply with not only Ockham's position, but also many post-Reformation and most post-Enlightenment views. It implicitly contradicts, for example, modern claims—traceable to at least Thomas Hobbes—that our identity is relatively unaffected by our free choices and actions, or that we know who we are through what happens to us in the sense of *experiencing feelings and urges* rather than through forming and carrying out *freely-willed acts*.

The beauty of the Catholic conception of human flourishing is that it endows human freedom with a significance that goes beyond simply exercising the will for the sake of exercising the will, or choice for choice's sake. Of course we *do* experience a type of liberty when we make a choice, willy-nilly, for something. For (if we might speak theologically for the moment) while grace actualizes our liberty, it doesn't eliminate our ability to resist God's love and the insights of natural reason. Five hundred years ago, the Council of Trent considered this such an important point that it even specified that our free will, moved by God, can still dissent if the person so wills.[18]

But what is our liberty *really* worth if it leads to one's inner disintegration, or if it reduces our reason to being nothing more than what the Scottish Enlightenment philosopher David Hume called "the slave of our passions"?[19] Two centuries before Hume, Saint Thomas More had pointed out that we all have the capacity to concoct many "worldly fantasies" of our own making.[20] Yet in More's words: "Is it not a beastly thing to see a man that has reason so rule himself that his feet may not bear him, but . . . rolls and reels until he falls into the gutter?"[21] More also knew that our capacity to sin is not, strictly speaking, included in the Catholic conception of freedom. As many a Catholic theologian has stressed, sin is properly understood as a *defectibility* of our liberty, just as our errors are a defectibility of our intellect. In this sense we can say that genuine liberty is *always* about willing the good rather than evil.[22]

In late 2012, Benedict XVI summed up this Catholic understanding of freedom and human flourishing in a beautiful reflection on the Ten Commandments:

> God has given us the Commandments to educate us to liberty and genuine love, so that we can be truly happy. They are a sign of the love of God the Father, of his desire to teach us the correct discernment of good and evil, of the true and the false, of the just and the unjust. They are comprehensible to all precisely because they establish the fundamental values in concrete norms and rules, in putting them into practice man can walk on the path of *true liberty*, which renders him firm in the way that leads him to *life* and *happiness*.[23]

Life, liberty, and the path to happiness are thus, for the Catholic, inseparable. Without the guarantee of life, freedom is impossible. Without liberty, one cannot pursue happiness. But happiness is not whatever we want it to be. Happiness has *content* to which the Commandments point: love of the one true God, love of knowledge of truth, respect for life, love of family, respect for property and the possessions of others. Divine Revelation tells us these things are good in themselves. So too does human reason. Who, after all, can *reasonably* argue that they prefer irrationality to reason, or ugliness to beauty?

Liberty and Pluralism

As anyone who has taught undergraduate students knows, any conversation about freedom and human flourishing inevitably generates the question of whether "thick" conceptions of human flourishing invariably leads to undue restraints on liberty. What space, for example, does the Catholic vision of liberty and happiness leave for individuality?

The answer to this question is twofold. First, the Church's view of human flourishing is indeed *non*-relativistic. Happiness is *not* to be found in hedonism or sheer willfulness. Yet each person's precise way of participating in all the goods at the heart of human flourishing *is* going to be different. It is partly determined by our particular talents, opportunities, and circumstances. The person with great musical talents has the possibility of being creative in ways that differ from those with a unique instinct for economic entrepreneurship. Dante was not a great artist, but he was an exceptional writer. Dante's precise way of participating in the good of beauty was thus different from Michelangelo's. But both were able to realize beauty.

Pluralism and difference need not therefore imply relativism about the good. *E pluribus unum* proclaims the Seal of the United States: "Out of many, one." There are as many individual paths toward freely realizing the one end of human flourishing and happiness as there are Americans. The precise way in which even quite similar people realize any number of virtues is often quite different. Yet none of this implies we cannot say *this* action is virtuous while *that* habit constitutes vice. Marital fidelity is *always* meritorious. Adultery is *always* sinful.

Human flourishing, however, is not a solitary exercise. Even the most radical individualist has to concede the truth of human sociability, whether in terms of civilizing children into responsible adulthood, or starting and growing a business.

Our need of others poses us with opportunities and challenges for freedom and human flourishing. How do societies preserve the space we all need if we are to make free choices for ourselves? How do we avoid the temptation to allow most of our choices to be made for us by other people? How do we address the fact that some people will always be tempted to think they can assume responsibility for others' well-being, if only they are given sufficient authority to arrange matters?

Establishing the precise conditions in a given society that promote the flourishing of thousands if not millions of free, social, sinful, creative, and therefore different individual human beings is thus an extremely delicate undertaking. This truth brings us straight to an important concept that has long formed a key element of Catholic reflection about the political, social, and economic order: the common good.

Freedom and the Common Good

When many Catholics hear this expression, they are inclined to imagine that it amounts to some type of a theological version of a "social contract" or a warrant for extensive economic intervention. The common good is not, however, a license for governments to do whatever they want.

Summarizing the Catholic understanding of this idea, the Second Vatican Council gave a very precise definition to the common good. It embraces, the Council Fathers wrote, "the sum of those conditions of the social life whereby men, families and associations more adequately and readily may attain their own perfection."[24]

Note carefully the words "attain their own perfection." That *is* the end of the common good: human flourishing. Promoting the common good must therefore be about *helping*—as opposed to attempting to realize directly—the flourishing of *all* human beings in a given society. Because no matter how conducive or difficult the conditions are to human flourishing, it will not occur unless people *freely choose* moral and spiritual goods through their actions.

The need for people to make free choices does not imply a government-free society. Many of the factors that constitute key conditions of the common good (such as the protection of all innocent life from arbitrary lethal force) necessitate an authority charged with unique responsibility for deterring and punishing certain choices (e.g., murder) that directly undermine these goods.

Sorting out the state's specific responsibilities vis-à-vis the common good and the flourishing of all members of a society is, however, far from a simple affair. For if governments constantly sought to predetermine our decisions, our scope for free choice would become unduly limited. On the other hand, the absence of certain prerequisites that rely heavily upon state authority for their effectiveness can drastically limit our opportunities for free choice and human flourishing.[25]

The situation is even more complicated once we recognize that while some conditions associated with the common good are essential for human flourishing, others are more relative. The rule of law, for example, is a permanent requirement of the common good. Everyone's opportunities for flourishing are dramatically undermined by its absence. Other conditions of the common good are more subject to circumstances. We permit governments to do things during natural disasters, for example, that we would never tolerate in normal circumstances.

A further wrinkle is introduced by a factor that our post-Enlightenment world has enormous difficulty getting its mind around: the reality of sin. While Christ saved us from the first sin of our parents, the effects of what the Church calls original sin remain everywhere. All of us (even the saints) subsequently often misuse our freedom in order to sin. That in turn means that while holiness is possible in this world, God-like perfection is not.

This has profound implications for how we understand the relation between freedom and the common good. As Benedict XVI wrote in his perhaps least-commented upon but arguably most insightful encyclical, *Spe Salvi*, Marxism could not help but leave behind "a trail of appalling destruction" precisely because Marx "forgot man and he forgot man's freedom."[26] In other words, once we accept the reality of human liberty, we know that our society or economy, local or global, can never be static, never perfect, never completely just. There is no human-engineered end of history.

One effect of this truth should surely be to inject a sober Augustinian realism into how we think about freedom and justice in the economy. Utopian thinking not only denies the reality of human sinfulness; it invariably suffocates human freedom in the name of justice. Hence while the common good partly involves striving to make economic life more just, we should be very wary of any impulse within ourselves that would lead us in the direction of attempting to use the state to realize the fullness of justice in the economy here and now.

There is, however, a positive side to this. The fact of sin and human imperfectability reminds us that the fullness of the flourishing we seek lies in *the world which is to come*, the gates of which have been opened for us by Christ's Resurrection. Secular utopians, deprived of such a hope, have no choice but to imagine that human perfection lies in a this-worldly future, and therefore can be attained by human means. But, as history tells us, such strivings *always* end in hubris and the creation of nightmares such as the class and race-based totalitarianisms of the twentieth century.

In our daily reality, we know that the economic goods produced through human minds, human initiative and human work have their own value. But such goods do not last. They eventually break down, malfunction, corrode, or find themselves being consumed, replaced or superseded. And like all worldly things, they eventually disappear from our lives when we die.

What *does* last, the Church teaches, is our participation in those moral goods which is realized through human free choice and action and which anticipate the Kingdom that is to come. At the Second Vatican Council, the Council Fathers made this very point in one of the most important conciliar documents, *Gaudium et Spes*:

> For after we have obeyed the Lord, and in His Spirit nurtured on earth the values of human dignity *[humanae dignitatis]*, brotherhood *[communionis fraternae]* and freedom *[libertatis]*, and indeed all the good fruits of our nature and enterprise, we will find them again, but freed

of stain, burnished and transfigured, when Christ hands over to the Father: "a kingdom eternal and universal, a kingdom of truth and life, of holiness and grace, of justice, love and peace."[27]

This is how Catholicism understands the ultimate significance of our flourishing in this world, including in the economy. Such flourishing contributes to building up the world that will be fully realized when Christ comes at the end of time. It's an understanding of human liberty and human flourishing that saves us from the dilemma of those Greek philosophers who posited human excellence for its own sake, but couldn't reconcile it with the pagan view of the gods as capricious, manipulative, and occasionally vicious creatures who used and abused human beings as mere toys. It also confers upon human choices, acts, and enterprises a significance that makes even some of the most apparently ordinary choices and actions potentially extraordinary, and which remind us of why human freedom truly matters in this life and its continuation in the next.

Liberty and a Republic of Virtue

With the exception of Charles Carroll, all of the American Signers of the Declaration of Independence were Protestants of various confessions, albeit with differing levels of commitment to their respective faiths. A good number of them were far removed indeed in their personal theological beliefs from the God revealed in the Scriptures and ultimately in the Person of Jesus Christ. Even among those who were active and convinced believers, few explicated in detail upon matters such as the relationship between reason and the will, let alone how these relate to human flourishing.

Nonetheless the vision of freedom outlined above is not utterly incompatible with the understanding of the nature and ends of liberty articulated by many of America's Founders; nor would it have seemed incomprehensible to them. In the first place, they appealed over and over again to "God" and "Providence." In the case of someone like Jefferson, these references can and perhaps should be read as reflecting the position of someone inclined to a version of Deism.[28] Yet such words also imply there *is* purpose and design in creation, including human beings, human reason, and human liberty. That alone provides something of a starting point for a genuine conversation between Catholicism and many of the ideas articulated in the American Founding.

On a number of occasions, Catholics have sought to initiate precisely such a discussion by drawing attention to parallel claims made by America's Founders and those of the Catholic Church. As John Paul II himself said in an address to the American ambassador to the Holy See in 1997:

> The Founding Fathers of the United States asserted their claim to freedom and independence on the basis of certain "self-evident" *truths* about the human person: truths which could be discerned in human nature, built into it by "nature's God." Thus they meant to bring into being, not just an independent territory, but a great experiment in what George Washington called "ordered liberty:" an experiment in which men and women would enjoy equality of rights and opportunities in the pursuit of happiness and in service to the common good.[29]

Several decades earlier, John Courtney Murray, S.J., had made a similar point. "The American Proposition," he explained, "rests on the . . . conviction that there are truths; that they can be known; for if they are not held, assented to, worked into the texture of institutions, there can be no hope of founding a true City."[30]

Some of the Founders were willing to affirm that this nexus between freedom and truth went beyond those moral truths about the person that the government is obliged to recognize and protect as rights. In the case of Charles Carroll, for example, one hears profound echoes of the Catholic vision of freedom. His father—Charles Carroll of Annapolis—

admonished the young Carroll to remember that "The rest of your Life will be a continued sense of ease and satisfaction, if you keep invariably in the Paths of Truth of Virtue."[31] Freedom, happiness, and the good life were thus, to Carroll senior's mind, inseparable.

Carroll of Carrollton himself had no doubt that the Christian God, rather than the Deists' anonymous Supreme Being, had charged man with using his freedom to realize the good. Writing to his only son, Charles Carroll of Homewood, a dissolute wife-beating alcoholic, not long before Easter in 1821, Carroll of Carrollton quoted Psalm 14:1 and told him:

> "The impious has said in his heart, 'There is *no God*.'" He would willing[ly] believe there is no God; his passions, the corruption of his heart would feign persuad[e] him there is not; the strings of conscience betray the emptiness of the delusion . . . [T]he heavens proclaim the existence of God and unperverted reason teaches that He must love virtue and hate vice, and reward the one and punish the other.[32]

Carroll's Catholicism meant that his vision of human liberty was never going to be precisely the same as that of a Deist like Franklin or even a Presbyterian like Witherspoon. But what the Catholic shared with the Deist and the Protestant was a notion of freedom as one of *liberty as self-government*. However debauched may have been the lives of particular Founders, it is hard to find eulogies to hedonism, let alone efforts to radically cordon off the claims that the truth known by reason make upon human freedom, in the Founders' writings. And for many of them, "unperverted reason" did indicate that our freedom found its apex in the realization of virtue.

For the Founders had little doubt that a *virtuous* citizenry was a prerequisite to the stability of a free republic. No one can seriously doubt that most of them would have regarded modern hedonistic accounts of liberty as not only intellectually shallow but also deeply corrosive of a society's capacity to remain free. James Madison, for example, informed the Virginia Assembly that limited republican government without a virtuous society was "chimerical."[33] Likewise Jefferson insisted without equivocation in his *Notes on the State of Virginia* that virtue "is the manners and spirit of a people which preserve a republic in vigor."[34] Inspired in many cases by reflection on the writings of Romans such as Cicero and eighteenth-century philosophers such as Montesquieu, they spoke of virtues such as honesty, trust, and industriousness, but also of marriage and religion.

Regarding the latter, they had few doubts about its centrality to free societies that took virtue seriously. In the year the American colonies declared independence, John Adams stressed in his correspondence that "Statesmen, my dear Sir, may plan and speculate for liberty, but it is religion and morality alone, which can establish the principles upon which freedom can securely stand."[35] Washington was thus hardly alone among the Founders when he proclaimed in his 1796 Farewell Address that public happiness could not be attained without religion or private morality.[36]

This doesn't mean that government and law have no role in shaping the moral order of free societies. The Founding Fathers never imagined that law could somehow be neutral or purely procedural. But a key insight of men such as Washington, Jefferson, Adams, and Madison was that if we are not willing to govern our free choices from "within," we should not be surprised if governments attempt to direct our choices from "without"—to the point whereby freedom itself gradually fades from our horizons and, along with it, our opportunities to partake of human flourishing.

Understood in this way, the ideal of liberty as self-government mitigates against not just self-enclosed individualism but also forced communalization from above. Charles Carroll understood this point extremely well. Commenting on the proposed Federal Constitution, he warned that once virtue ceases to prevail either as a reality or ideal in a free society, the laws would become "dead letters, their spirit and tendency being inconsistent with the general habits and disposition of such a People." Moreover, Carroll added, the potential for despotism becomes very real in such circumstances. "Such," he argued, "has been the destiny of every People, once free, but who knew not how to enjoy the blessings of freedom; who, suffering their liberty to become licentiousness . . . passed laws subversive of every principle of law and justice to glut their resentments and avarice."[37]

Some Catholics have expressed reservations about drawing too close a parallel between the Catholic vision of freedom and virtue with that of many of the Founders. As noted, the correlation is far from exact. Most of the Founders did not use the terminology employed by Aquinas and other scholastic writers. In some cases their understanding of natural law seems to owe more to figures like John Locke and his emphasis upon natural rights than the older, classical traditions of natural law reasoning. And while plenty of the overwhelming Protestant American colonists spoke of the New World in explicitly religious terms, their words were not precisely akin to the Second Vatican Council's particular description of the relationship between this world and the fullness of the Kingdom that will come at the end of time.

The thesis, however, that the Founders' vision of liberty is heavily rooted in Deism and scientific rationalism is much harder to sustain. The American Republic, John Courtney Murray noted, is simply incomprehensible without acknowledging its debt to the broader Western tradition that includes but also precedes the eighteenth century. That same tradition, Murray recognized, was decisively influenced by Christianity:

> The Bill of Rights was an effective instrument for the delimitation of government authority and social power, not because it was written on paper in 1789 or 1791, but because the rights it proclaimed had already been engraved by history of the conscience of a people. The American Bill

of Rights is not a piece of 18th century rationalist theory; it is far more the product of Christian history. Behind it one can see, not the philosophy of the Enlightenment but the older philosophy that had been the matrix of the common law. The "man" whose rights are guaranteed in the face of law and government is, whether he knows it or not, the Christian man, who had learned to know his own personal dignity in the school of Christian faith.[38]

As the political scientist Donald Lutz illustrated thirty years ago, of the 3,154 citations made in the writings of America's Founders, approximately 34 percent came from the Bible. William Blackstone[39] and Montesquieu[40] accounted for 7.9 percent and 8.3 percent each, while Locke and David Hume amounted to 2.9 percent and 2.7 percent respectively.[41]

Such facts should make anyone hesitate before subscribing to the notion that secular Enlightenment thought is the cornerstone of the American Founding. Though he recognized that they were "tinged with the philosophy of the day," the French Catholic philosopher Jacques Maritain's surveys of the Founders' writings quickly made it evident to him as an outsider that while "[t]he Founding Fathers were neither metaphysicians nor theologians . . . their philosophy of life, and their political philosophy, their notion of natural law and of human rights, were permeated with concepts worked out by Christian reason and backed up by an unshakeable religious feeling."[42]

Freedom, the Good Life . . . and the Economy?

The daily grind of life in a market economy seems far removed indeed from the noble vision of liberty, human flourishing, and the virtues sketched above. Yet the idea of regarding commerce and business as humdrum activities unworthy of men of their stature would not have occurred to most of America's founding generation. For all their interest in the world of ideas, neither politics nor political involvement was the all-consuming, even obsessive exercise for many of American Founders that it is for some Americans who choose to enter public life today.

No doubt this owed something to many of the Founders' fascination with inventiveness and that distinct Enlightenment concern for what was called "useful knowledge." Yet it also flowed from the fact that a good number of them were practical men of affairs pursuing business interests, with varying degrees of success. One area in which men like Washington, Jefferson, and Carroll differed from most of Western Europe's leading statesmen at the time was that they viewed commerce as entirely suitable for true gentlemen. For them, it was as much as a sphere for human endeavor as the arts, philosophy, astronomy, and letters. In short, business, economic liberty, and its supportive institutions constituted another realm of potential human flourishing—an insight that, to many people's surprise, is strongly affirmed by Catholicism.

Further Reading

Peter Berkowitz (ed.), *Never a Matter of Indifference: Sustaining Virtue in a Free Republic* (Stanford, CA: Hoover Institution Press, 2003).

Bradley J. Birzer, *American Cicero: The Life of Charles Carroll* (Wilmington, DE: ISI Books, 2010).

John Finnis, *Natural Law and Natural Rights* (Oxford: Clarendon Press, 1980).

Germain Grisez, *Fulfillment in Christ: A Summary of Christian Moral Principles* (Notre Dame, IN: University of Notre Dame Press, 1991).

Pope John Paul II, Encyclical Letter *Veritatis Splendor* (1993), http://www.vatican.va/holy_father/john_paul_ii/encyclicals/documents/hf_jp-ii_enc_06081993_veritatis-splendor_en.html.

Servais Pinckaers, O.P., *The Sources of Christian Ethics.* Translated by Sister Mary Thomas Noble (Washington, DC: Catholic University of America Press, 1995).

Chapter 2
An Economy of Liberty

Economic initiative is an expression of human intelligence and of the necessity of responding to human needs in a creative and cooperative fashion. . . . The sense of responsibility that arises from free economic initiative takes not only the form of an individual virtue required for individual human growth, but also of a social virtue that is necessary for the development of a community in solidarity.

Compendium of the Social Doctrine of the Catholic Church[1]

After all, the chief business of the American people is business.

Calvin Coolidge[2]

Alongside John Witherspoon, Charles Carroll has a good claim to being one of the best educated of America's Founders. Having spent time at the illegal Jesuit academy of Bohemia Manor in Maryland, he was sent by his father to Flanders in what is now Belgium to study at the English Jesuit College of Saint Omers. Here Carroll experienced the disciplined classical curriculum imparted by the Jesuits known as the *Ratio Studiorum*. Carroll then spent a year at the Jesuit college in Rheims before moving on to further study and eventually the presentation of a thesis (written in Latin) at the Collège Louis-le-Grand in Paris where he was granted his degree. This was followed by courses in law in Bourges and Paris, before five more years of law (but also surveying, geometry, trigonometry and what was known as the "Italian" method of double-entry bookkeeping) in London. Along the way, Carroll was exposed to classical minds such as Cicero, Virgil, and Horace; Roman and French civil law; English common law; Enlightenment thinkers (Montesquieu in particular, but also John Locke and Isaac Newton) as well as Thomistic scholars, most notably Aquinas himself and the sixteenth-century Jesuit Francisco Suárez. By necessity, Carroll acquired fluent French and a solid command of Greek and Latin.[3]

All this learning equipped Carroll superbly for life in Maryland and American politics. But his father had fully intended that such an education would also provide him with the moral and intellectual discipline as well as the practical business and financial skills needed to maintain and grow the Carroll family fortune.[4] And Carroll turned out, like his father and grandfather, to be a hardworking and immensely successful businessman—so much so that when George Washington thought of making him ambassador to France in 1796, he eventually decided not to do so. Carroll's devotion to his private economic affairs, Washington concluded, made it "morally certain he could not be prevailed on to go."[5]

Carroll's commercial interests extended far beyond those of the typical Maryland planter of the time. They ranged from grain products to livestock, small cloth factories, building crafts, cattle, mills, and orchards. Somehow he managed to combine this with land speculation and the expansion of an ironworks business created by his father and a consortium of Maryland businessmen—the Baltimore Company—which by 1770 was producing a then-incredible seventy tons of pig-iron each month. As well as investing and trading in domestic and European markets, Carroll engaged in loans to other planters and businessmen, charging them market interest rates. At one point, Carroll even authored a document defending the legality and morality of compound interest. And, it must be said, like many other Americans of the time, a portion of Carroll's assets consisted of slaves.[6]

His commercial success did not, however, mean that what Carroll often called the "habit of business" became suffocating for him. He would have thoroughly agreed with Calvin Coolidge that "the accumulation of wealth cannot be justified as the chief end of existence."[7] Though he worked incredibly hard at reducing costs, increasing his profit margins, and growing his business ventures, Carroll was also heavily involved in revolutionary-era politics in Maryland and the United States. Alongside these pursuits, Carroll was an active and generous philanthropist and a significant player in Catholic affairs in Maryland. In the midst of all this, Carroll also found time before, during, and after the Revolution to read the works of prominent *philosophes* such as Voltaire and Rousseau—and to find their critiques of orthodox Christianity thoroughly unconvincing.[8]

Carroll's catholicity of interests and endeavors prefigured the path of many other American business leaders. When the great French social philosopher Alexis de Tocqueville, author of perhaps the most important book on American political culture, *Democracy in America*, visited the United States in the early 1830s (during which visit he met Charles Carroll), he was stunned at the spirit of enterprise that characterized the republic. Americans, Tocqueville soon grasped, were a commercial people.[9]

At first Tocqueville thought Americans—particularly New Yorkers!—were obsessed by the pursuit of wealth. Yet after a few weeks, he noticed something else about American society. For all their apparent concern with acquiring riches, Tocqueville realized American merchants were quite religious, unfailingly polite, surprisingly well informed about foreign affairs, and possessed of strong philanthropic instincts, a respect for education, and a taste for fine art and good conversation.

Another feature of American life that profoundly impressed Tocqueville was the degree to which commerce was seen as integral to America's attachment to liberty. "Americans," he wrote in *Democracy in America*, "do regard their freedom as the best tool of and the firmest guarantee for their prosperity."[10] In that regard, Tocqueville noted, they reflected a more general pattern that had been underscored a century earlier by Montesquieu. "I doubt," Tocqueville stated, "if one can cite a single example of any people engaged in both manufacture and trade, from the men of Tyre to the Florentines and the English, who were not a free people. There must therefore be a close link and necessary relationship between these two things, that is, freedom and industry."[11]

Some may quibble about the general empirical applicability of that last statement. But in America's case, the concern and appreciation for commerce and economic freedom more generally has always formed a major part of the canopy of causes that associate themselves with movements to limit government power. The American revolutionaries especially resented the strictures placed upon economic life by Britain's adherence to the distinctly government-oriented economic system otherwise known as mercantilism. Perhaps it is not a complete coincidence that the Declaration of Independence and the book most associated with the modern case for economic liberty—Adam Smith's *Wealth of Nations*—were published in the same year. They partook of the dominant spirit of the time: a love for liberty.

Catholic thinkers have long seen the practical connection between the prospects of freedom and the habits and institutions of economic liberty. But the Catholic vision of economic freedom goes beyond this. The author of one of the most discussed books in recent times on the case for free markets, the philosopher John Tomasi, correctly points out that what he calls the Catholic free market tradition offers a particularly rich vein of *principled* arguments in favor of economic freedom and its political corollary of limited government.[12]

Catholics, Business, and Human Flourishing

A great paradox of the anti-Catholic laws which prevailed throughout Britain and its North American colonies for much of the sixteenth, seventeenth, and eighteenth centuries is that it left many talented Catholics with little else to do but make money. Until the Catholic relief laws began to be passed in Britain in the late eighteenth century, Catholics were barred from entering government service, much of the legal profession, the military, and political life. Many subsequently went into business and associated professions such as commercial legal practice. Unable to spend their wealth on acquiring political, civil, or military office, many such Catholic families grew rich.[13]

Charles Carroll, his father, and his grandfather were among the first of a long line of thriving Catholic American business leaders and entrepreneurs. They range from figures such as former Treasury Secretary William E. Simon (1927–2000), to former CIA director William Casey (1913–1987). Closer to Carroll's own time, there was the former slave and daily Mass attendee Pierre Toussaint (1766–1853).

Declared Venerable by the Church in 1996 and the first layperson to be buried in the crypt below the main altar of Saint Patrick's Cathedral on New York's Fifth Avenue, this former Haitian slave established his own hairdressing business, purchased the freedom of his sister and his wife, and generated enough wealth to become one of the most generous Catholic philanthropists of his time. A personally frugal man, Toussaint also created a credit bureau for the poor, helped Haitian refugees receive an education, assisted them in finding jobs, and took a special interest in aiding orphans.

One undoubted contribution of business to the common good are the resources created by commerce—which allows people like Pierre Toussaint to be generous with the less fortunate. To this, however, we should note some of the less-noticed benefits of the creation of wealth, such as providing people with jobs and wages, aspiring entrepreneurs with loans of capital, and governments with tax revenues.

Unhappily, the connection between business, economic freedom, and human flourishing has never been especially obvious for some Catholic Americans. Despite the long and honorable history of American Catholics in business, many American Catholics (especially intellectuals who have imbibed all the academy's longstanding prejudices against business) remain somewhat suspicious of private enterprise and the market economy more generally.

So why the wariness and misgivings? The story is complicated, but parts of it require unfolding so that the way can be cleared for explaining all the reasons why Catholics can and should emphasize the material and moral potential of free enterprise and the free economy, without falling into the heresy of the prosperity gospel that afflicts parts of Evangelical Protestantism in Africa, Latin America, and also, sadly enough, the United States.

The Social Question

At the time of the American Revolution, Catholics were a tiny percentage of the population of the thirteen American colonies. When Charles Carroll's cousin John Carroll was consecrated bishop of Baltimore in 1790, his flock numbered a mere 35,000 out of a total American population of something close to 4,000,000 souls.[14]

This situation was transformed by successive waves of immigration from European Catholic countries from the mid-nineteenth century onward, not to mention nations with large Catholic minorities such as Germany. Possessing little by way of formal education or technical skills, many of these immigrants gravitated to jobs in heavy industry such as mining. Some consequently found themselves working in the difficult conditions that were part and parcel of mid-to-late–nineteenth–century industrial capitalism.

The situation of these Catholic migrants was further complicated by the fact that they often did not speak English and regularly encountered considerable prejudice from many American-born Protestants. Though presumably preferable to the quasi-servitude many of them had endured in Europe, these conditions created fertile soil for many of these newly minted Catholic Americans to develop skeptical views about industrial capitalism, to become seriously attracted to possible alternatives, and to view trade unions and government intervention as ways of ameliorating their situations.

This development was set against a more general background of the Church, beginning with Leo XIII's famous 1891 encyclical *Rerum Novarum*, expressing serious critiques of nineteenth-century capitalism. Modern Catholic social teaching has always condemned Marxism and socialism outright. The popes have also offered defenses affirming the basic morality of institutions such as private property and processes such as free exchange. Nevertheless the Church has always criticized various abuses (worker exploitation, poor working conditions, etc.) that many regard as peculiarly characteristic of capitalism and which lay at the heart of what nineteenth-century European and North Americans referred to as the "social question."

The fact that such evils have occurred in many other economic systems such as the ancient world's slave-driven economies, not to mention socialist and communist systems, often goes unremarked. But notwithstanding these details, concerns about real and imagined abuses associated with capitalism have inspired many Catholics over the past 120 years to advocate heavy regulation of the economy, generous welfare states, and in some cases the idea of a "Third Way"—a form of economic life that sought to preserve the best of market economies while integrating them into a wider framework of extensive government intervention. One post-war Italian Prime Minister, Amintore Fanfani, exemplifies such thinking.

Like many European Christian Democrat politicians of the twentieth century, Fanfani came from an intellectual background, writing a number of influential works on economic history. His most read book, *Catholicism, Protestantism and Capitalism*, was published in 1935—a time in which the overwhelming majority of intellectuals from the European left, right, and center had one thing in common: the conviction that the capitalism of the pre-Great War world had run its course and needed to either be completely rejected or modified beyond recognition.

Fanfani was strongly anti-Communist and no advocate of collectivism. He never wavered, however, in his criticism of what he called the "capitalist spirit." Capitalism, Fanfani claimed, "requires such a dread of loss, such a forgetfulness of human brotherhood, such a certainty that a man's neighbor is merely a customer to be gained or a rival to be overthrown." As an economic system, he added, it holds "that wealth is simply a means for the unlimited, individualistic and utilitarian satisfaction of all possible human needs." These claims led Fanfani to conclude that there was "an unbridgeable gulf between the Catholic and the capitalist conception of life."[15]

Such ideas and sentiments were commonplace among twentieth-century European Catholic intellectuals and shared by many of their American brethren. Firm anti-Communism went hand in hand with considerable skepticism about many aspects of the market economy. The pervasiveness of such thinking was exacerbated by two factors: one secular, the other religious.

Liberalism, Protestant Ethics, and Mercantilism

The association of capitalism with what is often called liberalism has always created obstacles to Catholic engagement with the ideas and institutions of modern market economies. In this context, "liberalism" does not mean what most Americans associate with this phrase, that is, the New Deal, the Great

Society programs of the 1960s, and government's general expansion into economic life. Instead the word invokes particular forms of Enlightenment thinking as well as some of the intellectual and political movements that lead to and flowed from the French Revolution.

In many cases, European liberals advocated liberalizing markets through ending restrictive economic practices such as tariffs. The same liberals, however, were often quite anti-Christian and specifically anti-Catholic. For them, the Catholic Church was largely an obstacle to progress and greater illumination for all. Thomas Jefferson's reference in his letter of June 24, 1826 to Roger C. Weightman to "arousing men to burst the chains under which monkish ignorance and superstition had persuaded them to bind themselves" arguably contained more than a whiff of such thinking.

Nor can we ignore the fact that, for many Catholics, liberalism meant the French Revolution: the same Revolution that had guillotined an inept but arguably saintly Catholic king; promoted the mass murder of Catholic bishops, priests, and nuns; turned Catholic churches into temples through which prostitutes garbed as the "goddess of Reason" were paraded; looted church property; closed convents and monasteries; shuttered Catholic schools; and sought to separate the French Church from the See of Peter. And much of this was done in the name of "religious liberty"—understood as the state acting to "free" people from any religious beliefs that raised questions about the tenability of aspects of the Enlightenment project.

Given the post-Enlightenment linkage of free market ideas with liberalism, it's hardly surprising that many European and American Catholics had their suspicions about capitalism's intellectual associations. A second factor, however, made matters worse: the persistence in many Catholics' minds of the myth of a correlation between Protestantism and capitalism, a thesis whose most prominent proponent was the German sociologist Max Weber.

Weber is justly famous for many things, but especially for having developed a theory about the relationship between capitalism and religion. The influence of his *Protestant Ethic and the Spirit of Capitalism* (1905) remains considerable, not least because it has become a staple part of sociological literature on the subject.[16]

Based upon lectures he gave during a visit to America in 1904, Weber's *Protestant Ethic* maintained that capitalism's nature had to be understood as more than just producing and exchanging goods in a particular way (e.g., free exchange) within a particular institutional setting (limited government, rule of law, etc.). At its heart, Weber insisted, capitalism was a *state of mind*: the subordination of emotion, custom, tradition, folklore, and myth to the workings of instrumental reason.

The real controversy begins, however, with Weber's argument that the decisive linkage of this form of rationality with economic practices occurred primarily in Europe's predominantly Protestant areas. He especially was thinking of countries such as England and the Netherlands which were home to large numbers of Puritans and Calvinists, many of whom migrated to North America in the seventeenth century. These forms of Protestantism, Weber posited, engrained the belief among its adherents that they should avoid superficial hobbies, games, and entertainment. Instead Christians should commit themselves totally to whatever calling to which God had summoned them.

Weber believed these forms of Protestantism, especially their central doctrine of predestination, helped to foster the type of focused minds and disciplined work habits that are essential for capitalist economies. According to Weber, these ascetic Protestants didn't believe it was possible to do good works to attain heaven in the next world. Either you were among the elect, or you were not. Weber interpreted Calvin as suggesting that one indication of election was the acquisition of wealth. It followed—or so Weber's theory went—that the accumulation of wealth encouraged people to see themselves as destined to be saved. This in turn fostered a spirit among people that encouraged them to engage in growing ever greater amounts of wealth.

On the surface, Weber's proposition makes considerable sense. After all, many culturally Catholic countries like Portugal and Spain—not to mention almost all Latin American nations—*have* lagged behind other Western nations in terms of economic development. More careful analysis of Weber's claims, however, soon reveals them as less than adequate.

The accuracy, for instance, of Weber's interpretation of Calvinist theology is very much open to question. The Westminster Confession—the profession of faith that dominated Calvinist and Presbyterian theology from the sixteenth century onward, and upon which Weber drew in developing his ideas—indicates that the notion of "calling" in Puritan and Calvinist thinking is difficult to reconcile with the meaning given to it by Weber. The Confession clearly distinguishes between each person's worldly vocation and his ultimate calling. Moreover, the earthly calling of each individual is not considered to constitute a positive or negative contribution to that person's salvation.

The Westminster Confession also stresses that believers must ensure that their earthly vocation does not distract them from pursuing their heavenly calling. Weber by contrast seemingly conflates the two. And on the subject of vocation itself, the Confession insists that Christians choose "that employment or calling in which you may be most serviceable to God. Choose not that in which you may be most honorable in the world; but that which you may do most good and best escape sinning."[17] Nothing in the text suggests any particular emphasis on commerce, let alone the idea that acquiring material wealth was somehow a sign of being among the elect.

Second, the empirical evidence disproving Weber's connection between Protestantism and the emergence of capitalism is considerable. Even Catholic critics of modern capitalism—most notably Fanfani—have had to concede that "the commercial spirit" preceded the Reformation by at least two hundred years. From the eleventh century onward, the words *Deus enim et proficuum* ("For God and Profit") began to appear in the ledgers of Italian and Flemish merchants. This was not a medieval version of some type of prosperity gospel. Rather it symbolized just how naturally intertwined were the realms of faith and commerce throughout the world of medieval Catholic Europe. The pursuit of profit, trade, and commercial success dominated the life of the city-states of medieval and Renaissance Northern Italy, the towns of Flanders, not to mention the Venetian republic that exerted tremendous influence upon merchant activity throughout the Mediterranean long before Luther's Theses were posted in 1517.

Since Weber's time, much scholarly work has been done to illustrate the advanced state of market-driven economic development in the Middle Ages. Throughout the 1940s and 1950s, the Belgium scholar Raymond de Roover penned numerous articles demonstrating how during the Middle Ages financial transactions and banking more generally started to take on the degree of sophistication that is commonplace today.[18] Likewise in his magisterial *The Commercial Revolution of the Middle Ages*, the Italian-American historian of medieval European economic history, the late Robert S. Lopez, shattered the historical claims that formed much of the background to much of Weber's argument by demonstrating in detail how the Middle Ages "created the indispensible material and moral conditions for a thousand years of virtually uninterrupted growth."[19]

In more recent decades, the historians Edwin Hunt and James Murray have demonstrated just how much the medieval period was characterized by remarkable innovation in methods of business organization. They also suggest that the advent of modernity actually heralded the expansion of state economic intervention and regulation in an effort to constrain economic freedom.[20] In a similar fashion, the sociologist Rodney Stark has gathered together disparate sources of historical and economic analysis to illustrate the indisputable origins of capitalism and major breakthroughs in the theory and practice of wealth creation in the medieval period. Central to Stark's analysis is his highlighting of the way in which pre-Reformation Western Christianity saw the world as one in which humans were called upon to use their reason and innate creativity to develop the world—including economically.

Here one could add that, until Adam Smith, some of the most elaborate thinking about the nature of contracts, free markets, interest, wages, and banking that developed *after* the Reformation did not occur in those countries that, by and large, joined the Protestant revolt against Rome. The economist Alejandro Chafuen has written at length about the extent to which such thinking was articulated in the writings of Spanish Catholic scholastic thinkers of the sixteenth and seventeenth centuries. Theologians such as Francisco de Vitoria, O.P., Martín de Azpilcueta (otherwise known as Doctor Navarrus), Juan de Mariana, S.J., and Tomás de Mercado, O.P., anticipated many of the claims made by Smith two centuries later.[21]

To be sure, much of this thinking occurred by way of side effect rather than as a result of the systematic analysis embarked upon by Smith. As commercial relationships expanded throughout Europe in the centuries preceding and following the Reformation, there was a marked increase in the number of penitents asking their confessors for guidance about moral questions that had a strong economic dimension. What was the just price? When was a person no longer obliged to adhere to a contract? When was charging interest legitimate? When did it become usurious? As a result, priests looked to theologians for guidance on how to respond to their penitents' questions. Thus, as Jürg Niehans stressed in his *History of Economic Theory*:

The scholastics thus found it necessary to descend from theology into the everyday world of economic reality, of early capitalism, foreign trade, monopoly, banking, foreign exchange and public finance. What one knew about these things in the School of Salamanca was hardly less than Adam Smith knew two hundred years late, and more than most students know today.[22]

Even when we consider modern capitalism's emergence, a direct connection between this event and Protestantism is very open to question. In 1995, for instance, the economic historian Jacques Delacroix highlighted many facts about this period that Weber's theory simply cannot account for. "Amsterdam's wealth," Delacroix writes, "was centered on Catholic families; the economically advanced German Rhineland is more Catholic than Protestant; all-Catholic Belgium was the second country to industrialize, ahead of a good half-dozen Protestant entities."[23]

A better explanation for why some parts of Europe lagged behind others is to be found in the influence of absolutism and mercantilism. To our ears, "absolutism" is a word that contains echoes of despotic government. Yet the age of absolutism, which lasted throughout most of Europe from about 1600 until 1800, was a rather different phenomenon. Drawing heavily on the Divine Right of Kings (a theological doctrine always disputed by the Catholic Church) for legitimacy, absolutism was also associated with the rise of the nation-state that began before the Reformation, but which accelerated after 1517.

Absolutism's underlying motif was the conviction that centralizing state power was *the* path to stronger and wealthier societies.[24] In terms of commercial life, absolutism manifested itself in countries such as Lutheran Prussia, Catholic France, and Orthodox Russia in the form of ever-increasing restrictions upon economic freedom. Governments began assuming more top-down direction of economic activity through subsidizing exports, imposing tariffs upon imports, and mandating government monopolies of particular trade or products which were then sold or leased to groups of merchants. Adam Smith famously called this set of economic arrangements the *mercantile system*.

It is difficult to downplay mercantilism's effect upon modern economic development. From the Age of Discovery to the late nineteenth century (and in many cases beyond), Catholic Latin America was largely dominated by an absolutist, mercantilist economic culture. Therein lie, Stark contends, some of the fundamental causes of Latin America's slower economic development as compared to the United States.[25] Even the dominant eighteenth-century Protestant power, Britain, engaged in mercantilist economic practices despite having rejected a drift toward absolutism in the previous century. And as every student of the American Revolution knows, Britain's mercantilist economic policies contributed mightily to the outbreak of the War of Independence.

Much more could be said about these historical observations. The point, however, is that the widespread association of Catholicism with anti-capitalism is theologically dubious, empirically disprovable, and largely incidental. To make these observations is not to propose that modern capitalism was somehow constructed upon a "Catholic ethic." That would be equally false. It is simply to note that much of Weber's particular analysis is very questionable and that this should be acknowledged by economists, historians, and above all, by *Catholics*—American or otherwise. How ironic (and sad) it would be if the last people to believe in Weber's Protestant ethic thesis were Catholics!

Beyond Labor and Capital

How, then, might Catholics develop a vision for economic freedom consistent with its particular view of human freedom and human flourishing? One way forward is to begin with the same starting point with which the Church commences its discussion of human liberty: the nature of the human person.

Much modern Catholic reflection upon the economy has approached this subject through the categories of "labor" and "capital." These featured heavily in many secular (especially Marxist) approaches to addressing the same question during the nineteenth and twentieth centuries. Many Catholic scholars consequently considered it important to address capitalism using conceptual tools and frameworks familiar to non-Catholics.

Today, however, this framework's limitations are more obvious than ever. The juxtaposition of labor and capital sometimes encourages people to think that it is somehow only employees who work and whose labor creates economic value. This was central to Marx's argument about the exploitation of labor by those who owned capital.

A moment's reflection, however, soon makes one realize that *everyone* is a worker—not just employees but managers and owners as well. The work of a manager or owner or even investor is certainly different to that of an employee. But it is still work. It is also clear that, *contra* Marx but also Adam Smith, the economic value of a good or service is not determined by *how much labor* has been invested in it. The economic value of a good or service is reflected in its price, and natural law theory has generally regarded the normal measure of the value of an economic good to be the price it would be accorded in the settings of "the market" (*secundum communem forum*)—or so concluded Aquinas long ago.[26]

As for capital, we now understand that the concept can no longer be limited to the means of production or stored-up monetary resources. While people themselves are not capital (persons are ends in themselves—never mere means), the word "capital" can be used to describe non-material resources such as ideas, talents, education, and skills. Thus "labor" actually possesses its own "capital."

These insights directly challenge some of the ways many people have reflected upon modern economic life. Above all, they point to the fact that at the heart of free market economies is not so much labor or capital. Rather it is *creative* human beings who choose and act freely in the realm of supply and demand. In recent decades, the Catholic Church has not only had a great deal to say about this matter, but also linked it specifically to the end of human flourishing.

Humanity, Economic Creativity, and the Entrepreneur

Catholics have always given considerable attention to the theme of creativity. God's intelligence, the Church teaches, is the ultimate cause of every created good. It also holds there is an intelligent plan for the whole created universe. This schema is often referred to as "Providence." The Church views humankind as having a critical part in the unfolding of that plan through both extraordinary but also rather ordinary human choices and events. Hence while the Church teaches that the world created by God is a masterpiece, it also holds that the world can be made even better through human choice and action.

Modern Catholic social teaching has taken time to apply these theological insights to economic life. This is especially true regarding the significance of the entrepreneur and business more generally in fulfilling a role that might be described as one of "co-creativity." In 1969, the distinguished philosopher-economist who, by some accounts, helped to draft Pius XI's 1931 social encyclical *Quadragesimo Anno*, Father Oswald von Nell-Breuning, S.J., (who had his own criticisms of capitalism) made this theme a major element of his widely-read commentary on parts of the Second Vatican Council's *Gaudium et Spes*.

Given the Council's praise of the dynamism of modern economies as well as "an inventive spirit, and eagerness to create and to expand enterprises,"[27] Nell-Breuning thought it "all the more odd that the key-figure in this economy, *the entrepreneur*, is not mentioned in any way."[28] Businesses are, he noted, made up of people who contribute labor or capital. Nonetheless, Nell-Breuning insisted, the fact could not be ignored that "[w]ithout question, *intellectus* comes first, that is. . . initiative and enterprise."[29]

Prior to the 1980s, modern Catholic social teaching did make reference to the significance of economic freedom, albeit somewhat indirectly. In *Rerum Novarum*, Leo XIII insisted, against the prophets of socialism, that wage earners had the right to dispose of their earnings so that they had the chance to increase their wealth and improve their living standards.[30] The unstated assumption was that *everyone* had a right to use his or her economic resources in a creative manner, not simply business owners.

One suspects Nell-Breuning would be pleased to see just how far the Catholic Church has come over the past thirty years both in terms of underscoring the economic role of human creativity, but also in connecting these activities to human flourishing. Much of the credit here is due squarely to John Paul II.[31]

In his three social encyclicals—*Laborem Exercens*, *Sollicitudo Rei Socialis*, and *Centesimus Annus*—John Paul gradually unfolded a principled case for economic liberty. To be sure, he was not the first pope to describe economic initiative as a type of right. In 1963, for example, Blessed John XXIII stated in his encyclical *Pacem in Terris* that "man has the inherent right not only to be given the opportunity to work but also to be allowed the exercise of personal initiative in the work he does."[32] John Paul, however, significantly developed Catholic appreciation of this point in *Sollicitudo Rei Socialis*. Here it is worth citing his exact words:

[I]n today's world, among other rights, *the right of economic initiative* is often suppressed. Yet it is a right which is important not only for the individual but also for the common good. Experience shows us that the denial of this right, or its limitation in the name of an alleged "equality" of everyone in society, diminishes, or in practice absolutely destroys the spirit of initiative, that is to say *the creative subjectivity of the citizen.* As a consequence, there arises not so much a true equality as a "leveling down." In the place of creative initiative there appears passivity, dependence and submission to the bureaucratic apparatus.[33]

In these four compact sentences, John Paul II neatly summarized some major economic and political problems with the creaking, centrally-planned economies which dominated much of the world in 1987. But the pope was also making a moral point: economic initiative needs to be understood *as a right.* And the only being who possess rights is the human person—the being who exercises "creative subjectivity."

"Subject" here means the one who is creative and initiates free choices and free acts. This deepens our understanding of *why* economic initiative is a right. It expresses the truth that humans are, by nature, the initiators of economic acts. The phrase also indicates that economic initiative does more than create goods and services. As an act of the creative subject, economic initiative can involve humans freely choosing moral good. It is a way of realizing human flourishing.

In *Centesimus Annus*, John Paul is even more forthright on this matter. Deeper contemplation of how and why people actually work together in modern economies soon reveals to us some self-evident truths. For one thing, it illustrates the "increasingly evident and decisive" role of initiative and entrepreneurship.[34]

Two points are being made here. The first is economic. Entrepreneurship's centrality reminds us that, to cite John Paul's words, "besides the earth, man's principal resource is man himself. His intelligence enables him to discover the earth's productive potential and the many different ways in which human needs can be satisfied."[35]

Every human person is thus a potential entrepreneur, regardless of whether he works for himself or someone else. This puts human reason, human free will, and human creativity at the heart of the economy. Financial capital and technology certainly matter. But unless humans can deploy their reason to use financial capital, the means of production, and their own talents in creative ways, the economy will lack the dynamism it needs to sustain growth over time.

John Paul's second claim concerns the *non-material human development* that occurs through economic activity. Throughout his long life, Charles Carroll never ceased to emphasize the order and discipline which business and trade can introduce into people's lives. Over two hundred years later, John Paul affirmed that, through commerce, people can acquire "important virtues." These include "diligence, industriousness, prudence in undertaking reasonable risks, reliability and fidelity in interpersonal relationships, as well as courage in carrying out decisions which are difficult and painful."[36]

Reflection on the nature of prudence soon indicates to us just how central it is to everyday life in successful businesses. Contrary to what is often supposed, prudence is not simple pragmatism. Nor is it mere timidity or even shrewdness. In English, the word "prudent" implies cautiousness. The Latin *prudens*, meaning "wise" or "skillful," is closer to the true meaning of prudence, especially in commercial affairs.

But above all, prudence is first and foremost a virtue which involves three intellectual acts. The first is "counsel." This involves reflection and consultation as we study and identify the various means appropriate for realizing the end in mind. The second is "practical judgment": the formation of the actual choice to be made. The third is called *imperium*: directing the execution of the act. Aquinas specifies that living out all three aspects of prudence also requires people to learn and benefit from others' knowledge, to reflect with objectivity and without self-delusion upon their past choices, and to develop the ability to deal with unanticipated factors and situations—while simultaneously avoiding the temptations of being intemperate, timid, or unjust.[37]

Realizing the virtue of prudence is challenging, even at the best of times. It requires an understanding of principles (such as "one may never do evil that good may come of it"), open-mindedness, humility, foresight, and the willingness to research alternative possibilities. But though they may not think about it in these terms, many business executives and entrepreneurs have to act out the virtue of prudence all the time if they want their businesses to grow over the long term. Someone may stumble, for example, upon a new product or service which he instinctively grasps is going to be immensely attractive to consumers. But success in taking it to market, let alone sustaining sales or building a business around the product over the long term, requires *constant* decision making that follows the three acts of counsel associated with prudence.

Entrepreneurs and businesses unable to develop this habit will have great difficulty being successful. They also need the supplementary habits that Aquinas associates with prudence, so that it becomes "connatural" with their use of reason and exercise of free will. In markets which value business accountability and transparency, a succession of imprudent choices on the part of business leaders or even entire companies will simply not be tolerated for long periods of time. Imprudent executives soon find themselves looking for alternative employment. Likewise, companies that develop a reputation for making poor choices will have difficulty attracting investors and customers.

Business as Vocation, Free Enterprise as Calling

One welcome side effect of John Paul II's attention to entrepreneurship and business was the manner in which it encouraged greater reflection upon this subject throughout the Church. In one of the most penetrating of such analyses, Father Anthony G. Percy unfolds the positive affirmations of free enterprise and business which are found not only in modern Catholic social teaching but also in the Scriptures, the Church Fathers, the life of the medieval Church, as well as the post-Reformation period.

It is true, as Percy notes in his book *Entrepreneurship in the Catholic Tradition*, that Church Fathers such as Saint Basil and Saint John Chrysostom focused primarily upon questions of wealth distribution. Nor does it need to be restated that virtually every Catholic who has written about commerce has warned about the very real moral risks associated with life in business, such as the temptations of materialism and greed, or subordinating human dignity to profit. The same commentators also stress that those who create and possess wealth have, like everyone else, concrete obligations to those in need.

Alongside these caveats, however, Percy illustrates that many of the Church Fathers—including Basil and Chrysostom—showed "a remarkable capacity to appreciate the beauty and importance of entrepreneurial work."[38] Percy also surfaces a longstanding Catholic appreciation for the contribution of business and entrepreneurs to the common good. In one of the most interesting parts of his book, Percy explores Aquinas's counterintuitive explanation of how greed actually inhibits people involved in commerce from contributing to wealth creation. Summarizing Aquinas's reflections on this matter, Percy writes:

[I]f a man does not moderate his love for money, it would be highly unlikely that he would embark on a great and lofty undertaking. Motivated by an inordinate love for money, the immoderate man opts for a safer form of investment that would ensure returns and the protection of his original sum. No great projects would be undertaken as a result of his love for comfort and fear of risk. It is only the magnificent man, the man with the virtue of fortitude and a moderate love for money, who is capable of undertaking risks that will benefit the common good.[39]

Aquinas's analysis reflects closely one of the underlying themes of the Parable of the Talents. The lazy servant hid his talent because of *fear*. He clung to his money because he lacked the virtue of fortitude and consequently refused to take any risk whatsoever.

These are just some of the jewels uncovered by Percy in his study of how Catholicism has long affirmed entrepreneurship and business as morally worthy activities in themselves. In 2012, however, the conversation was taken to a new level when the Pontifical Council for Justice and Peace—a section of the Roman Curia that some associate with what is often called the "social justice" wing of the Church—produced one of the Church's finest statements about business.

Entitled the *Vocation of the Business Leader*, this document didn't shy away from making pointed criticisms of much contemporary business activity. It also stresses the importance of regulation, albeit without specifying its type or depth. Yet the *Vocation* portrays business as neither a necessary evil nor a mere means to an end. Instead it articulates—perhaps for the first time in the Catholic Church's history—a lengthy and thoroughly positive reflection from a body of the Roman Curia about the nature and ends of business.

Especially striking was the *Vocation's* insistence that business makes distinct contributions to the common good *precisely through business activity*. The *Vocation's* authors noted, for instance, that

> Businesses produce many of the important conditions which contribute to the common good of the larger society. Their products and services, the jobs they provide, and the economic and social surplus they make available to society, are foundational to the good life of a nation and of humanity as a whole.[40]

> Successful businesses identify and seek to address genuine human needs at a level of excellence using a great deal of

innovation, creativity and initiative. They produce what has been produced before but often—as in the arenas of medicine, communication, credit, food production, energy, and welfare provision—they invent *entirely new ways of meeting human needs*. And they incrementally improve their products and services, which, where they are genuinely good, improve the quality of people's lives.[41]

Entrepreneurs exercise their creativity to organize the talents and energies of labor and to assemble capital and other resources from the earth's abundance to produce goods and services. When this is done effectively, well paying jobs are created, profit is realized, the resulting wealth is shared with investors, and everyone involved excels.[42]

These are among *the* most significant arguments that pro-free enterprise Catholic Americans should articulate when explaining how businesses contribute to the conditions that help all of us to flourish. Their contribution is *not* first and foremost about how much they donate to this or that cause—even good causes. Instead their primary input to the common good occurs precisely by businesses doing what they are supposed to do *as businesses*.

Businesses are not the same type of community as, for example, a family or a charity. Unlike these forms of association, businesses are not ordered in themselves to their members' flourishing. Rather they are focused upon attaining a more limited set of goods, such as profit, wealth creation, and wages, which are some of the means that help us engage human flourishing.[43] That said, there are many opportunities for individuals—be they entrepreneurs, maintenance staff, board members, technicians, CEOs, accountants, managers, or researchers—to pursue human flourishing *within* a business, while simultaneously realizing specific common goals such as providing particular goods and services.

A similar argument manifests itself in the *Vocation's* analysis of business and entrepreneurship. As well as repeating themes articulated by John Paul II (the words "creativity" and "initiative" are repeated over and over again), the *Vocation* stresses the non-material good that can flow from business activity. Business, it states, makes "an irreplaceable contribution to the material and even the spiritual well-being of humankind."[44]

That is very powerful language. Not only is business the normal means by which many of our material needs and legitimate desires are satisfied, it is also a sphere in which people can participate in the goods that define our humanity.

Such a standpoint has enormous potential to move the wider defense of business away from narrowly utilitarian arguments. Generally speaking, business and free enterprise *are* more effective and efficient in providing any number of goods and services than planned economies. Christian faith, however, endows them with moral meaning and depth that is much harder to find in more secular defenses of economic liberty. Two sections of the *Vocation* spell this out:

[B]usinesses . . . continue to educate people in virtue, especially those young men and women who are emerging from their families and their educational institutions and seeking their own places in society.[45]

[C]reating wealth is not restricted to financial profit alone. The very etymology of the word "wealth" reveals the broader notion of "well-being:" the physical, mental, psychological, moral and spiritual well-being of others. The economic value of wealth is inextricably linked to this wider notion of well-being.[46]

These truths also point to another important point recognized by the *Vocation*. Real-life entrepreneurs "are motivated by much more than financial success, enlightened self-interest, or an abstract social contract as often prescribed by economic literature and management textbooks."[47]

Self-interest and profit certainly number among the reasons that people go into business. The Church itself has stated on numerous occasions that profit is essential if a business is to survive, let alone grow. But the reasons that people start or enter businesses are many. Some of them have less to do with money *per se* than with wanting to be creative, to realize an insight, and to exercise their initiative because such choices can be fulfilling in themselves.

None of this affirmation of business's moral import means that the Church regards each and every entrepreneurial choice and business act as somehow beyond reproach. There are many products and services produced by entrepreneurs which are unworthy of humanity. There is literally *nothing* redeemable about being the world's most successful brothel owner. The choice to create and provide pornography makes no contribution whatsoever to either the common good or human flourishing.

But perhaps one of the *Vocation's* most significant messages was indirect: direct recognition of—and a *mea culpa* for—the fact that many Catholic leaders have not always taken the world of business seriously. In some cases, they primarily viewed it as a source of funds for various Church projects. This has encouraged some Catholics to view business as merely instrumentally useful. More generally the *Vocation* acknowledges that business leaders have sometimes been confronted by "a civil or ecclesiastical culture hostile to entrepreneurship in one or more of its forms."[48]

It is difficult to read this as anything other than a firm rebuttal of the condescending view of business often adopted by some Catholic clergy and laity throughout history. To the credit of its authors, the *Vocation* represents a clear repudiation of such mindsets—something that will not only benefit business leaders but the Catholic Church as whole.

Freedom and the Ends of Property

Though indispensable, neither business nor entrepreneurship is enough for an economy that takes freedom seriously. Business can after all act in ways that diminish economic liberty. There is no dearth of businesses that follow up on their success by trying to block newcomers and potential competitors from entering the marketplace. To this end the *Vocation* even presses business leaders to ask themselves: "Am I creating wealth, or am I engaging in rent-seeking behavior? Am I engaging in anti-competitive practices?"[49]

To an extent, some business leaders' anti-market behavior is influenced by the economic environment in which they operate. If the incentives are weighted toward rent-seeking behavior, it is harder (though obviously not impossible) for business leaders to resist such temptations.

This in turn points to a wider issue: an economy's institutional settings. Certain economic settings translate into economic growth. Others do not. The first and most fundamental institutional arrangement of any economy—free or otherwise—concerns how the use and ownership of *property* is organized.

The laws and regulations about property that prevail in any society tell us a great deal about a society's economic priorities. A society that values economic liberty, for instance, is likely to be especially attached to private property and invest it with significant legal value. Societies firmly rooted in social democratic values typically accord property rights a low priority.

Property's unique capacity to identify the ownership of goods and services with particular individuals and groups makes it indispensable for free economies. It allows the coordination of billions of individual and group investments, purchases, and exchanges in the present and with an eye to the future. In a property-less world, people might be able to possess material things insofar as they exercise immediate control over such objects. But as one theorist of property notes, "they would have no right to exclude others and no normative power to transfer artifacts to others."[50]

For 2,000 years, Catholic theologians, moralists, and social thinkers have written thousands of pages on the rights and responsibilities associated with property use and ownership. Yet the teaching remains remarkably simple, even if the terminology is potentially confusing. It can be summed up in two expressions: *common use* and *private ownership*.

The idea of common use—otherwise known as the "universal destination of material goods" in Catholic teaching—has nothing to do with socialism or a planned economy. When popes, councils, and doctors of the Church use this expression, they are simply underlining the principle that the earth and *all* it contains are to be used by and on behalf of all people. This does not mean that in the beginning human persons somehow jointly owned the material world, with each having an equal share. Rather, as Grisez writes, it means nothing in "subhuman" creation ever comes with a label saying, "this good is meant for this person but not that one, this group but not that."[51] In the beginning and now, God provides material goods for the use of all.

The question then becomes one of *how* this universal destination is to be realized. The Commandment against theft points us toward private ownership. And over the centuries, the Church's position has been that private possession of property is not just licit, but usually necessary.

Aquinas, for instance, offers three reasons in favor of the private ownership of economic goods. First, he notes, people tend to take better care of what is theirs than of what is common to everyone, since individuals tend to shirk a responsibility which is nobody's in particular. Second, if everyone were responsible for everything, the result would be confusion. Third, dividing up things generally produces a more peaceful state of affairs; sharing common things often results in tension. Individual ownership, then—understood as the power to manage and dispose of things—is legitimate.[52]

Successive popes and councils have built upon these points to underscore the well-known problems of communal ownership. In 1961, for instance, John XXIII observed that "it would be quite useless to insist on free and personal initiative in the economic field, while at the same time withdrawing man's right to dispose freely of the means indispensable to the achievement of such initiative."[53] In other words, an economy marked by freedom and creativity means that people need considerable, even extensive space to use what they own in free and creative ways. To this, however, Pope John added the importance of private property for sustaining a free political order: "history and experience," he stated, "testify that in those political regimes which do not recognize the rights of private ownership of goods, productive included, the exercise of freedom in almost every other direction is suppressed or stifled. This suggests, surely, that the exercise of freedom finds its guarantee and incentive in the right of ownership."[54]

The arguments among Catholics about property usually start when it comes to the question of *how* we use our private goods. The Church is very clear that the private nature of our property does not mean we are justified in using it exclusively for ourselves, especially in the face of others' authentic needs. Private property is not an end in itself. It is *for* something. "Use," the Church specifies, remains common.

The Church therefore not only insists that we should use our "surplus goods" (what each person has left over once they have used their property to meet their own and their families' needs) to assist others, but that we should even be ready to use our non-surplus wealth to serve others. This is easier to realize in practice than many people might imagine. For most of us, for example, our houses are non-surplus assets. We truly need somewhere to live. But this does not prevent us from also using our houses to provide homes for our elderly parents, or for our older children as they make their first steps into adult life.

Over the past hundred years, many social justice Catholics have regarded the common use principle as a warrant for the state to engage in extensive redistribution in order to realize the universal destination of goods. Among other things, they have in mind high tax rates on those considered wealthy, specific taxes to fund parts of the welfare state (most notably Social Security and healthcare), and selective government ownership of particular industries. This is their prudential assessment of how the state can help realize the universal destination of goods.

But might they be mistaken? There is much that free enterprise Catholics can say that leads to rather different prudential conclusions. Certainly the Church does not exclude public ownership of particular goods in any circumstances. If this is necessary for realizing the principle of common use in specific cases, such forms of ownership and intervention are permitted. And although the Church has expressed many criticisms of the welfare state, it is not opposed to a state-provided safety net.

It is one thing, however, for governments to implement such policies on a selective basis, or even to do so in an expansive way in particular conditions (such as wartime). It is quite another to view the principle of common use as a mandate to march down the path of full-fledged social democracy. This becomes clearer when we factor the Catholic appreciation of the significance of liberty and human flourishing into the discussion.

In the first place, we need to recall that the goal of common use is not redistribution for its own sake. Nor is it the progressive *equalization* of social and economic conditions. The goods of the earth serve all of us by helping to facilitate human flourishing. It is precisely for this reason that the Church allows people tremendous scope—that is, freedom—in *how* they use their surplus and non-surplus wealth to serve others. As one of the early Church Fathers Saint Basil (who had *very* tough things to say about the wealthy Christians of his time) argued, one reason why superfluous goods are allowed to people by way of trust was precisely so that they should have the *merit* of discharging this trust well.[55] This is echoed by another Church Father, Saint Clement of Alexandria, in his famous homily, "What Rich Man will be Saved?" "How could," he wrote, "we ever do good to our neighbor if none of us possessed anything?"[56] Private ownership allows us to freely discharge this trust so that our use of the goods we own contributes not just to the common good but also our flourishing as humans.

One way we realize this trust is through charitable and philanthropic giving. The Church has always mandated almsgiving. But one of the geniuses of the free economy is that it provides everyone—be they ultra-wealthy, middle-class, or blue-collar—with ways to put their wealth, superfluous or otherwise, at the service of millions of others.

The person who, for instance, places his savings in a bank effectively contributes to the accumulation of capital that is turned into the investments and loans that allow others to buy houses, educate themselves, start businesses, invest in new technology, grow existing enterprises, and employ people. Is the depositor earning interest in doing so? Of course. But putting your wealth at the disposal of others through this particular means doesn't mean you are forbidden from being compensated for the risk you are taking in placing your wealth in a bank. Indeed, such risks were one of the factors identified by scholastic thinkers in identifying those instances in which interest-charging did not constitute usury.[57]

In *Quadragesimo Anno*, Pius XI—also quite critical of the capitalism of his time—made similar arguments: "the investment of superfluous income in developing favorable opportunities for employment, provided the labor employed produces results which are really useful, is to be considered according to the teaching of the Angelic Doctor an act of real liberality particularly appropriate to the needs of our time."[58] This reference to the habit of "liberality"—or what Aquinas[59] calls the *virtue* of "magnificence" or the doing of great things (*magna facere*) indicates that through freely using and investing our resources we not only contribute to others' well-being, but also help actualize our own flourishing.

Free Association, Free Exchange, Free Trade

Beside entrepreneurship and property, there is a third way in which the free economy allows us to contribute to the common good and human flourishing. This is the space it creates for individuals and communities to enter into economic exchanges with one another.

In his Farewell Address as America's first President, George Washington urged the young Republic not to meddle in international commerce, "neither seeking nor granting exclusive favors or preferences." He also maintained that the government's involvement in trade should be limited to ensuring that the rules of commerce were followed and the rights of merchants were upheld.[60] Twenty years earlier, the economic case for freedom of exchange within and among nations had been stated in detail by Adam Smith in his *Wealth of Nations*. But it was also incorporated into a broader American agenda for freedom when the Declaration of Independence's list of condemnations of King George III included an indictment for "cutting off our Trade with all parts of the world."

At the time, mercantilism was the reigning economic orthodoxy. Part of the mercantilist argument was that one country could only become richer at other nations' expense.

This zero-sum view of wealth led countries to aim, as Smith noted, "at the impoverishment of all our neighbors."[61] By contrast, Smith's argument for free trade was premised on the notion that individuals, groups, and even nations needed to be able to discern their comparative economic advantage and that open global markets were the setting that best allowed that process to occur. As Smith put it, "If a foreign country can supply us with a commodity cheaper than we ourselves can make it, better buy it of them with some part of the produce of our own industry employed in a way in which we have some advantage."[62]

It was certainly possible, Smith's argument goes, for a country like Scotland to grow grapes. The financial cost, however, of doing so compared to, for example, growing grapes in Italy, made that an economically foolish choice for Scots. Conversely, individuals, businesses, and countries in a cross-border free market would be encouraged to focus on doing what they did best and would not be incentivized by protectionism into developing industries that, in the long run, couldn't compete in the marketplace, even with extensive tariff protection.

Smith's reasons for advocacy of free trade are now commonplace. Less well-known is Smith's *moral* critique of mercantilism. In Smith's words: "It is the industry which is carried on for the benefit of the rich and powerful, that is principally encouraged by our mercantile system. That which is carried on for the benefit of the poor and indigent, is too often, either neglected or oppressed."[63] The mercantilist system, Smith maintained, allowed the already rich to collaborate with government officials to develop very detailed regulations that helped them maintain their dominant position by locking everyone else out of the marketplace.

Smith was not the first to emphasize the economic benefits of, and moral case for, free exchange within and among nations. Almost one hundred seventy years earlier, the Protestant theologian Hugo Grotius underscored, for example, free trade's moral dimension in his famous 1609 book *Mare Liberum* (*The Free Sea*). Even more surprising is the fact that over two hundred years before Smith and several decades before Grotius, some *Catholic* theologians were describing free exchange and free trade as a "right." The first to do so was the sixteenth-century Dominican scholar Francisco de Vitoria.

Vitoria's argument for free trade begins with the insight that humans are by nature social beings. This means they must be free to associate with each other if they are to flourish as human beings. From this is derived the right of free association enjoyed by all people. Such a right, Vitoria argued, translated into people being free to choose with whom they associate and for what ends.

While Vitoria did not regard freedom of association as absolute (no one is free, for example, to associate together for criminal purposes or to abandon their children), he did not think there were many reasons why national boundaries should limit freedom of association. Significantly, Vitoria developed this line of argument in the context of claiming that the native peoples of the New World should not be prevented from freely trading with European merchants by either their indigenous rulers or European monarchs. Natural justice, Vitoria stated, required rulers to allow people to enter their lands in order to trade.

Such were Vitoria's convictions against mercantilist policies that he described laws unduly limiting free trade between nations or which sought to exclude well-intentioned strangers from trading as "iniquitous and against charity." Vitoria was so insistent on this point that he actually described denial of free trade as a legitimate *causa bellum*—a legitimate cause for war![64]

Over two hundred years after Vitoria's death, Charles Carroll stood out, even among the American colonists, in his opposition to import and export duties imposed by the British Parliament. Carroll always thought the American colonies should *never* have agreed in the first place to Britain imposing *any* import and export duties on American merchants.[65] This position was not common among Carroll's contemporaries in the 1760s.[66] As a close student of European politics, however, Carroll understood that Britain's policies in this area owed much to the efforts of Britain's prime minister, William Pitt, to curry favor with English and Scottish merchants, many of whom exerted enormous influence upon British political life. British merchants, Carroll well knew from his years in France and England, *feared* competition from America. It threatened the comfortable market niches that they maintained through government privilege rather than hard work and competition in the marketplace.[67]

But Carroll then went another step. He insisted that British regulation of the colonies' commerce was simply another form of taxation imposed upon Americans without their consent. Though Britain repealed the Stamp Act in March 1766, Carroll was among the first to point out that the Declaratory Act of 1766 that accompanied the Stamp Act's repeal provided the legal basis for the ongoing restrictions on American commerce within, between, and outside the American colonies.[68]

Carroll's ultimate objective was to break mercantilist policies and replace them with free trade. On a domestic level, Carroll worked strenuously to eliminate tolls within Maryland's jurisdiction, and sought to make the border riverways free to travelers and merchants.[69]

Nor was Carroll afraid to appeal to justice in his efforts to overturn what he considered unjust impositions upon American colonists. He saw no reason why he or anyone else should be forced by law to trade many of his goods with English merchants alone.[70] Nor did Carroll think it fair that anyone should be forced to forgo their comparative advantage in the marketplace because of mercantilist policies. "If," Carroll wrote in 1766, "I could make a coat of my own wool, much better and cheaper than what I could have from

England, would it not be the highest injustice to force me to forego such an advantage: would it not be raising a very heavy tax upon my property without my consent?"[71]

Such policies amounted, Carroll patiently explained to the less-economically informed Benjamin Franklin, to nothing less than price controls—something that he regarded as "destructive of that freedom in dealing which is the life and soul of trade."[72] "Every regulation of price," Carroll wrote, "is an acknowledgement that the price allowed is not equal to the value of the commodity on which it is fixed."[73] The only place, Carroll insisted, in which the value could be fairly established was in a marketplace characterized by truly free exchange. Here Carroll stood squarely with not only Adam Smith but also, as he most likely knew, with Aquinas and the vast majority of scholastic writers on the subject of the just price.

This generally favorable view of free trade prevailed in Catholic teaching for centuries. As recently as 1941, Pius XII stated, Vitoria-like, that the "free reciprocal commerce of goods by interchange and gift" was intimately linked to the institution of private property and, like private property, was immediately derived from the natural law.[74]

Some twenty-six years later, however, Paul VI expressed significant reservations in his encyclical *Populorum Progressio* about the extent to which free trade could be viewed as the preferred norm for international economic relations.[75] More radical reservations about free trade were articulated in those Catholic circles influenced by liberation theology. On questions of international trade and development, most liberation theologians embraced what was known as "dependency theory": the claim made by some twentieth-century economists that resources flow from a "periphery" of poor nations to a "core" of wealthy countries, enriching the wealthy at the poor's expense. It followed, so the theory went, that poorer nations should erect barriers that limited and restricted trade with foreigners, and discourage if not prohibit foreign direct investment.

In many respects, dependency theory was nothing more than a thinly-disguised neo-mercantilism vested in the liberationist rhetoric and neo-Marxist theory that proliferated throughout the West in the 1960s and 70s. Today it is more widely grasped that, contrary to dependency theory, free trade is *not* a race to the bottom. The decision of India and China to open themselves to the global economy has helped millions of people to escape levels of poverty almost all Americans would consider unbearable. Both countries have seen the rise of a commercially-oriented middle class. And in China's case, it is a middle class that has proved remarkably open to the Gospel, despite strong reservations from China's Communist rulers. After all, once you concede liberty in one sphere (such the economy), it is very hard to constrain it in other areas—such as the freedom to think about and ask questions concerning life's ultimate meaning.

During the pontificates of John Paul II and Benedict XVI, Catholic social teaching witnessed a return to the older tradition of generally portraying free trade in favorable terms, while also underscoring protectionism's injustice and relative inefficiency. In *Caritas in Veritate*, for example, Benedict stressed that "The world-wide diffusion of forms of prosperity should not . . . be held up by projects that are self-centered, protectionist or at the service of private interests."[76] Likewise John Paul took the opportunity in *Centesimus Annus* to stress the folly of developing countries isolating themselves from the world market. Such policies had only led to "stagnation and recession." Those economies which had entered global markets, the pope added for good measure, had grown.[77]

But what about those people who lack the talents and skills which allow them to participate in open global markets? Shouldn't they be accorded special assistance or even protection so that they too can live a dignified life?

John Paul II acknowledged this as a genuine challenge: "many people," he wrote, "do not have the means which would enable them to take their place in an effective and humanly dignified way within a productive system in which work is truly central."[78] Yet the pope did not view this as a mandate to return to a type of economic nationalism, let alone a warrant for subsidies to particular businesses or tariffs being established to protect politically well-connected industries. For John Paul, the issue was how we help people "acquire expertise, to enter the circle of exchange, and to develop their skills in order to make the best use of their capacities and resources."[79]

The Church's high regard for free trade and free exchange doesn't mean these are absolute rights. Certain things, the Church insists, should never be economically traded or subject to monetary prices. Sexual relations and human organs are prominent examples.[80] The Church also maintains that employees are owed certain things as a matter of justice in the labor market. Catholic social teaching thus places considerable emphasis upon securing laws that protect employees from inhumane working conditions, as well as outlining principles that should inform the legal treatment of wage-fixing.[81]

But these caveats aside, if, as Vitoria claimed, the freedom to associate and exchange in the marketplace is a type of right, then the reasons to restrict freedom of exchange and trade within and among nations need to be very serious indeed. The onus falls squarely upon the person or industry *requesting limits* to freedom of trade to explain why others' freedom of association and right to free trade should be restricted. Certainly free trade, like private property, is ordered to the end of realizing the universal destination of material goods. But the very nature of free trade is such that it helps to realize the principle that the goods of the world are to be used for the well-being of all rather than just one community or one particular nation.

What about Justice?

The Church's invocation of the language of rights with regard to free trade and economic initiative is something with which many Americans, Catholic or otherwise, are likely to resonate. In 1987, for instance, Ronald Reagan argued that America's Founders had placed economic freedoms on a par with other rights, "as sacred and sacrosanct as the political freedoms of speech, press, religion, and assembly." Among the rights listed in what he called "America's Economic Bill of Rights," Reagan included the freedom to work, to own and control property, to participate in a free market, and to enjoy the fruits of our work.

Reagan did not suggest these rights were somehow unconditional. Nor did he claim that they somehow nullified the legitimacy of any regulation or taxation whatsoever. Reagan did, however, maintain that there were limits to the extent governments could regulate the exercise of these rights—"not only because excessive taxation undermines the strength of the economy but because taxation beyond a certain level becomes servitude." Economic liberties, Reagan added, help to link "life inseparably to liberty, what enables a person to control his own destiny, what makes self-government and personal independence part of the American experience."[82]

Attaching the language of rights to concepts of economic freedom and the free market remind us that these are not simply bulwarks of freedom. Rights are also a matter of justice. This is significant, because a common criticism of limited-government Catholics by their social justice brethren is an alleged overemphasis on freedom at the expense of justice.

The question of justice in the economy has of course been a major subject of attention for modern Catholic social teaching. In a post-Great Recession era, the contour of some of the questions has changed. How, for example, should Catholics respond to proposed reductions in the size of the welfare state in the wake of high levels of government expenditures that many consider unsustainable? Does opposing the expansion of government welfare programs mean that a Catholic is somehow betraying the poor's well-being?

Limited-government Catholics can and should point out that market economies have been very successful in reducing poverty and raising living standards, especially in America. Here they echo Ronald Reagan who asked in 1966: "Have we in America forgotten our own accomplishments? For 200 years we've been fighting the most successful war in poverty the world has ever seen."[83]

Such ripostes are part of a measured response. The free enterprise system *has* lifted millions of people out of poverty in a way that command economies and socialism manifestly failed to do so. Yet appeals to economic effectiveness cannot constitute the only response or even the primary answer articulated by those who ground their position in favor of economic liberty and limited government on the basis of the common good and human flourishing. In the following chapter, we consider Catholic arguments for constraining the state's economic reach on precisely such foundations.

Further Reading

Francois Michelin, *And Why Not? The Human Person at the Heart of Business* (Lanham, MD: Lexington Books, 2003).

Richard John Neuhaus, *Doing Well and Doing Good* (New York: Doubleday, 1992).

Michael Novak, *Business as a Calling: Work and the Examined Life* (New York: Free Press, 1996).

Anthony G. Percy, *Entrepreneurship in the Catholic Tradition* (Lanham, MD: Lexington Books, 2010).

Pontifical Council for Justice and Peace, *Vocation of the Business Leader: A Reflection* (Vatican City: Pontifical Council for Justice and Peace, 2012).

Robert A. Sirico, *Defending the Free Market: The Moral Case for a Free Economy* (New York: Regnery, 2012).

Chapter 3
Solidarity, Subsidiarity, and the State

Having thus taken each citizen in turn in its powerful grasp and shaped him to its will, government then extends its embrace to include the whole of society. . . . It does not break men's will, but softens, bends, and guides it; it seldom enjoins, but often inhibits, action; it does not destroy anything, but prevents much being born; it is not at all tyrannical, but it hinders, restrains, enervates, stifles and stultifies so much that in the end each nation is no more than a flock of timid and hardworking animals with the government as its shepherd.

Alexis de Tocqueville[1]

When Alexis de Tocqueville wrote these words in *Democracy in America*, he was trying to imagine how the republic which he had painstakingly studied in the 1830s might come undone from within. At no point did Tocqueville use the expression "welfare state." Yet many have identified modern regulatory and welfare systems as embodying the essence of his warning.

From a Catholic standpoint, there is nothing intrinsically problematic about governments seeking to regulate the economy. Modern Catholic social teaching also recognizes that the state should exercise a number of welfare functions. By no stretch of the imagination can the Church be regarded as opposed in principle to governments seeking to help those in need.

But alongside these axioms, the Church continually reminded Catholics that as *individuals* and as a *religious community*, they have concrete responsibilities to their neighbor which are not fulfilled by voting for expansive welfare programs or even paying the taxes that fund such activities. Hence, from the beginning of the Church's presence in North America, its life has been marked by an ongoing outreach to those in need: the unborn and their mothers, the materially poor, the sick and elderly without family, the mentally ill, orphans, abandoned women, the unemployed, the disabled, and immigrants to name just a few. Whether as generous financial contributors to such initiatives or by directly working with those in need, Catholic Americans were involved in these concrete expressions of love of neighbor long before federal, state, and local governments began assuming an ever-expanding role in the provision of welfare services.

But while few Catholic Americans believe our responsibilities to the less well-off are limited to "do no harm," there is intense disagreement today among Catholics about *how* Americans fulfill their responsibilities as citizens to those in need should be realized. Four factors appear to be driving this debate.

The first is the disturbing size now assumed by the American welfare state. The Heritage Foundation's *2012 Index of Dependence on Government* illustrated, for example, that, by 2010, 70.5 percent of total federal government spending was being consumed by welfare programs. The equivalent figure in 1962 was 28.3 percent, while the number in 1990 was 48.5 percent.[2] Are Americans supposed to wait until the figure approaches 100 percent before becoming worried about this?

This brings us to the second factor in play: the incredible number of Americans receiving some type of welfare support. In 2011 alone, approximately one-third of Americans received some form of welfare assistance from one or more of the over eighty means-tested federal government programs. Note that this figure actually *excludes* Social Security and Medicare.[3] In raw numbers of Americans, this meant the number of people receiving benefits from the federal government in the United States has grown from under ninety-four million in 2000 to more than one-hundred twenty-eight million in 2011.[4]

Is *this* what the American dream is supposed to be about?

A third factor animating the welfare state debate among Catholics concerns its impact on poverty alleviation. In 2008, for example, total welfare spending amounted to approximately $16,800 per person in poverty. That equates to $50,400 per poor family of three. As the policy analyst Peter Ferrara notes, this was four times as much as the figure estimated by the Census Bureau to raise all of America's poor up to the poverty level, thus technically purging all poverty from America.

But has this spending actually made a difference? According to Ferrara:

> Poverty fell sharply after the Depression, before the War on Poverty, declining from 32% in 1950 to 22.4% in 1959 to 12.1% in 1969, soon after the War on Poverty programs became effective. Progress against poverty as measured by the poverty rate then abruptly stopped.[5]

Leaving aside the welfare state's disappointing record vis-à-vis poverty reduction, a fourth issue should be of even greater concern for Catholics. This is the welfare state's worrying effects on America's moral culture. Social scientists rightly remind us that correlation isn't causation. Nevertheless, studies authored by commentators ranging from the late Democratic Senator Daniel Patrick Moynihan, to rather more conservative scholars such as Charles Murray, James Q. Wilson, Michael Novak, and Nicholas Eberstadt have provided overwhelming evidence of how welfare programs have contributed to disturbing social trends such as the decline of able-bodied men actively participating in the workforce, and a rise in the number of unwed mothers and fatherless children throughout America.[6]

These background considerations present Catholics with significant dilemmas. In a 2012 interview, Archbishop Charles Chaput of Philadelphia memorably outlined the moral challenge of poverty for Catholics in the following manner:

Jesus tells us very clearly that if we don't help the poor, we're going to go to hell. Period. There's just no doubt about it. That has to be a foundational concern of Catholics and of all Christians.

No faithful Catholic can disagree with this statement. No one who has read the Gospels can have any illusions about Christ's insistence upon his followers loving and caring for the poor and the consequences of not doing so. But then Chaput added words that some social justice Catholics will find difficult to read:

> But Jesus didn't say the government has to take care of them, or that we have to pay taxes to take care of them. Those are prudential judgments. Anybody who would condemn someone because of their position on taxes is making a leap that I can't make as a Catholic.[7]

Here Chaput is stressing that *how* we help the poor is *prudential* in ways that Catholic teaching regarding something like the obligation to oppose each and every attempt to legalize euthanasia is not.

Nevertheless, the fact that Catholics can disagree about the best means of addressing poverty doesn't absolve them from thinking about *how* they do so in ways consistent with the protection of human liberty, the development of human flourishing, and the promotion of the common good. This in turn directs attention to the meaning and implications of two key principles of Catholic social teaching: solidarity and subsidiarity.

Solidarity: Love and Freedom

When Catholics above the age of forty hear the word "solidarity," many recall the popular movement of that name— *Solidarność*—which, inspired by John Paul II's 1979 visit to Poland, played a major role in confirming that Communist regimes fundamentally relied upon lies and coercion to maintain their power. For other Catholics, solidarity evokes a long history of Catholic support for trade unions dating back to Leo XIII's *Rerum Novarum*.

While these are important reference points, the word solidarity has a relatively simple and much older meaning in Catholic teaching. Solidarity is nothing more and nothing less than the commandment to love our neighbor as we would want to be loved ourselves. As the Second Vatican Council recalled, Christ "clearly outlined an obligation on part of the sons of God to treat each other as brothers." Solidarity may therefore be said to involve fulfilling the basic duty to be just to each other and love one another. The Council then defines solidarity as the rendering of "mutual service in the measure of the different gifts bestowed on each."[8] This suggests people should meet their obligation of brotherhood by serving each other through using their specific talents and resources.

That in turn underscores a very important point: there is not always a single right way for people to give positive expression to their concern for each other. So that we understand this clearly, consider the following two cases.

Giving effect to solidarity means that any Catholic is bound to resist the imposition or expansion of laws that, for example, allow the intentional application of lethal force against innocent human life from conception to natural death. Why? Because the *negative* precepts of the natural law and the Commandments, such as "don't lie" or "don't commit adultery," *always* bind. They are truly absolute, and admit of no exception. This has *always* been among the most crucial elements of Catholic moral teaching, and it was reiterated in decidedly unambiguous terms by John Paul II's *Veritatis Splendor*.[9] The point of such negative precepts is to protect what *Veritatis* Splendor calls "fundamental goods,"[10] without which our neighbor's human flourishing is impossible.

But when addressing a question such as "how can I contribute to the reduction of poverty?," living out solidarity does *not* mean that I *must* support, for example, *this* particular welfare program. Why? Because the Gospel's *positive* precepts (such as love of the materially poor) can be often lived out in a variety of ways. Much depends on my particular talents, the resources at my disposal, and my preexisting obligations. Other factors in play include my prudential assessment of what I think I can reasonably contribute in this particular instance, not to mention whether I believe a given program will actually serve the common good or undermine it.

Too many social justice Catholics are prone to implying that if a fellow Catholic declines to support particular government programs which *they* think benefits the poor, then such a person is somehow shirking his responsibilities to those in need. That might be the case, but not necessarily so. It could simply be that other Catholics think the suggested program is counterproductive, or they are living out Christ's call to love the poor by contributing elsewhere and in different ways.

One particular element that limited-government Catholics can emphasize in discussions of solidarity is its attention to freedom. In *Sollicitudo Rei Socialis*, John Paul II devoted considerable attention to this dimension of solidarity.

John Paul II used the word "solidarity" to describe a person's chosen commitment to the good of others as a specific moral *attitude* and *virtue*. It cannot therefore be mistaken for vague sentimentalism. Instead, the pope specified, "it is *a firm and persevering determination* to commit oneself to the *common good*; that is to say to the good of all and each individual, because we are *all* really responsible for *all*."[11] Solidarity thus finds its ultimate end not in some earthly Rousseauian utopia of universal brotherhood, but rather in promoting the conditions that facilitate human flourishing.

The word "virtue" implies that solidarity needs to become as much a moral habit as something like courage or temperance. Virtues, moreover, are only realized when a person *freely* commits himself to acting consistently for the good. This is why John Paul stressed that "an essential condition" for living out the virtue of solidarity "is autonomy and free self-determination."[12] To realize solidarity as a *good* thus means I must *decide freely* to commit myself to my neighbor and to the common good—and I must do so continuously.

This does not mean that the state and law has no role whatsoever in encouraging people to embrace the moral life, including the virtue of solidarity. The question, however, is *how* we build a concern for liberty and human flourishing into the way that all institutions and communities help to promote solidarity in a given society. At this point, we begin to see how solidarity relates to that other great principle of Catholic social teaching: subsidiarity.

Subsidiarity: Operationalizing Solidarity

Between 2005 and 2013, anyone looking at the website of the United States Conference of Catholic Bishops—specifically the section marked "Themes of Catholic Social Teaching"— would have found a helpful page listing various principles of Catholic social doctrine. These included the option for the poor, the dignity of every human *life*, care for creation, the intrinsic worth of human labor, and the rights of workers.[13] Strangely missing, however, was one of *the* most important themes of Catholic social doctrine: the principle of subsidiarity.

Within Catholic circles in America (and elsewhere), solidarity is often seen as the principle of the "Catholic left," while subsidiarity is considered something to which the "Catholic right" is especially attached. The truth, however, is that the two principles are bound to each other, and the glue consists of three things: the *goal* of human flourishing; the *responsibilities* we have for our neighbor; and our *respect* for the dignity and liberty of others—including those we seek to help.

The beginnings of a formal articulation of the principle of subsidiarity may be found in Aquinas's insistence that, with the exception of particular emergencies, justice itself requires that individuals in a community be free to carry out their duties and obligations via their own free choices and actions.[14] Several hundred years later, a fuller definition of subsidiarity was articulated by John Paul II in *Centesimus Annus*:

> [A] community of a higher order should *not* interfere in the internal life of a community of a lower order, depriving the latter of its functions, but rather should support it in case of need and help to co-ordinate its activity with the activities of the rest of society, always with a view to the common good.[15]

As if to clarify a point about the scope and length of such support and coordination, John Paul insisted in the same paragraph that:

> Such supplementary interventions, which are justified by urgent reasons touching the common good, must be as brief as possible, so as to avoid removing permanently from society and business systems the functions which are properly theirs, and so as to avoid enlarging excessively the sphere of State intervention to the detriment of both economic and civil freedom.[16]

The interventions of "higher" communities (such as governments) in the activities of "lower" bodies (such as families and civil associations) are thus justified by reference to the common good. But that same common good also provides limits to intervention by telling us that assistance is meant to help people to make choices for the good—not supplant their need and ability to do so. Hence whenever a case of assistance and coordination through the state proves necessary, as much space as possible should be accorded to the rightful liberty of the person or community receiving help.

Subsidiarity is often referenced by some of its advocates for the efficiency which its application introduces into our approaches to social and economic problems. There are good reasons for this. One might be called the "knowledge problem." People closer to a problem afflicting, say, Albuquerque, New Mexico usually have a better sense of all the issues involved than government officials who rarely venture out of Washington, D.C.

We need to remember, however, that subsidiarity has less to do with efficiency than with the moral imperative of people realizing human flourishing under their own volition. One requirement for realizing this flourishing is *to do things for ourselves*—as the fruit of our own reflection, choices, and acts—rather than to have others do those things for us that we are indeed capable of doing.

There are, however, four other insights that arise from reflection upon how subsidiarity fits into the Catholic vision of living out the command to love our neighbor.

The first is that subsidiarity reminds us of a wider sociological fact which limited-government Catholics should always emphasize: that there are literally thousands of free associations and communities which establish many of the conditions that assist people to realize human flourishing. They thus have a primary responsibility to give others what they are objectively owed in justice.

To this extent, subsidiarity points toward *limited* government. Though an important form of social organization, government is only one of a number of communities and should not therefore displace or absorb the responsibilities properly assumed by individuals, families, churches, clubs, businesses, and other forms of non-state association. Subsidiarity thus tells us we should not *automatically* look to government when a community experiences problems. When a family seems unable to meet, for example, particular responsibilities (such as caring for an aging relative), extended family, neighbors, and churches should usually be the first to render assistance. When no other group can render the appropriate form of help, the state may need to become involved.

This logic of assistance extends into the economy proper. John Paul II noted, for instance, that one of the state's tasks "is that of overseeing and directing the exercise of human rights in the economic sector." Immediately, however, the pope added that "primary responsibility in this area belongs not to the State but to individuals and to the various groups and associations which make up society." His reasons for making this point are found squarely in the Church's concern for freedom. "The State," the pope wrote, "could not directly ensure the right to work for all its citizens unless it controlled every aspect of economic life and restricted the free initiative of individuals."[17]

The second matter highlighted by subsidiarity is that certain aspects of the common good can only be secured by the government. Only the state can, for instance, conduct foreign policy, provide national defense, and maintain the rule of law. Sometimes the common good requires governments to go beyond these and other core government functions, though normally on a temporary basis. Government disaster programs, for example, are designed to address natural disasters—their implementation should cease once a natural disaster's effects are overcome.

Third, subsidiarity suggests that different forms of wisdom apply in different realms as we seek to live out the virtue of solidarity. "The good of individuals, the good of families, and the good of *civitas*," Aquinas wrote, "are different ends; so there are necessarily different species of *prudentia* corresponding to this difference in their respective ends."[18]

One way of prudentially applying subsidiarity is to ask ourselves what different communities normally do well, and what they are not so good at doing. Though there are circumstances in which the intervention of others—including governments—may be necessary, the family is the place where children are normally raised. In short, just as political wisdom ought to reign at the level of government, domestic wisdom—and authority—should normally prevail in family matters.

Last, subsidiarity indirectly indicates something about the nature of government that many are prone to forget. People who hold elected office or occupy positions of state authority aren't perfect. They too are fallen creatures. They are as prone as anyone else to making mistakes, of being incompetent, or even abusing their position for personal interest.[19] A major difference, however, between ordinary citizens and government officials is that the latter's errors, incompetence, or sins often acquire the force of government authority and can even become embedded in law. Thus to the extent subsidiarity restrains the government, it helps to protect everyone against sin's effects upon the state.

Justice, Love, and Government

In *Deus Caritas Est*, Benedict XVI wove many of these points into a profound reflection which drew attention to the role played by the virtue of love in addressing our neighbors' needs, while subtly underscoring the limits of state power. The state is, Benedict wrote, indeed primarily concerned with the realization of justice. But then the pope affixed a significant caution:

> There is no ordering of the State so just that it can eliminate the need for a service of love. . . . There will always be suffering which cries out for consolation and help. There will always be loneliness. There will always be situations of material need where help in the form of concrete love of neighbor is indispensable.[20]

Justice matters, but not every human problem or need is a question of justice.

This has direct implications for how Catholics think about government. On a practical level, *Deus Caritas Est* explains that a state attempting to take care of all problems would inevitably degenerate into a soulless bureaucracy that treats people as things rather than persons. And a "mere bureaucracy," the pope writes, is "incapable of guaranteeing the very thing which the suffering person—every person—needs: namely, loving personal concern."[21] Efforts to realize justice that deny the ultimate horizons revealed by divine love can easily degenerate into a harsh impersonal formality, which considers forgiveness and redemption to be essentially irrelevant, while also darkening our ability to see the one whom we help as truly our flesh-and-blood neighbor, weak and fallible like ourselves.

This doesn't mean, Benedict hastened to add, that society can dispense with any government welfare function whatsoever. Rather his point was that "[w]e do not need a State which regulates and controls everything."[22] Instead society requires "a State which, in accordance with the principle of subsidiarity, generously acknowledges and supports initiatives arising from the different social forces and combines spontaneity with closeness to those in need."[23]

In other words, subsidiarity is at least partly about providing space for human beings to demonstrate in *personal* word and *personal* deed their love for each other, thereby highlighting the truth that all of us are truly brothers and sisters by virtue of having the same God as the Father who commands us to love one another. It follows, as Benedict stressed elsewhere, that "By considering reciprocity as the heart of what it is to be a human being, subsidiarity is the most effective antidote against any form of all-encompassing welfare state."[24]

As the Scriptures constantly emphasize, the Christian God is most definitely a God of Justice. Christ Himself assures us there *will* be a final reckoning. All of us *will* be judged. Not everyone will enter heaven (Matt 25:31–46). Christ is certainly Love. But as Benedict explained, justice is "an integral part of the love 'in deed and in truth.'"[25] That said, love "transcends justice and completes it in the logic of giving and forgiving."[26]

Strictly speaking, the logic of giving and forgiving can only be lived out by free persons and free communities. Neither gifts nor forgiveness can be compelled from without. To have any significance for human flourishing, they must arise from "within." Moreover, this free self-giving is a way of giving effect to the *mercy* that is at the heart of the Christian message, and which serves to correct the very human tendency to imagine that meeting the formal requirements of justice is enough. A God who was simply Justice rather than Love would, after all, never have condescended to enter into human history in the Person of Jesus Christ to rescue us from our own folly. God owed us *nothing*. In that sense, it is *divine mercy* rather than justice that truly saves us.

Freedom and Social Justice

How then should these reflections shape the approach of limited-government Catholics to realizing our concrete obligations to the poor?

One lesson is that free enterprise Catholics need to engage questions of welfare reform from the standpoint of *both* fiscal rectitude *and* human flourishing. Many advocates of limited government focus heavily upon the welfare state's financial costs. Obviously a concern for good stewardship of taxpayers' money is economically and morally essential. But Catholics anxious to reform the welfare state also need to link such reform to facilitating conditions that foster integral human development.

In 1996, the Clinton Administration and the Republican-controlled Congress implemented significant changes to America's welfare system. Among other things, these reforms demonstrated that America *could* transform its welfare state without thrusting thousands of people into poverty and despair.

There was, however, something else these changes achieved. As one politician who contributed to that reform, former

United States Senator Rick Santorum, wrote sixteen years later:

> It replaced a permanent entitlement with temporary assistance, and it block-granted money to the states, giving them the power to design and deliver welfare as long as they adhered to federal work-requirement rules.
> The law transformed the lives of those who were in or near poverty. Welfare rolls dropped by more than 50%. The work requirements provided a path toward self-respect, work skills and a ladder to success. Poverty levels and unemployment also declined.[27]

Santorum's point was not only that the 1996 welfare reform helped reduce costs and get people back to work. His other insight was that encouraging people to find work, even imposing work requirements, helped people to choose work and experience the human flourishing—the self-respect—that comes about through work.

A second lesson is that any streamlining, or fiscal capping of the American welfare state must be accompanied by Americans stepping into the breach to help their neighbors in need. Subsidiarity does not mean leaving individuals and communities on the margins to fend for themselves. Nor can the *subsidium* offered by Catholics degenerate into creating situations whereby people's undue dependency on the state is simply transformed into overreliance upon the Church and other non-state actors. Obviously there are many people such as the chronically ill or the profoundly disabled whose capacity to live independent lives is much more limited than most other people. But the general point should be to help people in need of genuine assistance, as far as possible, to choose and act in ways that allow them to flourish as human beings.

This becomes even more important to consider when we realize that poverty is more than a material phenomenon.

People are more than just mouths. Poverty consequently has moral and spiritual dimensions. Pope Francis himself underscored this point in one of his first formal addresses to the representatives of the world's temporal powers:

> But there is another form of poverty! It is the spiritual poverty of our time, which afflicts the so-called richer countries particularly seriously. It is what my much-loved predecessor, Benedict XVI, called the "tyranny of relativism," which makes everyone his own criterion and endangers the coexistence of peoples. And that brings me to a second reason for my name. Francis of Assisi tells us we should work to build peace. But there is no true peace without truth! There cannot be true peace if everyone is his own criterion, if everyone can always claim exclusively his own rights, without at the same time caring for the good of others, of everyone, on the basis of the nature that unites every human being on this earth.[28]

The meaning of Pope Francis's words is unambiguous. Spiritual poverty today involves the embrace of relativism and the corresponding denial of moral truth. Unfortunately such language is not easily found in the thought and literature of a good number of those who purport to be fighting poverty today.

Catholics are often surprised to learn that Saint Francis of Assisi's own understanding of poverty had nothing to do with class warfare or even envy of those who possessed wealth. According to the author of perhaps the best biography of the saint, Augustine Thompson, O.P., Saint Francis actually wrote very little about poverty, and when he did, it was primarily with reference to the fact that the Second Person of the Trinity humbled Himself by taking on human form in the Incarnation and sacrificed Himself for humanity by dying on the Cross.[29] Francis's conception of poverty was thus primarily about "renunciation of one's own will," service of God, and

111

obedience to the Gospel and, yes, the Church.[30] In that sense, Francis's ideas about poverty, Thompson adds elsewhere, "are not political." They are about attaining the spiritual wealth that is found in the embrace of Christ. Indeed, Francis regarded beautiful churches as a way for humans to give glory to God and for the same reason directed his followers to ensure that churches and liturgical vestments be aesthetically pleasing and that the vessels used at Mass be made of precious metals.[31]

The Gospels never stop insisting that moral and spiritual poverty can be as devastating (if not more damaging for humans from the standpoint of their salvation) as material deprivation. Yet these are precisely areas of human life that government welfare programs have never been especially adept at addressing. Instead these human realities require the "loving personal concern" to which Benedict referred.

A third lesson is the need for Catholics to ask ourselves how Americans addressed social and economic problems before the welfare state's growth acquired full steam in the United States in the 1960s.

Here our best eyewitness is Tocqueville. The nineteenth-century Americans portrayed in *Democracy in America* generally dealt with most social and economic problems through the habit of free association—especially through the medium of churches and other religiously-based associations—rather than immediately looking to the government. For Tocqueville, the contrast with France, where a highly centralized state was seen as the first port of call for help, was astounding:

> Americans of all ages, all conditions, and all dispositions constantly form associations. They have not only commercial and manufacturing companies, in which all take part, but associations of a thousand other kinds, religious, moral, serious, futile, general or restricted, enormous or diminutive. The Americans make associations to give entertainments, to found seminaries,

to build inns, to construct churches, to diffuse books, to send missionaries to the antipodes; in this manner they found hospitals, prisons, and schools. If it is proposed to inculcate some truth or to foster some feeling by the encouragement of a great example, they form a society. Wherever at the head of some new undertaking you see the government in France . . . in the United States you will be sure to find an association.[32]

The same phenomenon was noted 120 years later by another famous French Catholic. The United States studied by Jacques Maritain in the 1940s and 50s was very different to that analyzed by Tocqueville, not least because of the New Deal's economic and social effects. Yet despite these changes, Maritain observed that

one of the most striking characteristics of the picture is the infinite swarming, on the American scene, of private groups, study clubs, associations, committees, which are designed "to look out for one aspect or another of the common good". . . . The effect is a spontaneous and steady collective regulation and prodding of the tremendous effort of the whole country, which is of invaluable importance.[33]

This seemingly endlessly varied web of associational activity was matched by a financial generosity that astonished Maritain:

Americans like to give. Of course, there is the exemption from taxes for gifts directed to the common welfare; but this very law about taxes would not have been possible if the astute legislator did not know that as a rule the American people are aware of the fact that it is better to give than to receive. Not only the great foundations, but the ordinary course of activity of American institutions and the innumerable American private groups show us that the ancient Greek and Roman idea of the *civis praeclarus*, the dedicated citizen who spends his money in the service of the common good, plays an essential part in American consciousness. . . . There is no materialism, I think, in the astonishing, countless initiatives of fraternal help which are the daily bread of the American people, or in the profound feeling of obligation toward others which exists in them, especially toward any people abroad who are in distress.[34]

Alongside these specifically American reference points, there are older examples for Catholic Americans to follow in living out the virtue of solidarity in accordance with the principle of subsidiarity and the demands of freedom. The ancient Church is an obvious case. The first Catholics did not imagine that lobbying Roman senators to implement welfare programs was the way to show how much they loved their neighbor. Instead, to the pagan world's amazement, Christians—bishops, priests, and laity—helped *anyone* in need in very direct, practical ways.

As anyone who has read the Church Fathers knows, the first generations of Christians went out of their way to *personally* care for the poor, abandoned women, the incurably sick, and the disabled—the very groups who were sub-human to the pagan mind. When plagues came and everyone else fled, the Romans were amazed that Christians generally stayed behind, putting their own lives at risk by refusing to abandon those in distress, regardless of their religion.

If fiscal realities mean the United States is facing what might be called a post-welfare state world, the time may have come for Catholic Americans to radically rethink the *whys* and *hows* of loving those to whom Christ Himself devoted special attention. That would certainly require a significant shift in habits of thought and action on the part of those Catholics accustomed to thinking primarily about solidarity in terms of state intervention. But it *also* entails a willingness on the part of limited-government Catholics to lead by example in developing associational solutions to those problems that aren't resolvable by either markets or the state. The moral, spiritual, and material well-being of the least among us surely demands nothing less.

The Good of Health, the Challenge of Health Care

Virtually all observers of America have remarked upon its inhabitants' remarkably practical instincts. Most Americans are consequently bound to ask how pursuing the end of human flourishing according to principles such as solidarity and subsidiarity might apply to those challenges with not only a heavy economic dimension but in which many people also believe the state, in the name of justice, *must* play a major role in addressing. What, for instance, do these ideas apply to as convoluted a policy challenge as universal healthcare?[35]

As noted in chapter one, health is a vital concern for Catholics because it is an intrinsic part of the good of life. And while there is much exaggerated talk about healthcare as a "right," health as a fundamental good does give rise to certain types of rights.

One is a species of *negative rights* associated with health. Other people have a duty not to intentionally damage our health. Thus the state has a direct responsibility, for example, to punish doctors who intentionally prescribe their patients with the wrong medicine in order to "see what happens." In such instances, governments must act directly to deter and punish such actions, not least because of the grave damage caused by such choices to the common good.

The picture becomes more complicated, however, when we consider the positive rights that arise from the good of health. All of us have some positive duties to the healthcare of others. Sometimes these duties are very clear. Parents, for instance, have a positive duty to provide their children with their healthcare needs, consistent with the use of family resources to promote the overall flourishing of all its members.

But, we inevitably ask, precisely *what* and *how much* does everyone in a given society owe to everyone else when it comes to their often very different and changing healthcare needs? Must, for instance, a family sacrifice everything to provide a dying relative with a specific treatment that has a 5 percent success rate at keeping patients alive for another two months, even if it involves severely undermining that family's long-term ability to support its other members' participation in goods such as education? Or at an even further distance: What does someone living in Maine who has consciously chosen to lead a healthy lifestyle owe to the alcoholic in Nevada whose own actions have directly contributed to the destruction of his health?

In short, complications for any reasonable discussion of possible options arise from:

- the practical fact of a scarcity of resources in any community;
- the need for the same resources to serve as a means for people to participate in other goods besides health;
- the reality that some people will make unreasonable choices that damage their health and the health of others; and
- the inevitability that death comes to everyone.

To this we should add Grisez's comment that consideration of the empirical merits of different proposals is entirely appropriate in such a discussion. He points, for example, to the manner in which public healthcare programs have embodied significant dysfunction because of such policies' distorting impact upon the workings of financial incentives on people's decision making concerning their perception of their needs and its relationship to the consumption and allocation of resources.[36]

Taken as a collective whole, all such factors indicate that while it's possible to affirm "a right to healthcare," there are many questions that even a well-founded recognition of a right to healthcare cannot resolve by itself.

The Catholic understanding of human flourishing, solidarity, and subsidiarity would appear to suggest that proposals which seek to realize positive health rights more or less exclusively through a state-administered system (such as Britain's National Health Service) normally constitute a violation of these principles. It doesn't exclude the possibility that, where no other community is capable of fulfilling particular healthcare requirements, the state might act to meet directly certain essential needs. But in most circumstances, these principles exclude the state's assumption of near-total control—direct or indirect—of a given nation's healthcare system.

Subsidiarity particularly implies that much of the state's contribution to actualizing positive healthcare rights should usually be indirect. These might include policies such as tax breaks for healthcare research or the provision of healthcare services for those without any other means of securing basic healthcare needs. More remote (albeit arguably essential) assistance might involve enacting laws that establish the basic requirements of public order, without which any provisions of healthcare by private or public means is extremely difficult. Another could be the state's maintenance of a system of rule of law and enforcement of property rights and contracts, without which market-oriented approaches to healthcare, for instance, cannot function.

The same principles, however, suggest that efforts to give effect to a positive right to healthcare ought to lie primarily with those associations *closest* to the person in need. The first community that ought to address the sickness of a child in most cases should be the child's family. It is not the government's primary responsibility to ensure that a child with a bad cold receives sufficient rest or that an elderly person with walking difficulties can go grocery shopping. Their children, relatives, and friends should be the first to assist.

But as stressed by the Catholic philosopher Christopher Tollefsen, "the state properly has within the scope of its concern all persons within its borders. Consequently it falls to the state to correct for the inevitable gaps in the scope of concern of voluntary associations."[37] The state may therefore intervene directly, but only when there is clearly no other association in closer proximity to those with a particular healthcare need, or when all other communities have failed or proved unable to realize the need.

Even in those instances when government appears to be the only institution capable of meeting the need, subsidiarity suggests that once a non-state community has emerged that is capable of addressing the healthcare need, the government ought to begin devolving many of its responsibilities to the new association (or to a community that has recovered its capacity to meet the need). For if a government sought to continue exercising primary responsibilities in light of such developments, it would significantly impede the capacity of individuals and communities to promote or directly participate in the good of health. In Tollefsen's words, "Such a state seems, to that extent, unjust."[38]

Debt and Deficits

During the healthcare debates that preoccupied millions of Americans between 2009 and 2012, it became clear that it was not simply Obamacare's expansion of state power that bothered many Americans. At a more mundane level, the debate was also about money. The provision of healthcare and welfare more generally is not and cannot be "free." Attention to this question of cost has no doubt been sharpened by many

Americans' concerns about the nation's public debt level and the size of government deficits.

On May 1, 2013, the total public debt held by the United States totaled $16.805 trillion.[39] In 2012, the Congressional Budget Office (CBO) warned America's political leaders that unless there were significant changes to current tax and spending policies, America would attain a national debt-to-GDP ratio of 93 percent by 2022 and a disturbing 199 percent of GDP by 2035.[40] In a subsequent update, the CBO confirmed the United States would end fiscal year 2012 for "the fourth year in a row with a deficit of more than $1 trillion." As if that was not enough, the CBO stated that the end of the 2012 fiscal year had seen federal debt held by the public reaching 73 percent of GDP. This was the highest level since 1950 and about twice the share that it measured at the end of 2007.[41]

So why has the United States accumulated such levels of public debt? The answer lies in a long-term imbalance between spending and revenue. In 2012, taxes and other revenue paid for approximately two-thirds of federal government expenditures. The remaining balance was covered by borrowing.[42] This pattern has been in place for a long time.

Today the bulk of federal government spending is dominated by welfare programs. In 1967, federal spending on what are formally described as "human resources"—Social Security; Medicare; Health-expenditures; Education, Training, Employment, and Social Services; Veterans benefits; and Income Security (i.e., unemployment benefits)—constituted 32.6 percent of the federal budget.[43] The equivalent percentage in 2009 was 61.3 percent.[44] These figures give us some sense of what happens, fiscally-speaking, when governments try to assume prime responsibility for giving direct effect to the principle of solidarity and pay lip-service, at best, to subsidiarity.

Part of the Catholic response to this situation should surely be to examine America's welfare programs at whatever level of government they occur and to ask (1) whether the design of these policies truly reflects the principles of solidarity and subsidiarity, and (2) whether they are helping to realize human flourishing. Programs failing to meet such criteria should either, at a minimum, be significantly reformed or abolished altogether.

Aside, however, from addressing the immediate issues, America's fiscal challenges provide an opportunity for Catholics to seriously reflect on the ethics of debt: public and private.

Such an endeavor is long overdue. In spite of the pivotal role that has long been played by debt and deficit spending in modern economies, contemporary Catholic social teaching generally has relatively little to say about these questions. Even the very comprehensive *Compendium of Catholic Social Doctrine* confines itself to very broad statements about finance, and never really addresses the moral dimension of private and public debt.

This absence of sustained modern Catholic reflection on financial questions is puzzling. After all, most of the practices of modern finance and banking first assumed concrete and increasingly-sophisticated form in the Catholic world of medieval Europe. For centuries, Catholic bishops and theologians invested considerable energy in understanding the world of money and banking. They were driven to do so because of the usury issue, which raised questions about the legitimacy of charging interest on loans.

In his two-volume study of Catholic social doctrine, perhaps the most authoritative twentieth-century English-speaking commentator on Catholic social teaching, the late Rodger Charles, S.J., illustrated that the Church understood usury as a *loan for subsistence* (as in the case of a wealthy person who loans money to a starving man to buy food instead of simply helping the distressed individual with no expectation of financial return) as opposed to a *loan of capital*.[45] In other words, the Church has long understood, to quote the fourteenth-century theologian Bernardino of Siena, that "[m]oney has not only the character of money, but it has beyond this a productive character which we commonly call capital."[46] This distinction is crucial, as it does not appear that the Church ever had any serious objections to people lending others capital.[47]

Having examined authoritative patristic, medieval, and early modern Catholic commentaries on this subject, the historian Werner Sombart remarks:

> The very simple formula in which ecclesiastical authority expressed its attitude to the question of profit making is this: Interest on a pure money loan, in any form, is forbidden; profit on capital, in any form, is permitted, whether it flows from commercial business, or from an industrial undertaking . . . or from insurance against transport risks; or from shareholding in an enterprise . . . or however else.[48]

A welcome side effect of Catholic analysis of these questions was that Catholic theologians were consequently among the first to identify money's primary functions, illustrate how money in the conditions of economic freedom could assume the form of capital, demonstrate the moral legitimacy of charging interest on money as capital, and assess the moral status of different debts in different contexts.

Today it is much harder to find Catholic contributors commenting on the moral and economic issues associated with debt (private and public) and deficits who go beyond broad admonitions to put the poor's interests first in an age of austerity. Several years ago, however, one prominent Catholic proved willing to engage some of the deeper background of these matters.

In 2010, Benedict XVI indicated that a deeper moral disorder may underlie the running up of high levels of private and public debt in many developed nations. While avoiding entering into the technicalities of whether or not high levels of public debt and government deficit spending helps or hinders long-term economic growth, Benedict suggested that the willingness of so many people and governments to incur what many regard as extraordinary levels of indebtedness may mean that "we are living at the expense of future generations."[49] On the face of it, that would appear to constitute a rather flagrant violation of intergenerational solidarity.

But Benedict then sharpened his argument. This apparent choice on the part of governments, communities, and individuals to increasingly live off debt means that people are "living in untruth." "We live," Benedict stated, "on the basis of appearances, and the huge debts are meanwhile treated as something that we are simply entitled to."[50]

In fact, we can go further and argue that casual attitudes toward debt may well reflect a mindset of practical atheism: living and acting as if God does not exist, as if the only life is this life, as if the future does not matter. Only people who have no hope—no hope in God, no hope in redemption, no hope for the future—will think and act this way.

The economist John Maynard Keynes once famously wrote, "In the long run, we are all dead." To be fair to Keynes, he was making a specific point about monetary theory. Yet his words are evocative of an outlook that should trouble Catholics. For if we choose to allow our governments' fiscal policies to be dominated by short-term perspectives, we should not be surprised to see governments taking on ever-escalating levels of public debt and running year after year of trillion-dollar deficits. Likewise, if individuals and families want to engage in levels of consumption that are beyond their means, then recourse to loans for consumption is one way to realize that goal. But what do such choices say about a society's priorities and conception of human flourishing?

For governments, businesses, families, and individuals to take on debt is not intrinsically problematic. It is often an entirely reasonable choice—ethically and economically. A good example might be a government deciding to borrow money in order to fulfill an urgent need for public infrastructure: a function that no less than Adam Smith thought *was* a government responsibility.

Likewise the choice of an individual to take on a loan to start a business is surely uncontroversial in itself. Nevertheless it remains that a culture of inexorably-increasing levels of public and private debt and a failure to confront its moral and economic causes can slowly corrode the sense of responsibility on the part of governments and individuals for their freely-undertaken financial obligations and severely tempt them—and the rest of us—to live in a fantasy world of moral and fiscal unreality. In such a world, true freedom becomes a chimera.

Money, Money, Money

Another aspect of the government's role vis-à-vis the economy that has received relatively little attention in modern Catholic social teaching is the question of monetary policy. Inasmuch as the Church's social teaching discusses this issue, the emphasis has been upon the government's responsibility to maintain a *stable* currency: the requirement that money has a stable *internal* value in the sense of price stability. This in turn translates into a stable *external* value of the currency vis-à-vis other currencies. To the extent that governments can realize and maintain monetary stability, they make an important contribution to the economic dimension of the common good.

In terms of the technicalities of realizing this end, the Church doesn't endorse any one approach. The different political and economic trade-offs associated with, for instance, central banking versus the gold standard are a subject that Catholics are free to argue about among themselves.

But this leaves unanswered the issue of *why* the Church emphasizes the importance of monetary stability. While this is not spelled out in official Catholic social teaching, the reasons are not hard to discern. Monetary *instability* damages the common good in numerous ways. Inflation is a good example of this.

When the general price of goods and services rises rapidly over time, there is a decline in a currency's purchasing power.

Those who suffer are people who live off accumulated savings, or those on fixed incomes such as pensioners, the elderly, and the poor. In that sense, inflation effectively redistributes resources from these people, to those whose incomes have more chance of keeping pace with inflation. The ability of those on fixed incomes to maneuver in the face of inflation is far more limited than those who are younger, healthier, and possess more disposable wealth to invest.

Part of the argument for allowing a central bank to follow policies of low-but-persistent levels of inflation is that it boosts employment. The problem, however, is that such policies are like taking a stimulant. While inflation may have a short-term positive impact upon unemployment, the effect is only short-term. Maintaining the "high" requires another stimulant.

Moreover, as Sean Fieler observes, the subsequent rising prices associated with this stealth inflation have actually eroded many Americans' standard of living over the long term. If the purchasing power of a currency is devalued by, say, 2 percent in a given year, that effectively cancels out half of the benefit of a 4 percent wage increase in that same year. Part of the insidiousness of even a relatively low inflation level is thus the way it anesthetizes wage earners to gradual declines in their wages' purchasing power.[51]

A second effect of inflation is that it thrusts more and more people into higher tax brackets while simultaneously decreasing their money's spending power. Thanks to inflation, an American family which fell into a low income tax bracket in 1980, for example, would almost certainly fall into a higher tax bracket in 2013. Inflation, it might be said, thus allows governments to avoid the requirement of natural justice concerning gaining the people's consent before increasing taxes.

Then there are the effects of monetary instability upon people's ability to engage their right of economic initiative. Inflation impairs the ability of entrepreneurs, businesses, and consumers to make sound decisions concerning whether or not to launch a new product, expand their business, or make particular investments. In an economy in which high inflation levels prevail, for instance, it's much harder for businesses to discern whether their cost increases are real, or if they reflect inflation.

When all these elements are combined, they increase uncertainty—something that discourages economic creativity, prudent risk-taking, and investment. But the subsequent damage to the common good is magnified by the fact that a government's failure to maintain monetary stability may well constitute an act of injustice. Historically speaking, governments have proved very susceptible to manipulating monetary policy for self-interested short-term reasons (such as their reelection) or to benefit particular interest groups (such as those who vote for them) at the cost of long-term monetary stability.

Catholic thinkers were among the first to identify such developments as unjust. In the fourteenth century, for example, Bishop Nicole Oresme of Lisieux (1320–1382) assailed the widespread practice of currency debasement among European monarchs of the time in his *Tractatus de origine, Natura, Jure et Mutationibus Monetarum* (1355). The king, he insisted, did *not* "own" the kingdom's money. Rather he was its custodian, and the crown's responsibility was to maintain the stability of the currency's value.[52]

In the early seventeenth century, the Spanish theologian Juan de Mariana, S.J., wrote an entire treatise, *De monetae mutatione*, which was highly critical of those governments that depreciated currencies in pursuit of dubious ends.[53] For his pains, Mariana was charged with treason and sentenced to life imprisonment in a Franciscan monastery. One-hundred fifty-two years after Mariana's death, Adam Smith indicated little had changed in the way governments treated money. He lamented that "in every country in the world . . . the avarice and injustice of princes and sovereign states abusing the confidence of their subjects, have by degrees diminished the real quality of the metal, which had been originally contained in their coins."[54]

Across the Atlantic just one year later, America's most prominent lay Catholic had the distinction of being the only member of the new Senate of Maryland to vote against a legal tender law that allowed Marylanders to pay their debts in fiat paper money issued by either the Continental Congress or Maryland. The crux of Charles Carroll's argument was as much moral as economic. Such a law (which he described as "a most infamous action"[55]) meant, Carroll maintained, that the government was effectively allowing debtors who had been lent money in pounds-sterling to repay their loan in a paper currency that, thanks to wartime inflation, was becoming worth less and less by the day. This meant no current debtor would have to repay the full real value of what they owed.

Alongside this basic injustice, Carroll observed such measures meant that creditors (of whom, it must be said, he and his father, were among Maryland's most prominent) would be less trusting in the future, thereby limiting access to credit for those who needed and merited it. It also opened the door to what Carroll called "the secret workings and devices of the avaricious and the artful."[56] By this, he seemed to have had in mind not only less-than-scrupulous debtors, but also governments who issued fiat currency. Carroll was especially scathing in his criticisms of the monetary ideas of the Scottish-French financier John Law, whose attempt to solve the French government's fiscal imbalances by indulging in the wholesale issue of paper money eventually produced a financial bubble and the crash of France's *Banque Générale* in 1720.[57]

More generally, Carroll viewed monetary instability as extremely dangerous for the republic in both the short and long term. Among the weaknesses undermining the Revolutionary War effort, Carroll repeatedly insisted to his fellow Americans with a weaker grasp of economics than himself, was the absence of sound money.[58] In more general terms, Carroll was convinced that sound money was indispensable for independence and the future well-being of Maryland and the United States.[59] Carroll's own preference was for a metallic standard. He reasoned that the scarcity of precious metal for minting would make it a natural stabilizing force in the economy.[60] But however the new American republic decided to address the issue, Carroll argued, America's experiment in freedom *would* falter in the absence of sound money. In short, for Charles Carroll, monetary stability was about the common good.

The Economy and Religious Liberty

From the beginning of America, many of its citizens have worried about the expansion of the government's involvement in the economy. Many Catholic Americans have shared that concern. But, as demonstrated, the Church's vision of the nature of human freedom means that Catholic worries should be driven as much by moral qualms as by worries about the economic impact of such expansionism.

Unfortunately for the Church in America, it is now apparent that the effects of excessive government economic intervention go beyond Americans' ability to engage their economic liberty in the pursuit of human flourishing. It is now directly impacting a freedom that has always been central to the achievements of the American Revolution and to which the American republic has always accorded a high priority: the right of religious liberty.

Further Reading

James Bartholomew, *The Welfare State We're In* (London: Politico's Publishing, 2004).

Philip Booth (ed.), *Catholic Social Teaching and the Market Economy* (London: IEA, 2007).

Joseph Boyle, "Fairness in Holdings: A Natural Law Account of Property and Welfare Rights," *Social Philosophy and Policy* 18, (2001), 206–26.

Stephen Grabill (ed.), *Sourcebook In Late-Scholastic Monetary Theory* (Lanham, MD: Lexington Books, 2007).

Samuel Gregg, "Money and its Future in the Global Economy," in Samuel Gregg and Harold James (eds.), *Natural Law, Economics and the Common Good* (Exeter: Imprint Academic, 2012), 169–92.

Chapter 4
The First Freedom

To obtain religious, as well as civil liberty, I entered zealously into the Revolution . . . God grant that this religious liberty may be preserved in these States to the end of time.

Charles Carroll, 1827[1]

[I]t is imperative that the entire Catholic community in the United States come to realize the grave threats to the Church's public moral witness presented by a radical secularism which finds increasing expression in the political and cultural spheres. The seriousness of these threats needs to be clearly appreciated at every level of ecclesial life. Of particular concern are certain attempts being made to limit that most cherished of American freedoms, the freedom of religion.

Benedict XVI, 2012[2]

Any regime seeking to establish authoritarian control over a society knows that extinguishing political, civil, and economic freedom is never quite enough. Whether it is those relatively rare outright efforts to destroy religion *per se*, or the more subtle, occasionally vicious, but nevertheless relentless harassment such as that experienced by the Catholic Church in Germany between 1933 and 1945, *all* such governments know that religious freedom seriously limits their power. Robust conceptions of religious freedom diminish their capacity to interfere with people's ability—including the liberty of non-believers—to think and draw conclusions about religious truth, to make choices consistent with their religious beliefs, and to organize their religious community's external activities and internal life. All these liberties make a truly authoritarian state that much harder to realize.

The significance of religious liberty—and, more particularly, *libertas ecclesiae*—for freedom more generally has been well-understood for centuries. The famous words recorded in Luke's Gospel—*Reddite ergo, quae Caesaris sunt, Caesari et, quae Dei sunt, Deo* [render to Caesar what belongs to Caesar, and to God what belongs to God] (20:25)—were revolutionary in their implications for how the West and therefore America subsequently understood the nature and boundaries of government. No longer could the state claim the divine characteristics with which it was invested by the pre-Christian pagan world. Instead the state and its rulers were now, like everyone else, *sub Deus*.

The Greek phrase for church, *ekklesia*, comes from combining the word *kaleo* (to call) with the prefix *ek* (out). This particular aspect of Christianity irked the Roman authorities so much that they accused the early Christians of atheism. To belong to the Christian church meant that while you were a member of a community which respected the state's authority, you did not practice the religion of the state. To the Roman mind, that meant you were effectively godless.

Throughout the centuries, there were many instances when the Catholic Church associated itself to varying degrees with the exercise of temporal power. That produced many entanglements between Catholicism and the state that took the Church centuries to escape. Yet despite this association, the crucial distinction between the claims of God and those of Caesar, with its implicit limiting of government power, has persisted in Catholic belief and action in ways less obvious in some other Christian communities.

In the West, the doctrine of the Divine Right of Kings enjoyed considerable favor in Anglican communities and some Lutheran confessions. It even received support from some absolutist Catholic monarchs. This doctrine, however, found few advocates and many critics among Catholic clergy and bishops precisely because of the way it diminished the Church's autonomy from the state. The Jesuit scholar Francisco Suárez wrote powerfully against the idea.[3] Another sixteenth-century theologian and Doctor of the Church, Saint Robert Bellarmine, not only refuted divine right arguments; he also attacked the French monarchy's efforts to exercise more control over the Catholic Church in France.[4]

At first glance, this background seems far removed from the world of twenty-first–century America: a society in which most people describe themselves as Christian, but in which Catholics, Eastern Orthodox, Protestants, Jews, Mormons, Muslims, Hindus, Buddhists, and non-believers live side-by-side in a generally peaceful manner. Part of this relative peacefulness flows from a certain confidence on the part of Americans that their religious freedom receives considerable protection under the First Amendment's Establishment and Free Exercise clauses: "Congress shall make no law respecting an establishment of religion, or prohibiting the free exercise thereof."

The history of religious liberty in America and its relationship to Catholicism is, however, more complicated than even many Catholic Americans realize. Even less well understood is how the growth of government's involvement in economic life not only provides a means for the state to unreasonably constrain Catholics' ability to live their faith, but also tempts many Catholic Americans to constrain their own appreciation of religious liberty's full meaning. For religious freedom is not simply about tolerance and peace. At a deeper level, religious liberty is really about human flourishing.

America, Catholics, and Religious Liberty

One reason why some of the first Catholics migrated to Britain's American colonies from the seventeenth century onward was to escape religious persecution in England, Scotland, and Ireland. Almost a hundred and thirty years before Thomas Jefferson drafted the Statute of Virginia for Religious Freedom in 1777, the early Maryland colony established by Lord Baltimore and other English Catholics in the 1630s was specifically committed to a high degree of religious freedom by the Maryland Toleration Act of 1649. This stated: "No person or persons . . . . professing to believe in Jesus Christ, shall from henceforth be any waies troubled, molested or discountenanced for or in respect of his or her religion nor in the free exercise thereof."[5]

Toleration was thus plainly limited to Christians. Excluded were those (such as Jews) who denied Christ's divinity. That Maryland's Toleration Act was sufficiently controversial, however, is attested by the fact that it was repealed five years later by a combination of Anglicans and Puritans—a legislative action accompanied by provisions specifically banning Catholics from publically practicing their faith, voting, or holding public office.

In 1658, the Act itself was restored. But following Britain's Glorious Revolution in 1688, Maryland's limited experiment in religious liberty came to end. The Toleration Act was rescinded in 1692 and the public practice of Catholicism was once again banned. Maryland Catholics such as the Carrolls gradually found themselves subject to various disabilities on account of their religious beliefs, not least among which (alongside being forbidden to vote or hold public office) was the double taxation levied upon the property of Catholics living in Maryland in the 1750s during the French and Indian Wars. Between 1720 and the outbreak of the Revolution, Maryland's Catholics had no success in diminishing the laws that robbed them of many of the freedoms enjoyed by their fellow colonists. By 1756, legalized anti-Catholic discrimination had become so bad in Maryland that Charles Carroll of Annapolis seriously contemplated leaving the province altogether and removing his family and wealth to the French (and therefore Catholic) colony of Louisiana.[6] The historian James Hutson does not exaggerate when he writes that "Until the American Revolution, Catholics in Maryland were dissenters in their own country, living at times under a state of siege."[7]

No doubt these circumstances created an extra incentive for Charles Carroll and other Catholic colonists to view the break with Britain as a once-in-a-lifetime opportunity to overturn the discrimination that Catholics endured as a matter of law in many American colonies. Writing the fourth of four letters published in the *Maryland Gazette* under the pseudonym of "First Citizen" in 1773, Charles Carroll made it politely but abundantly clear that any society that took freedom seriously must embrace a robust measure of religious liberty because freedom itself was indivisible.[8] And in his many conversations with his friend and political ally George Washington, Carroll never ceased to insist that the constitutional arrangements of the new United States had to exclude religious tests for public office.

His time spent in France, Carroll wrote in 1759, made it evident to him that the world's strongest Catholic power lacked at the time what Carroll called "that greatest blessing [,] civil liberty."[9] Living in Britain had made it equally obvious to Carroll that religious liberty certainly didn't exist in the world's strongest Protestant nation. Carroll nevertheless concluded that the existence of civil liberty in Britain and its colonies not only made life in Maryland preferable, it might also provide the foundations for the eventual realization of substantive religious freedom in America.[10]

One major cause of religious intolerance, Carroll believed, was the way in which the state's establishment of religion invariably resulted in governments using religion for narrow political advantage, thereby weakening religion's beneficial moral effects upon society. "Ye savage wars, ye cruel massacres, ye deliberate murders committed by law, under sanction of Religion," Carroll exclaimed in correspondence, "have no reformed ye morals of men. They have indeed answered ye purposes of ambition, they have abetted ye Revenge of an enraged Party and sometimes too they have served ye cravings of Lust."[11]

Nor could Carroll help highlighting that there was often an *economic* motive to religious intolerance. "Selfish men," he commented, "invented the religious tests to exclude from posts of profit & trust their weaker or more conscientious fellow subjects."[12] Hence it should be no surprise that Carroll later concurred with the vote of Maryland's House of Delegates in favor of allowing Quaker merchants to make a simple affirmation rather than being required to take the oath required of all merchants when disclosing their cargoes in Maryland ports.[13] Carroll was also conscious that his family's commercial success (and that of the other Maryland Catholics who, despite being a minority, together made up half of the colony's twenty largest fortunes) created, perversely enough, an economic incentive for both private individuals and government officials to invoke anti-Catholic laws against them in order to remove Catholic competitors from the marketplace or simply confiscate the wealth of Catholics.[14]

An even worse effect of state-sponsored religious intolerance, according to Carroll, was the way in which it shut down debate and discussion about religious truth. "Were an unlimited toleration allowed and men of all sects were to converse freely with each other," he argued, "their aversion from a difference of religious principles would soon wear away."[15] The point of religious tolerance was, to Carroll's mind, not the promotion of religious indifferentism (the self-evidently false position that all religions are basically the same and therefore equally meaningful or meaningless). Rather it was to create conditions in which people could argue about their respective religions' claims of truth without such differences leading to tragedies that did so much damage to Christianity's credibility, such as the Wars of Religion that gripped Europe from the Reformation until the mid-seventeenth century.

Religion and Liberty

These and similar questions were of intense interest to Alexis de Tocqueville during his visit to America in the early 1830s. Though Tocqueville struggled for most of his adult life with the claims of the Catholic Faith, he could not help but be fascinated by how his fellow Catholics fared in the United States. Tocqueville's France was, after all, a society in which Catholicism had long been intimately involved in politics. And while the Church in France had fought many political and legal battles with the monarchy during the age of absolutism, Catholicism in late-eighteenth century France emerged as perhaps the strongest bulwark of opposition to the French Revolution and its invocation of *liberté, égalité, fraternité*.

Tocqueville was deeply conscious that the Catholic Church in France and other countries had endured savage persecution at the hands of France's revolutionaries. The *Constitution civile du clergé* passed by France's National Assembly on July 12, 1790 represented an attempt to control the Church's inner life that went far beyond anything attempted by the Bourbons. As if overnight, the Civil Constitution created a basis for mass resistance to the Revolution on the part of devout French Catholics. Catholics in France also found it hard to forgive, let along forget, the mass killing of Catholic bishops, priests, and religious by revolutionaries who professed to be promoting liberty, not to mention the thousands of Catholics slaughtered in the Vendée region in what some have described as a genocidal effort to exterminate opposition to the Revolution.

Given this background, it is understandable Tocqueville was so surprised to find that Catholic clergy and laity in America numbered among the strongest defenders of America's commitment to religious liberty. "In France," he wrote, "I had seen the spirits of religion and of freedom marching in opposite directions. In America I found them intimately linked together in joint reign over the same land."[16] When Tocqueville asked one American Catholic priest (who made no effort to disguise his antipathy toward Protestantism) for his opinion on whether the civil power should lend its support to religion in the sense of European-like establishment arrangements, Tocqueville was taken aback to hear the priest say:

> I am profoundly convinced it is harmful. I know that the majority of Catholic priests in Europe have a contrary belief; I understand their point of view. They distrust the spirit of liberty whose first efforts have been directed against them. Having, besides, always lived under the sway of monarchical institutions which protected them, they are naturally led to regret that protection. They are therefore victims of an inevitable error. If they could live in this country, they would not be long in changing their opinions. . . .[17]

This Catholic American commitment to non-establishment represented no concession to the idea that it was best to marginalize or exclude religion from the American public square or that the state should be neutral about religion. Catholic Americans favored the strong distinction between the temporal and spiritual realms precisely because they believed it allowed religion to exert a civilizing influence upon American society.

After hearing these views expressed by priest after priest during his time in America, Tocqueville concluded that continental Europe had something to learn from the American approach toward religious freedom. In our own time, the same claim was made by no less than Benedict XVI.

Pope Benedict was far from uncritical of contemporary American culture.[18] Nonetheless he repeated on many occasions that one reason why America has avoided many of the disputes between Christians and non-believers that have plagued continental Europe since the various Enlightenments was the American Republic's decision to have no established church. Interestingly Benedict also specifically invoked

Tocqueville's claim that one of the reasons that "the unstable and fragmentary system of rules on which . . . this democracy is founded" somehow managed to work was the commitment to Christian religious and moral convictions that permeated American society.[19]

Part of the genius of America's religious arrangements, Benedict argued, was the insight that "the State itself had to be secular precisely out of love for religion in its authenticity, which can only be lived freely."[20] Truth, religion, and liberty were consequently reconciled in America in a manner that remains incomprehensible to some Europeans, even today. When Jacques Maritain visited the United States, he instantly noticed the difference between American and French understandings of the distinction between the spiritual and temporal realms. Maritain subsequently pleaded with Americans to "not let your concept of separation veer round to the European one."[21]

Such historical experiences make comprehensible the contribution of Catholic Americans to a document of the Second Vatican Council that repays careful rereading: the Declaration of Religious Liberty, *Dignitatis Humanae*. Reflecting one year after the Declaration's formal promulgation, the future Pope Benedict stressed that the initiative on this issue was taken by American bishops at the Council,[22] many of whom worked closely with key bishops from Eastern Europe—most notably, Archbishop Karol Wojtyła of Krakow, Poland—in an ultimately successful effort to bring the document to fruition.

American bishops were, for instance, among the most prominent in urging the Council not to incorporate a statement about religious freedom into the document on ecumenism. Instead they pressed for a separate text. They also focused the Council's attention upon how the Church could endorse religious freedom in ways that avoided accepting the view that individuals or governments could be indifferent toward religion. This was particularly important given that the phrase "religious liberty" had often been used in previous Church teaching as a way of describing the problem of indifferentism.

Religious Liberty and the Dictatorship of Relativism

American Catholicism's long appreciation of religious liberty's benefits makes more comprehensible the Church's reaction against efforts to circumscribe its freedom to live in accordance with its beliefs. Arguably the most serious infringement in recent decades was the January 2012 decision of the Obama Administration to require the insurance policies of most Catholic institutions to include coverage of abortion-inducing drugs, sterilizations, and contraception.

There was a religious exemption provided by this Health and Human Services (HHS) mandate. It specified that a "religious employer" was one which (1) had the inculcation of religious values as its purpose; (2) primarily employed persons who share its religious tenets; and (3) primarily served persons who share its religious tenets. The narrowness of this criteria, however, effectively *excluded* most Catholic universities, hospitals, schools, and charities from being covered by the exemption, despite the fact that the Church has always understood activities of helping the poor, educating people, and providing care for the sick—regardless of the faith of those being assisted—as flowing directly from its central mission.

Leaving aside the fact that the Catholic Church—and many others—has *always* regarded intentional abortion, sterilization, and contraception as intrinsically immoral acts (meaning they are incapable of being ordered to the good), the original HHS mandate was also based on two especially troubling assumptions. One is that the state was somehow in a position to tell the Catholic Church what constituted a Catholic religious activity and what did not. Consider the first of the conditions for an exemption identified by the first version of the mandate: the inculcation of religious values. Where, it might be asked, does the federal government derive the authority—let alone the competence!—to decide which values are religious and which are not?

The second assumption informing the mandate was that freedom of religion was essentially about freedom of worship. The implication was that religious liberty was limited to what you said and did inside a church, synagogue, or mosque. As we will see, a coherent conception of religious liberty goes beyond this rather limited definition.

But perhaps the HHS mandate's strangest aspect was the fact that it is not as if contraceptive devices, abortion-inducing drugs, and sterilization procedures are somehow in short supply throughout America. There are numerous ways for people who want these things to access them relatively inexpensively, such as through *publically* funded entities like Planned Parenthood. So why was the federal government so determined to force Catholic organizations and Catholic-owned businesses to pay for such things?

Part of the answer is ideological. While the Obama Administration spoke of a commitment to women's health, pregnancy does not qualify as a disease outside the ghoulish world of Planned Parenthood. Instead the ideological agenda at work was, first, the absolutization of choice for the sake of choice and, second, the desire to create a society in which any discussion of the actual ends we choose is increasingly considered unacceptable in public debates about law and morality.

Modern liberalism has a long history of trying to exclude consideration of the proper ends of human action from public discourse in the name of tolerance. But neither liberalism nor secularism are as neutral about such matters as they pretend.

Self-identified liberals (and secularists more generally) typically insist that justice and tolerance demand that government should not privilege any conception of morality—religious or secular—in framing its laws. Unfortunately for liberals, this position, outlined in excruciating detail by the seer of modern secular liberalism, the late John Rawls, is self-refuting. Why? Because it *privileges* a legal and political commitment to relativity about moral questions. It is the same absurdity underlying the philosophical skeptic's claim that there is no truth—except for *the* truth that there is no truth. But these little inconsistencies have never stopped liberals and secularists from using conceptions of tolerance and justice as weapons for terminating any contribution to public debate informed by the propositions that moral truth exists, that we can know it through revelation and/or reason, and that it is unjust to cordon off these truths from the public square.

Here we come face-to-face with the essence of what Benedict XVI famously described in a homily delivered just before his election as pope in 2005 as "the dictatorship of relativism." Most people think of tyrannies as involving the imposition of a defined set of ideas upon free citizens. Benedict XVI's point was that the coercion at the heart of the dictatorship of relativism derives precisely from the fact that it "does not recognize *anything* as definitive."[23]

In this world, tolerance is no longer about creating the space for us to express our views about the nature of good and evil and its implications for law and public morality, or to live our lives in accordance with our religious beliefs. Instead tolerance serves to banish the truth as the reference point against which all of us must test our ideas and beliefs. The objective is to reduce everyone to modern Pontius Pilates who, whatever their private beliefs, wash their hands in the face of obvious injustices such as what the Obama Administration inflicted upon the Catholic Church and, by extension, *anyone* whose convictions about the truth require them to abstain from cooperating in acts they regard as evil *per se*.

Secularists and liberals *do* of course have their own preferred ends. Here they embrace Hume's view that reason should be our passions' lackey. Reason's role, in other words, is not to identify what is rational for people to choose. Instead reason is reduced to merely devising the means for realizing whatever goals that people "just feel like" choosing.

On this basis, utilitarians such as Jeremy Bentham concluded that life was really about nothing more than the experience of sensations. Hence the goal of life was to maximize pleasure and minimize pain. But having repeatedly failed to construct a coherent hedonistic calculus of utility (even Rawls concluded it was a doomed endeavor[24]), the "ultimate goal" of liberalism and secularism now "consists," as Benedict noted in 2005, "solely of one's own ego and desires." That in turn reduces life and my choices to ensuring I am among those who are powerful enough to get to indulge my ego and my desires, sophistical enough to produce rationalizations for doing so, and strong enough to trample over anyone whose existence or beliefs might limit my ability to do whatever I just happen to "feel like" doing.

Here liberalism's essentially illiberal nature reveals its true face. Because if your theological or philosophical convictions get in the way of your employee's desire to avoid the "disease" of pregnancy, then too bad. Desire plus autonomy trumps all. Considered from this perspective, Obamacare was not just about socialized medicine. It also reflected, as one commentator wrote, "the principle that the comprehensive definition and delivery of human physical and emotional well-being is a responsibility of the liberal secular state."[25]

The Catholic Church and its teachings about good and evil go back 2,000 years. During that time, it has weathered the savage persecutions of the Roman Empire, the proclivities of absolutist monarchs, the terrorism of the French Revolution, the systematic harassment of National Socialism, and the all-out assault of Communism. And, perhaps most telling of all, it has managed to survive the many sins and often terrible faithlessness of its own members.

The Church's struggle with the dictatorship of relativism may, however, prove one of its most difficult challenges. It is a subtle form of oppression that trades off words like "choice" that strongly resonates in Western nations like America; the same societies in which many secularists all too quickly equate any religion's claim to teach the truth with murderers who fly planes into buildings.

But while battles such as those concerning the HHS mandate are certainly important for the Church's daily life in America, there is at least one possible benefit flowing from the mandate controversy. It may help Catholics remember *why* religious liberty is important and *how* it relates to the wider struggle for liberty. Close attention to this subject reveals some curious parallels with the struggle for economic liberty.

Why Religious Liberty Matters: The Limited State

In the ancient pre-Christian world, Judaism always implied some limits upon the authority of temporal rulers. It was, however, with Christianity's advent that the question of religious liberty—in the sense of the limits on state coercion regarding the religious beliefs and practices of individuals and organizations—started to assume profound significance.

Jesus Christ's words about Caesar were literally revolutionary in their implications for how most people (including non-Christians) subsequently understood the state. With good reason, Luke's Gospel records that Christ's "answer took [his questioners] by surprise" (20:26). For, as observed by the nineteenth-century English historian Lord Acton, "in religion, morality, and politics, there was only one legislator and one authority" in the pre-Christian ancient world: the *pólis* and later the Roman state.[26] Separation of the temporal and spiritual was incomprehensible to pagan minds because a distinction between the "temporal" and "spiritual" did not exist in European pre-Christian culture.

Throughout the Greco-Roman world, the widespread ascription of divine characteristics to the *pólis* and the Roman state was often paid lip service. Recognizing the strength of Jewish resentment concerning the token emperor worship required of the Empire's subjects, the Roman authorities generally exempted Jews from such acts. Yet there were times when the pagan synthesis of religion and state created immense difficulties for people. They could not, for instance, appeal to a divine law that transcended the state.

By universalizing the Jewish belief that those exercising legal authority were as subject to Yahweh's law as everyone else, Christianity achieved the hitherto unthinkable: the state's desacralization. Christianity remained respectful of the Roman state's authority. The writings of Saint Paul and Saint Peter underlined the divine origin of the state's legal authority.[27] Nevertheless Judaism and Christianity also quietly insisted that Caesar was not a god and may not behave as if he was god. Though Jews and Christians would pray *for* earthly rulers, it was anathema for them to pray *to* such rulers. As one early Christian martyr cried out before his execution, "*Deus major est, non imperatores*" [God is the greater One, not the emperors]! While Christians regarded the state as the custodian of social order, they did not consider the state itself to be the ultimate source of truth and law.[28] Christians thus viewed the state as an order that found its limits in a faith that worshiped not the state, but a God who stood over the state and judged it.[29]

This set the stage for ongoing confrontations between the state and the Catholic Church across the globe that persists until today. These embrace numerous questions ranging from the legitimacy of religious belief as a foundation for activity in the public square, blasphemy laws, religious tests for public office, and religious education in private and public settings, to state funding of religious activities. It need hardly be said that denial of religious liberty has resulted in the coercion of millions over the centuries, the worst in sheer numbers being that inflicted by Communist regimes upon Christians throughout the twentieth century.

When the Second Vatican Council declared that people have a right to religious freedom, it implicitly criticized any political system that unreasonably denied this freedom either as a matter of principle or substantially in practice. The political order that acknowledges religious liberty in the sense outlined in *Dignitatis Humanae* is thus by definition a restricted state. That in turn creates space for the Catholic Church—and other religious groups—to live out their freedoms.

Obviously religious freedom is not a catch-all basis for preventing the application of just law or tolerating terrible crimes committed in the name of faith. A government can, according to *Dignitatis Humanae* itself, act "against possible abuses committed in the name of religious freedom." This, however, must be done "in accordance with legal principles which are in conformity with the objective moral order."[30] By "objective moral order," the Church means the knowledge of good and will knowable by reason because it is inscribed into reason itself: that is, the natural law.

If, for example, a group of Hindu Americans attempted to revive the practice of *suttee* (the Hindu practice of a widow immolating herself on her husband's funeral pyre which was banned by the British throughout India in 1826), state officials may intervene to stop the practice. Religious liberty, grounded upon the good of religion, is no defense of one person's choice to intentionally kill himself or another person, for such an act would involve violating the good of life.

But the Church's conception of religious liberty also cuts the other way inasmuch as it clashes with those who view religious tolerance as a basis for the state to unreasonably circumscribe the freedom to act on the basis of their faith. The Catholic vision of religious liberty has, for instance, little in common with skeptical understanding of tolerance. These suggest that the soundest basis for tolerance is to not have robust beliefs about good and evil, right and wrong; in short, the more skeptical someone is, the greater his commitment to tolerance.

Such notions of tolerance are highly problematic. If we really believe the goal of tolerance is tolerating, we should accept even intolerance. Likewise, if someone considers that the greatest underpinning for tolerance is to avoid any strong belief, he should not strongly deem intolerance to be mistaken. The paradox from such understandings of tolerance cannot escape their inability to respond to the question "Why be tolerant?" without committing themselves to particular *goods* such as social peace. The idea that tolerance must be established upon value-neutrality is thus fallacious.[31]

This language of goods and the good is significant because Catholicism does not believe in religious liberty just because it helps limit the state's coercive powers. *Dignitatis Humanae* makes clear that something else is at stake: the common good and human flourishing.

Why Religious Liberty Matters: Human Flourishing

The centrality of religious liberty to human flourishing becomes more apparent when we ask ourselves what distinguishes religion from, say, politics or culture. In the end, what makes religion different, even unique, is that it's ultimately concerned with one's search for and conclusions about the truth concerning the transcendent.

The word "religion" is itself derived from the Latin *religionem*. Broadly speaking, this meant reverence for the gods, respect for what is sacred, and the bond between man and the gods. In writings penned by figures ranging from pagans such as Cicero to Catholics such as Saint Augustine, such reverence, respect, and bonds are clearly understood as implying the living of our lives in accordance with knowledge of the truth about such things.

In that sense, religion is one of the key goods at the heart of human flourishing.[32] Religion and religious organizations are directly concerned with knowing the truth about the divine (including whether or not there is a God); and, second, the meaning of that truth for human choice and action in a way that, for instance, political beliefs, ideological convictions, and non-religious forms of human organization are not.

Particular political or ideological convictions may imply or reflect commitment to specific religious positions. From its very beginnings, Marxism was deeply committed to and reliant upon atheism from its adherents. Likewise National Socialism embodied an ill-disguised pagan vision of the universe. But political philosophies such as liberalism, socialism, and conservatism are not immediately concerned with attempting to know and then express and live the truth about the divine and the transcendent in the ways that atheism, Christianity, Islam, Judaism, or Hinduism most certainly are.

Note that the particular understanding of religion outlined here does not in itself require the assent of the mind and will to any specific religious claim. An atheist is one who has presumably thought seriously about and found unconvincing all religions' claims to embody a divine revelation, as well as the many arguments for the existence of a divinity which have and continue to be made on the basis of reason unaided by revelation.

But what atheists and others can share with Catholics is an understanding of the point of considering (1) whether there is some ultimate, more-than-human source of value and meaning, (2) of using one's intellect to discern the truth of this question, and (3) then trying to order our lives on the basis of our judgments about this matter. For what is at stake is knowledge of the truth and our ability to arrange our lives on the basis of what we discern to be the truth, consistent with the freedom of others to do the same.[33] Truth is thus the foundation of religious liberty, but truth is also the goal of religious liberty.

This understanding of religion's nature as an element of human flourishing has several effects. First, it creates the grounds for religious tolerance without conceding that everyone must embrace relativism about religion. That is why *Dignitatis Humanae* was able, on the one hand, to affirm religious liberty by stating that "The truth cannot impose itself except by virtue of its own truth, as it makes its entrance into the mind at once quietly and with power,"[34] while simultaneously insisting that nothing in the Declaration contradicted the Catholic Church's unchanging teaching that the "one true religion subsists in the Catholic and Apostolic Church."[35]

Second, this conception of religion underscores the element of free choice which must be operative in any act that facilitates human flourishing. The good of religion can only be actualized by each person's free choice to seek the transcendent and then order his life to it. Such freedom of choice is crucial for the *integrity* of our religious beliefs. As Saint Augustine wrote: "If there is no assent, there is no faith, for without assent one does not really believe."[36] Coercion for the sake of religious belief destroys people's understanding of the very point of freely exploring such questions.

Third, the Catholic understanding of religion bolsters the case for religious liberty as an immunity from coercion in respect of religious belief, expressions of religious belief, and other acts of putting one's religious belief into practice (compatible with the rights of others, public peace, and public order). For if *religion* is conceptualized in this manner, then religious *liberty* must be about seeking to guarantee that all are *free to consider* whether or not there is an ultimate transcendent being whose existence provides a compelling explanation of life, and to *assent freely* and *act upon* the conclusions of their reason, provided justice and morality are respected.

Religious liberty thus goes far, far beyond the freedom to worship. It affects matters such as fasting or not fasting at particular times of the year; whether we dress in particular ways; if we choose to educate our children in a certain fashion;

how we understand and live the moral life; and even whether we convert to another religion or abandon our religion. All such liberties allow everyone to order their lives on the basis of their answers to these questions, consistent with the rights of others and public order.

This also tells us that religion is not a purely "private" good and therefore cannot be "privatized." Addressing this very point, *Dignitatis Humanae* states that our "own social nature requires that man gives external expression to his internal acts of religion, that he communicate with others on religious matters, and profess his religion in community."[37] Since all people think, act, and communicate in relationship with others at different points of time, it follows that their profession and practice of a religion is naturally expressed through a series of acts, individual and collective, private and public, which create and sustain human communities. Religious liberty thus also goes beyond protecting individuals' choices. It also safeguards the beliefs and acts of those communities that people form on the basis of common beliefs about the transcendent and how such communities should live their lives.

Religious Liberty and the Limited Government Movement

Part of the distinctiveness of the Catholic vision of religious liberty is that you don't have to be Catholic to accept *Dignitatis Humanae's* account of the meaning of religious freedom. It is after all an argument based on reason and a reasoned account of human flourishing and the ends of human freedom. That said, we still face the question of how Catholics can make the Church's conception of religious liberty a living force in the movement to push back the encroachments of the state in America.

The first step is to be very clear that the Church is not seeking "establishmentarianism." Catholicism does not expect the government to aggressively promote an official national religion, let alone the Catholic Faith. Not only would that be contrary to the historical experience of Catholic America, it is also not *Dignitatis Humanae's* stance.

From this flows a second step: which is to insist that it is not the business of governments or officials acting in their name to formally or informally promote a brand of secularism as an unofficial state faith that seeks to restrict the exercise of religious liberty to religious worship.

Here we should be clear about the various meanings of the term "secular." The word itself was originally used by Catholics to signify the affairs of this world or the daily life of any human society. When used in this way (including by no less than Aquinas himself), the expression did not necessarily have negative connotations.[38]

"Secularism" today, however, often denotes a distinct set of beliefs which hold that *any* religious-motivated action is unacceptable in the public square. Such secularism has nothing to do with maintaining a healthy distinction between spiritual and temporal authority. Rather it is about the state effectively prohibiting or unduly restricting religiously-motivated acts outside the freedom to worship.

Taken to its logical conclusion, what might be called "doctrinaire secularism" can easily amount to the not-so-covert promotion of atheism or skepticism as an unofficial state religion. In this scenario, the government insists that anyone contributing, for example, to political discussion *must* act as if there is no God; or if there is a God, then this *ought* to have no bearing whatsoever upon their choices and actions in the public square. This is, more or less, the view expressed at different times by John Rawls.[39]

These are most certainly *not* religiously neutral positions. As John Finnis writes, both standpoints are derivatives of two of the three variants of atheism identified long ago by Plato (though he does not use the word): there is no God; or no God which has any concern with human affairs; or any such divine concern with the human is easily appeased by a superficial piety and requires no demanding reform of human vices.[40]

Needless to say, these forms of atheism rest on theological and philosophical arguments just as debatable (and, in fact, considerably weaker) as those underlying Judaism and orthodox Christianity. Not least among the controversial premises of such secularist thought are three often unspoken claims. One is the notion that all religion must necessarily be contrasted with reason. Obviously this conflicts with the entire Catholic tradition of understanding reason as capable of providing the preambles to Catholic faith.

A second unstated assumption is that religion is essentially a historical avatar which, in the interests of a peaceful transition to the better world that will be revealed to us by the sciences, must be accorded some token respect. To hold this position, however, is to essentially privilege a secularist understanding of history that is by no means undisputed.

A third and especially worrying presumption often underpinning secularist thinking is that human self-determination essentially concerns each individual's epicurean satisfaction of their desires. This implies that society must dramatically limit the influence of any religion which suggests that authentic human flourishing involves one's free conformity to moral truths knowable by reason but which receive confirmation from what different religions regard as direct revelations from God. Again, that is to promote a view of human liberty and fulfillment that has been rigorously disputed since the time of the Greeks.

The Non-Confessional Option

Against these claims, there is a principled position that Catholic Americans can articulate: one consistent with the history of religious freedom in America and the teaching of

Dignitatis Humanae—that the government's position vis-à-vis religion may be one of *non-confessionalism*. This is a state of affairs in which federal, state, and local governments refrain from according formal legal recognition to any one view of religion in the sense of formally establishing any one religion. It also genuinely seeks to treat members of all religious groups, including non-believers, fairly. This arrangement seeks to guarantee the freedom of all religious communities and non-believers within a free society, consistent with the liberties of others and the legitimate demands of public order.

Understood in this way, non-confessionalism doesn't translate into the government regarding religious liberty as a mandate to free people "from" religion. Nor does it mean denying a nation's religious heritage in the name of tolerance. To pretend, for example, that Christianity has not exerted tremendous influence upon the formation and history of America or Europe is as ahistorical as trying to deny the influence of Judaism in Israel, Hinduism in India, Islam in Saudi Arabia, Shintoism in Japan, or Buddhism in Thailand. It is perfectly possible for a nation to affirm historical truths about a religion's influence upon a nation while also insisting that a robust conception of religious freedom is a right enjoyed by every member of society, regardless of their faith or non-belief.

But here Catholics must remember that the case for non-confessionalism is a *principled* argument rather than one based on pragmatism. There may well be other supplementary reasons (immediate concerns, for example, about preserving civil peace) for states to tolerate a plurality of religious beliefs and religiously-motivated actions within their borders. The difficulty with relying, however, upon pragmatic rationales is twofold.

First, pragmatism provides no *principled* basis to protect the religious liberty of others if a group with little respect for religious liberty becomes the majority and establishes political dominance over that society. Being "pragmatic" in such circumstances could easily lead to the conclusion that suppressing some or all religions is "the pragmatic thing to do."

Second, the absence of a principled defense of religious liberty makes it easier for governments to act in ways that unreasonably suppress the religious liberty of individuals and organizations. Almost all Communist states were formally committed by their constitutions to religious liberty. Yet the same regimes regularly invoked "pragmatic" concerns to unreasonably infringe, corrode, or suppress the religious liberty of individuals and organizations. By contrast, if religious liberty is grounded on the idea of human flourishing, then the burden of proof for the state's legitimate coercion of religious believers in countries that take the rule of law seriously is much, much higher.

Government as Trojan House

Pressing the case for non-confessionalism in the terms described above is only part of the Catholic American contribution to limiting government's reach through making the Church's robust argument for religious liberty. Catholic Americans also need to ask themselves some very hard questions about how government funding of any number of church-managed programs has not only made such institutions unduly susceptible to secularist ways of thinking, but also elicited a willingness on some Catholics' part to unreasonably compromise their religious freedom.

As the funds from state contracts begin constituting a significant part of Catholic organizations' financial resources, their culture can easily change. Reliance on such support creates incentives to avoid potential confrontations with state authorities about how they do what they do and why they do it. It is not unknown for Catholic organizations in receipt of—or seeking—government contracts to subtly (and sometimes not-so-subtly) downplay their Catholic roots, mission, and identity. They slowly cease to be institutions that partake of the *libertas ecclesiae*. Instead they start morphing into what George Weigel aptly describes as "mere vehicles for the delivery of state-defined and state approved 'benefit,'"[41] rather than seeking to live out Christ's commandment to love our neighbor in ways consistent with the fullness of the truth revealed by Christ to His Church.

Then there is the depressing fact that acceptance of state funding by Catholic bodies can encourage many people working in such organizations to begin viewing the state as their primary master. Again, this should not be surprising. If 80 percent of a Catholic charity's income comes from government contracts, the government *has* effectively become their paymaster. Even more disturbing is the prospect of the leadership of some Catholic organizations using the fact of state funding to legitimate their *own* desire to dilute such institutions of any concrete Catholic commitments beyond vague appeals to social justice that are impossible to distinguish from the programs of left-wing social movements.

On other occasions, such subtle cultural shifts can reflect Catholic organizations embracing, unconsciously or otherwise, an understanding of the First Amendment far more narrow and restrictive than what's actually embodied in existing legal precedent. This situation was experienced by a priest who, at the beginning of a psychology internship at a Catholic Charities clinic in 2001, had to undergo routine tests to ascertain his ability to address some difficult situations:

> The clinic supervisor tested [the priest] on three hypothetical counseling situations: a depressed pregnant woman who wants to abort her child; two homosexuals seeking advice on their relationship, and a divorcing couple asking for counseling. In keeping with Catholic teachings, the priest advised against the abortion, refused

to endorse homosexual unions, and encouraged the divorcing couple to save their marriage. He failed the test. The supervisor explained: "We get government funds, so we are not Catholic."[42]

At the time, it was not at all clear that receipt of public funding would require this Catholic organization to act in ways so clearly contrary to Church teaching. What was clear is that the culture of this agency had plainly drifted from its Catholic moorings.

The Church has nothing in principle against Catholic organizations collaborating with governments for purposes such as outreach to the poor or the provision of healthcare and education. Nor does it regard being a recipient of public funding as intrinsically problematic.[43] It is, however, worth considering that the more the state takes in the way of taxes to pay for its often ineffective and socially-dysfunctional welfare programs, the more the financial ability of many Catholics to directly support Catholic outreach to those in need is diminished. That is not an argument for Catholics to be less financially supportive of the Church. But it is an economic reality that many Catholic leaders need to reflect upon more deeply.

Whatever view a Catholic organization adopts of government funding, the moment receipt of public funding requires a Catholic institution to compromise its freedom to teach and live the fullness of the Catholic Faith, it ought to rigorously contest such provisions. If these battles are lost in legislatures and the courts, then such organizations should dispense with public funding.

This especially matters with regard to the welfare state because, as James Hitchcock observes, the modern American welfare state is now more or less imbued with secularist assumptions about human beings. Why else would secularist thinkers insist, for example, that access to abortion-inducing drugs is a "human right" and that the welfare state should therefore cover the costs?

For if the secularist vision of freedom is one of progressive liberation through state action from what secularists typically regard as irrational constraints (such the Catholic conception of morality) upon human beings, it makes no sense for governments to exempt Catholics and the Catholic Church from the duty of conforming to secularist expectations when carrying out various outreach functions. Notions of sin or intrinsically immoral acts mean very little to most secularist commentators when it comes to the values they believe should be propagated through government and the welfare state. For them, religious liberty is at best a third or fourth-level concern compared to the specific rights associated with modern secularism, which, at its heart, embodies a hedonistic conception of human existence.[44]

And that creates a huge challenge for the Catholic Church in the future. Because the more the modern state associates itself with such visions of the person, the harder it will be for Catholic agencies to avoid tacitly buying into promoting such visions if they continue accepting funding from such a state. It may be that this reality was in the mind of the drafters of one of Benedict XVI's last teaching documents that, with regard to the issue of funding of Catholic charitable works, stated the following:

> [T]he diocesan Bishop is to ensure that charitable agencies dependent upon him do not receive financial support from groups or institutions that pursue ends contrary to the Church's teaching. Similarly, lest scandal be given to the faithful, the diocesan Bishop is to ensure that these charitable agencies do not accept contributions for initiatives whose ends, or the means used to pursue them, are not in conformity with the Church's teaching.[45]

No doubt many Catholic charities will protest that this provision will unduly limit their options for seeking funding.

But at least part of the point of religious liberty in general and *libertas ecclesiae* more specifically is for Catholics and Catholic organizations to be able to live the Catholic Faith with minimal interference from the state. If that means the Church must, as Ismael Hernandez memorably wrote, "tell Pharaoh to keep his money,"[46] then so be it. To sacrifice the Church's liberty to preach the Gospel and live out the meaning of Christ's message in order to receive state funding is more than a betrayal. It is patently absurd. Of course the Church's choice to decline government financial assistance is unlikely to stop determined secularists from trying to limit religious liberty in order to promote secularism as America's unofficial religion. It will, however, diminish their opportunities to do so.

For Our Liberty . . . and Yours

It would be easy to dismiss Catholic agitation about something like the Obama Administration's HHS mandate as a narrowly Catholic concern of marginal relevance for the overall struggle to maintain a free society in America. The truth, however, is that the Catholic struggle for robust religious liberty protections is *not* a peculiarly Catholic issue.

On one level, it is a matter of numbers and strategy. A federal government that successfully emasculates the Catholic Church's liberty in America—a Church that formally counts over seventy million Americans as members; which operates the largest number of religiously-based schools and universities, hospitals, and welfare services throughout America; and which has a long history of resisting assimilation by governments—will find other religious organizations in the United States to be easy game. The suffocation of substantive religious liberty for the Catholic Church in America means the marginalization of substantive religious freedom for *everyone*: Christian, Jew, Muslim, Buddhist, agnostic, or atheist.

Furthermore, a government that successfully undermines robust conceptions of religious liberty is more than capable of expanding its writ into other realms. That is a message that limited-government Catholics need to repeat over and over again—including to those in the broader movement for liberty who fail to grasp why religious freedom is so important.

This in turn raises other questions. How does the Catholic case for freedom, the free economy, and limited government relate to those ideas and groups who seek to defend human freedom on the basis of claims about the person that the Church regards as, at best, tenuous? And, others will ask, does the Catholic case for freedom in America outlined thus far downplay important principles highlighted by Catholic social teaching, such as the preferential option for the poor and the demands of social justice? These and other critiques deserve a careful response.

Further Reading

John Finnis, *The Collected Essays of John Finnis*, vol. V, *Religion and Public Reasons* (Oxford: Oxford University Press, 2011).

Robert P. George, *Making Men Moral: Civil Liberties and Public Morality* (Oxford: Clarendon Press, 1995).

George Pell, *God and Caesar: Selected Essays on Religion, Politics and Society* (Washington, DC: CUA Press, 2007).

Second Vatican Council, Declaration on Religious Liberty, *Dignitatis Humanae* (1965), http://www.vatican.va/archive/hist_councils/ii_vatican_council/documents/vat-ii_decl_19651207_dignitatis-humanae_en.html.

Chapter 5
But What About . . . ?

For it is not a sin to have riches, but to love riches.

Saint Thomas More[1]

Man, who was created for freedom, bears within himself the wound of original sin, which constantly draws him towards evil and puts him in need of redemption. Not only is this doctrine an integral part of Christian revelation; it also has great hermeneutical value insofar as it helps one to understand human reality.

Blessed John Paul II[2]

2008 was *not* a good year for the cause of economic liberty. Whether it was the financial system's implosion, the collapse of housing prices, the bailing out of banks and car companies, or the sharp increase in unemployment, many Americans' faith in the free enterprise system was severely shaken by the seemingly endless cascade of events which suggested that free markets were not working and that government needed to assume a larger role in economic life, perhaps permanently.

In retrospect, we now know that government policies themselves played a role in precipitating many of these events. In the housing industry's case, the unsustainable boom was partially fueled by the Federal Reserve keeping interest rates at artificially low levels for too long. Then there were the dysfunctional effects of Fannie Mae and Freddie Mac's lending policies. We should never forget that these were *government-sponsored enterprises* and that their irresponsible lending policies were *always* predicated, as the Nobel Prize economist

Vernon Smith warned in 2007, on the presumption they would be bailed out by the government if they got into trouble.[3]

In one sense, however, this context is irrelevant. The 2008 financial crisis and recession were, understandably enough, the cause for the revival of longstanding critiques of free markets. And, in addressing these critiques, many defenders of free markets answer all too often with the response: "compared to what?" By that, they mean that while free markets and limited government are not perfect, every other economic system is worse.

Less than perfect social, political, and economic arrangements are of course to be preferred to those which are catastrophically bad for human beings. But no one would describe the position that "the profoundly-flawed market economic system should be preferred because everything else is inferior" as an inspiring defense of free enterprise. Not only is its ability to win converts rather limited; it also downplays the many opportunities for human flourishing that, as demonstrated, *do* exist in societies that value business, commerce, and limited government.

These factors indicate the need for limited-government Catholics to articulate answers to those who worry about things ranging from the implications of free markets for social justice, to the ways in which free enterprise and free markets rely on people pursuing their self-interest. In this chapter, my intention is not to try to address every single criticism directed at free enterprise and the free economy by Catholics. Instead, the focus is upon those key concerns especially prevalent among Catholic Americans in the wake of the Great Recession. And one such concern is surely the vexed question of self-interest.

Self-Interest and Sin

"It is not from the benevolence of the butcher, the brewer, or the baker, that we expect our dinner, but from their regard to their own interest. We address ourselves, not to their humanity but to their self-love, and never talk to them of our own necessities but of their advantages."[4] Few sentences have proved the subject of more sustained controversy. Many have interpreted Adam Smith's words as implying "greed is good." Following the 2008 Recession, worries about the workings of greed and self-interest in the conditions of a market economy have only grown.

Not surprisingly, this issue of self-interest features heavily in many Catholic critiques of capitalism. On the face of it, Smith's description of a fundamental motivating force underlying free markets seems to fly in the face of Christ's call to love of neighbor and God. And greed is after all one of the seven deadly sins. The Scriptures, writings of the Fathers and Doctors of the Church, and constant teaching of the popes and councils are replete with condemnations of greed, especially love of money. Early in his pontificate, Pope Francis reminded Catholics that, from the Christian standpoint, there is something profoundly irrational about "greed for money that you can't take with you and have to leave" when you die.[5]

Smith's words hark back to claims made by the Dutch-born English philosopher, economist, and satirist Bernard de Mandeville (1670–1733) that are apparently even more offensive to Christian ethics. In his famous *Fable of Bees*[6] Mandeville portrayed a community of bees which positively thrived—that is, until its members suddenly decided to act virtuously. As a result of the disappearance of their pursuit of personal gain, the bees' world implodes. The surviving bees find themselves surviving in a hollow tree living rather uninteresting lives.

The less-than-subliminal message underlying Mandeville's tale was that public benefit flows, paradoxically enough, from allowing people to indulge their vices. Thus the decadent but wealthy hedonist who spends all her time indulging her senses may well be living a life of vice. Yet in doing so, she unintentionally provides incomes for numerous hoteliers, make-up artists, hairdressers, travel agents, winemakers, bartenders, and restaurant owners.

Leading scholars of Smith's thought, such as James Otteson and Ryan Patrick Hanley, have demonstrated that Smith's conception of self-interest can neither be reduced to self-interest narrowly understood nor conceptualized in purely Mandevillian terms. They also observe that Smith's *Wealth of Nations* should be situated in the wider corpus of his work, such as his *Theory of Moral Sentiments* (1759) which discusses the virtues and the moral life at length.[7]

Whatever the nuances of Smith's own position, the issue of self-interest does create particular intellectual challenges for pro-market Catholics. In many ways, the free economy *does* rely upon people pursuing their self-interest rather than being immediately focused upon promoting the well-being of others.

One response to this challenge is to recognize that fallen humanity cannot realize perfect justice in this world. "We can try to limit suffering, to fight against it," Pope Benedict wrote in *Spe Salvi*, "but we cannot eliminate it."[8] This Christian truth helps us to understand, like Saint Augustine, that what fallen humanity can achieve "is always less than we might wish."[9]

But long before Smith penned his *Wealth of Nations*, the Catholic Church acknowledged the role played by self-interest in generating, and, to an extent, *legitimizing* arrangements that bolster and incentivize economic liberty. Part of Aquinas's defense of private ownership involves, for example, recognizing the unreasonableness of expecting most people to assume responsibility for the use of communally-owned economic goods.

In *Centesimus Annus*, John Paul II developed similar insights but made specific reference to self-interest. In practical terms, the pope noted, violently suppressing self-interest results in its replacement with burdensome state bureaucracy that slowly drains creativity out of society. To this hard-to-deny historical observation, John Paul added the following insight from Christian anthropology. "Man," he wrote, "tends towards good, but he is also capable of evil. He can transcend his immediate interest and still remain bound to it. The social order will be all the more stable, the more it takes this fact into account and does not place in opposition personal interest and the interests of society as a whole, but rather seeks ways to bring them into fruitful harmony."[10]

The market economy is one way of realizing this harmony, albeit often indirectly. If, for instance, a business fails to produce new or better products at lower prices, it risks disappearing altogether, along with the jobs and capital it creates. Entrepreneurs and businesses consequently have to identify the needs and wants of consumers and then work out how to meet such needs and wants in a faster, less expensive manner. A certain alignment is thus established between a business's pursuit of its self-interest and other people's economic well-being, without anyone actually intentionally choosing such harmonization as their primary goal. Consumers receive a product at a progressively lower cost while businesses make a profit. This enables commercial enterprises to pay back loans, employ more people, engage in research and development, expand their size, and produce new and better products at often progressively-lower costs which in a competitive environment lowers prices.

None of this means that the pursuit of self-interest in the marketplace is cost-free. Sometimes a business is so successful that its competitors go out of business altogether. A certain degree of disruption (what Joseph Schumpeter famously called "creative destruction") is constant in a market economy. As a result, some people *do* lose their jobs. Some businesses *do* go bankrupt. And some people *do* have to retrain and start all over again.

Some defenders of markets are reluctant to acknowledge that embracing free enterprise, free markets, and liberty does mean trade-offs. Stability, for example, *is* sacrificed for mobility. Allowing people to pursue their economic self-interest *does* bring with it with many risks. The resulting wealth does create numerous resources that help literally billions of people to meet their needs, satisfy their wants, and potentially flourish precisely as humans should. Yet, as we will see, the same pursuit brings with it enormous spiritual and moral challenges—challenges that some free marketers deny at the risk of putting in peril the market economy itself.

Self-interest and the Common Good

For all the turmoil caused by markets, the creativity and competition flowing from people's pursuit of their self-interest in the marketplace contributes in many tangible ways to the common good. People, for example, often move to industries where they receive better pay. Others find themselves working in more personally satisfying occupations which provide more scope for human flourishing. Much-needed competition is introduced to parts of the economy where some businesses hitherto enjoyed a monopoly. Indeed it is hard to find a better description of free competition's beneficial effects than in the *Compendium of the Social Doctrine of the Church*:

> *A truly competitive market is an effective instrument for attaining important objectives of justice*: moderating the excessive profits of individual businesses, responding to consumers' demands, bringing about a more efficient use and conservation of resources, rewarding entrepreneurship and innovation, making information available so that it is really possible to compare and purchase products in an atmosphere of healthy competition.[11]

Observe here how the *Compendium* frames these issues as a matter of *justice* rather than efficiency. In other words, truly competitive markets—as opposed to crony capitalist arrangements—help deliver to consumers, businesses, and entrepreneurs many of the things they are owed as a matter of right, albeit in often indirect and unintended ways.

Market competition is not of course sufficient. As the *Compendium* goes on to say, market competition is a *means* rather than an end in itself.[12] Nor does the pursuit of self-interest in the economy always align individual well-being with the common good. Businesses, trade unions, and other groups have not proved shy about seeking to enlist state power to pursue their self-interest. Adam Smith himself emphasized the propensity of many businesses to try to rig the system in their favor. "People of the same trade," Smith wrote, "seldom meet together, even for merriment and diversion, but the conversation ends in a conspiracy against the public, or in some contrivance to raise prices."[13] In such cases, these businesses have ceased to be economically entrepreneurial. Instead they turn out to be adept *political* entrepreneurs: experts at gaming the system rather than meeting consumer needs.

The injury done to the common good in these instances is considerable. This includes the basic injustice of governments according *privileges* to particular industries. In economic terms, it reduces the incentives for businesses to be *economically* creative and competitive, while increasing their incentives to curry favor with politicians and government officials. Certainly a type of "harmony," in the sense of diminishing competitive turmoil, is temporarily established. But the long-term damage to many of the preconditions of human flourishing is difficult to underestimate. Note, however, that the problem is not the pursuit of self-interest *per se*. Rather it is the confluence of some people's self-interest with state power.

Rational Self-Interest and Virtue

Another part of the response to the self-interest question is to distinguish between greed and what might be called rational self-interest.

Greed implies a desire to possess something—power, wealth, sex, position—at virtually *any* cost and beyond what each

165

of us reasonably might need. Greed, like covetousness and avarice more generally, is thus the sin of excess. It perverts, for instance, the principle of ownership into a principle of egoism, whereby I prioritize my possession of things over my family, church, and even my own flourishing. It changes the business leader from someone who contributes to the material and moral well-being of himself and others through his work, into a selfish monopolist who preserves his possessions by enlisting government power to deter potential competitors.

The pursuit of rational self-interest is quite different. Playing off Adam Smith, Michael Novak explains this idea in the following way:

> We imagine that self-interest sets man against man, and flights individuals apart in centrifugal directions. We forget that human action is full of intelligence. Action is not random, wholly undirect. Free persons are intelligent and self-correcting. They have an interest in order. . . . What actually moves them is their own practical intelligence.[14]

No less than Aquinas insisted there *is* a reasonable love of self. That was how he understood the Second Commandment which instructs one to love our neighbor *as oneself*. This, Aquinas suggested, meant that people should be *reasonably* concerned for their self-preservation and their own participation in the good.[15] Indeed, as Germain Grisez observes, "Faith in Jesus is in human persons' ultimate self-interest" because "it holds out the hope of everlasting joy in heaven."[16]

These words remind us that much depends on *what* the "self" is interested in and *why* he is interested in it. I may, for instance, be interested in acquiring wealth because I simply want to possess more stuff for the sake of possessing more stuff. Not only is that greed, it is also thoroughly irrational inasmuch as it cannot be reconciled with the Catholic conception of true freedom.

Another person, however, may want to acquire wealth because his intention is to fulfill his responsibility to take care of his family's needs. Yet another individual may be anxious to trade and barter because he wants to build some of the material resources that he and others may need if they are going to be able to participate in any number of non-material goods. In these cases, the "interest" of the "self" cannot be classified as greed. The "self" in these examples has a rather more robust conception of human flourishing than Mandeville's hedonist.

Of course the pursuit of rational self-interest can and often does degenerate into greed (just as the pursuit of social justice often degenerates into the promotion of envy). People in the marketplace can forget their competitors are real human beings. For this reason and others, Smith did not hesitate to point to the need for market economies to be immersed in a culture of virtues in order to civilize our pursuit of self-interest.

Smith understood that virtues like prudence, temperance, thrift, promise-keeping, honesty, and humility—not to mention a willingness not to do to others what we wouldn't want them to do to us—are absolute necessities for a community that values economic freedom. If markets are going to work, the pursuit of self-interest harmonized with the common good, and appropriate limits on government power maintained, society requires substantial reserves of what might be called "moral capital."

At the end of his life, Smith added an entirely new section entitled "Of the Character of Virtue" to the sixth and final edition of his *Theory of Moral Sentiments*. His reasons for doing so are much debated. But perhaps Smith decided that he needed to reemphasize the importance of sound moral habits for societies that aspired to be both commercial and civilized.

Though his reference points and sources are quite different, Benedict XVI articulated analogous thoughts in *Caritas in Veritate*. "In and of itself," the pope wrote, "the market is not . . . the place where the strong subdue the weak. Society does not have to protect itself from the market, as if the development of the latter were *ipso facto* to entail the death of authentically human relations."[17]

For Benedict, any society which commits itself to human flourishing *must* allow market-oriented relationships of self-interest to be supplemented and undergirded—but not replaced—by relationships based on charity. Ultimately "if it is to be authentically human," Benedict stated, "economic, social and political development . . . needs to make room for the principle of gratuitousness as an expression of fraternity."[18]

What might this mean in practice? As an example, consider the workings of contracts. Contractual arrangements are an indispensable mode of interaction for free markets. They allow two or more people and organizations to align their respective self-interests in such a way that the fulfillment of the contract allows all its participants to benefit. Such relationships may well be the first (and sometimes the only) way in which many people in the marketplace encounter others.

Contracts in Catholic teaching are primarily subject to the demands of what the Church calls "commutative justice." This requires me to fulfill all the implied, formal, and reasonable promises I freely make when I enter into contracts with others. Fulfilling the demands of commutative justice is essential if contracts are to coordinate different people's self-interests.

But there is a sense in which I can fulfill the demands of a contract in a legalistic manner whereby I do the bare minimum of what is required. If, however, I strive to fulfill the commandment to love my neighbor, I will see I have many opportunities to go beyond these minimal requirements and give to the persons with whom I am contracting something that is in fact "mine" to gift them.

In real life, this occurs on a regular basis in many contractual arrangements. I might, for instance, voluntarily assume an extra cost and not even mention this to those people with whom I contracted. Even the most tightly-written contract presumes the contracting parties are willing to extend each other the gift of trust that no amount of expectation of commutative justice through courts can generate on its own. As Benedict stressed, "*Without internal forms of solidarity and mutual trust, the market cannot completely fulfill its proper economic function.*"[19]

For Benedict, it was not a question of somehow attempting to legislate the logic of gift into market transactions based on self-interest. No true gift can be compelled. Benedict's prime interest was in helping to make the economy a realm in which the virtuous habits associated with love of neighbor can be exercised in conjunction with and alongside people's pursuit of self-interest.

Naturally no amount of generosity makes up for basic violations of justice, such as failing to keep one's promises without reasonable cause. Hence Benedict insisted that "I cannot 'give' what is mine to the other, without first giving him what pertains to him in justice. If we love others with charity, then first of all we are just towards them."[20] At the same time, what Benedict called "relationships of gratuitousness, mercy and communion"[21] can exist alongside and even moderate relationships characterized by self-interest.

This is more often the case than we realize. People's words don't always reflect the real reasons they do things. Not everyone who says he is being charitable is actually concerned about his neighbor. And sometimes the inverse is true. Many who claim to be acting on the basis of self-interest aren't in fact doing so. This was quite characteristic of the Americans observed by Tocqueville:

> Americans enjoy explaining almost every act of their lives on the principle of self-interest properly understood. . . . I think

they often do themselves less than justice, for sometimes in the United States, as elsewhere, one sees people carried away by the disinterested, spontaneous impulses natural to man. But the Americans are hardly prepared to admit that they do give way to emotions of this sort. They prefer to do more honor to their philosophy than to themselves.[22]

Americans, at least from Tocqueville's perspective, were much less self-interested than they presented themselves. The disinterestedness of which Benedict spoke in *Caritas in Veritate* one hundred and sixty-nine years later was far more part of their lives than Americans admitted.

Morality and Regulation

Discussion of alignments between self-interest and the common good inevitably raises questions concerning the role of regulation in keeping the pursuit of self-interest in the economy from getting out of control.

As previously noted, the Church has always taught the state does have regulatory responsibilities. Laws prohibiting and punishing fraud and theft are, for instance, indispensable. The notion of a regulation-free economy is thus not at all consistent with Catholic teaching. To imagine, however, that regulation can somehow prevent all forms of greed or irresponsible behavior, or that regulation is *the* key to addressing such problems, is simply mistaken.

The 2008 financial crisis, for instance, owed much to widespread moral lapses that manifested themselves just as much on Main Street as on Wall Street. One example was the subprime mortgage fiasco. Today we know that thousands of Main Street borrowers simply *lied* about their income, assets, and liabilities when applying for subprime loans. One study, for instance, estimated there was some degree of deliberate misrepresentation by borrowers concerning their assets, income, and liabilities in as many as *70 percent* of

American early-payment defaults in approximately three million loans originated between 1997 and 2006.[23] On the other end of the transaction, many lenders failed to do even rudimentary checks on borrowers' credit history. On Main Street, thousands of investors mortgaged themselves to the hilt on the highly-imprudent assumption that house prices could only continue to soar. Meanwhile on Wall Street, investment banks overleveraged themselves, sometimes at ratios of 30-to-1.

Then there was the rampant materialism that had apparently permeated Main Street and Wall Street to equal degrees. The thrifty, even parsimonious Adam Smith would have been appalled by the "I-want-it-all-now" mentality that helped the personal savings rate in America to hover around 0 percent between 2005 and 2008—the lowest rate since the Depression years of 1932–1933. The same mindset may have also encouraged many Wall Streeters anxious to enhance their bonus prospects to sell securities which they *knew* were based on shaky subprime foundations to Main Street buyers blinded by the prospects of quick profits.

But is ever-increasing regulation the primary answer to such problems? In 2010, one group of Catholic bishops offered a surprising answer to this question.

In a document entitled *Choosing the Common Good*, the Catholic bishops of England and Wales noted that while the financial crisis's causes were complex, the crisis partly flowed from many irresponsible choices (especially a willingness to betray people's trust) made by many people working in the financial industry. Nevertheless, the bishops added, there was also plenty of irresponsible behavior by others— including politicians and ordinary folk—that contributed to the meltdown. It followed, the bishops stated, "that new and sweeping regulation [will not] of itself solve these deep-seated problems."[24]

The bishops then pointed to a problem with excessive reliance upon regulation. "In place of virtue," they contended, "we have seen an expansion of regulation. A society that is held together just by compliance to rules is inherently fragile, open to further abuses which will be met by a further expansion of regulation."[25]

No one familiar with the Catholic bishops of England and Wales would describe them as closet Thatcherites. In *Choosing the Common Good*, however, they hit upon some important truths concerning regulation and greed, virtue and self-interest. Regulation by itself is insufficient, and excessive reliance on regulation can have counterproductive effects. The lying and misrepresentation that characterized, for example, much of the mortgage business in America prior to the housing market's implosion was already illegal, so it is unclear how extra regulation would deter such behavior in the future. That suggests the only way to address this problem over the long-term is for people to stop lying. And even beyond this melancholy fact, there is no dearth of empirical studies illustrating the ways in which regulations can be counterproductive, and even incentivize people into making morally erroneous and economically dubious choices.[26]

More important, the bishops' statement underscored the fact that the desire to regulate often reflects an unwillingness to accept that the deeper problem is *people making imprudent and often immoral choices*, not to mention a reluctance to acknowledge that certain choices are by their very nature incapable of being ordered to the good. Such is the fruit of societies that embrace ethical relativism. Regulation does have a role to play in combating greed and its effects. But it's no substitute for millions of well-formed consciences that help people to pursue their self-interest in the marketplace in ways which are prudent and cognizant of the responsibilities we owe to our neighbor that go beyond the requirements of justice.

Selling out Social Justice?

The issue of justice raises the question of whether I am underplaying the Catholic commitment to what is often called "social justice."[27] Doesn't, some might suggest, less government economic intervention mean less social justice?

To answer this, let us first ask a vital question that often isn't posed: how *does* the Church—as opposed to secular-minded liberals—actually understand social justice?

Prior to 1993, precision was occasionally lacking in the term's formal use in official Church teaching.[28] The *Catechism of the Catholic Church*, however, provided a very concise definition. "Society," it states, "ensures social justice when it provides the conditions that allow associations or individuals to obtain what is their due, according to their nature and their vocation. Social justice is linked to the common good and the exercise of authority."[29]

Social justice is thus another way of describing our obligation to contribute to the common good, with the emphasis being upon people receiving what they are owed. Obviously the state has a role in this—hence the reference to authority. Equally significant, however, is the emphasis upon *society* pursuing this end. It follows that social justice is not and cannot be the government's exclusive concern. Social justice is *everyone's* concern: not every or even most actions seeking to contribute to its realization should be the state's.

This becomes more evident in the paragraphs in the *Catechism* immediately following this definition.[30] In the first place, the *Catechism* states, social justice involves respect for human rights that society recognizes rather than creates. Such rights, we may reasonably surmise, include, among others, the right to life, religious liberty, and economic initiative. Second, the *Catechism* stresses that social justice underscores the basic equality of all people that is theirs by virtue of being made in God's image. This is obviously crucial for the working of institutions such as rule of law.

Third—and in a move that will surprise many—the *Catechism* specifies that pursuing social justice requires us to acknowledge the *differences* and even *inequalities* that are legitimate and even necessary in any society. Many of these differences exist, the *Catechism* states, because God wills that we need each other. Such variations enable us to use our disparate talents and resources to meet others' needs. Last, the *Catechism* states that social justice embraces the idea of solidarity. Revealingly, the *Catechism* emphasizes that solidarity cannot be reduced to a single-minded focus on material goods. Rather it involves "the sharing of spiritual goods even more than material ones."[31] Human flourishing is, after all, more than just material well-being.

None of the *Catechism*'s treatment of social justice conflicts with the case for limited government and the free economy. Social justice is a way of expressing *every* Catholic's obligation to help his or her neighbor that has been part of the Christian message since the time of Christ. By no stretch of the imagination can this be read as requiring Catholics to automatically support one political program or another aimed at achieving greater equality of material wealth.

The common good—the goal of social justice—entails the integral human development of each and every person. There are numerous ways in which Catholics can contribute to this end, and many of them do not involve supporting government welfare programs. In the case of those welfare programs that undermine human flourishing, there is a strong case to suggest that Catholics should actually *oppose* them in the name of social justice. The question that "limited government Catholics" should politely address to their "social justice" brothers and sisters in America is why so many of them persist in seeing social justice as a blank check for expanding government intervention and why they often portray any retraction of government involvement in the economy as socially unjust. This is especially pertinent in light of the American associational approach that figures such as Tocqueville and Maritain highlighted as the distinctly American way of living out many of the moral commitments underpinning the principle of social justice.

And the Option for the Poor?

Like the term social justice, the phrase "preferential option for the poor" is now part of the everyday lexicon of many Catholic Americans and the Church more generally. Such language is also often invoked to imply that Catholics should generally be supportive of interventionist economic policies. Again, however, careful attention to the meaning of the expression clarifies matters.

The term itself gained traction in Catholic thought and writings in the late 1960s and 1970s. Many have traced its impact to the influence of various forms of liberation theology throughout this period. Such claims, however, tend to downplay the fact that the Catholic Church has *always* maintained a special outreach to those who are enduring poverty. It is an idea that finds resonance in the Old Testament prophets who spoke so clearly against the oppression of the poor, not to mention Christ's statements that He Himself may be recognized in the poor, in those who suffer, or who endure persecution.

The Christian understanding of poverty doesn't, however, make the mistake of imagining that poverty can be reduced to issues of material deprivation. In the 1980s, in the midst of the Church's sharpest articulation of its critique of Marxist-influenced versions of liberation theology, the Congregation for the Doctrine of the Faith (CDF) reminded Catholics that poverty had a rather more expansive meaning in Christian belief, thought, and action.

From Christianity's standpoint, *everyone* is poor inasmuch that *all of us* are deeply inadequate in the face of God's justice and mercy. Why else would Christ need to come into the world to save us from our sins and flaws? Moreover, the Christian embrace of poverty, the CDF stated, involves *everyone*—rich and poor—exercising detachment from material wealth: "It is this sort of poverty, made up of detachment, trust in God, sobriety and a readiness to share, that Jesus declared blessed."[32]

What does living out the option for the poor mean in practice? In the first place, we must engage in works of charity; in short, those activities that often address specific dimensions of poverty in ways that no state program ever could. And this means giving: the giving of our time, energy, and human and monetary capital in ways that bring Christ's light into some of the darkest places on earth.

This does not, however, mean that Catholics are required to give something to everything, or even that every Catholic must give away everything they own to everyone else. Moreover, as James Schall, S.J., emphasizes, "if we all stay at home and help the poor, just what do we do? If we take all the existing world wealth and simply distribute it, what would happen? It would quickly disappear; all would be poor."[33] Put another way, living out the option for the poor may well involve those people with a talent for creating wealth doing precisely that. In material terms, we cannot help others suffering from material deprivation unless material wealth is constantly being created.

This insight points to a second aspect of giving effect to the option for the poor. Obviously it is concerned with shaping the economy and society in ways that address problems of material deprivation and oppression. This does not rule out any form of government assistance to those in need. Yet lifting people out of poverty—and not just material poverty but also moral and spiritual poverty—does not necessarily mean that the most effective action is to implement yet another welfare program. There is no reason to assume that the preferential option for the poor is somehow a preferential option for big government. Often, being an entrepreneur and starting a business which brings jobs, wages, and opportunities to places where they did not hitherto exist is a greater exercise of love of the poor than government welfare initiatives.

The Catholic understanding of the option for the poor also means recognizing that those who suffer from material deprivation are human beings graced with reason and free will. Hence, like everyone else, they are also capable of engaging in some form of integral human flourishing. Sometimes a welfare program or new regulation is not the best way of helping those in need toward realizing this end, especially when such measures actually impede or discourage people from using their initiative and/or choosing to work.

Though we rarely think about it this way, deregulation is often a very concrete way of attempting to promote the option for the poor. Living out the option for those in need could be manifested, for example, in working to remove the tariffs that block people in poverty from entering into the circles of exchange at the heart of global markets, or which encourage people to stay in industries in America which are becoming uncompetitive in a global economy. It might also involve making the process of creating a business faster, or providing more transparent, less bureaucratically burdensome ways for people to migrate to countries where there are more opportunities.

Unions, Free Association, and the Common Good

In Catholic social teaching, questions surrounding the option for the poor and social justice have invariably touched upon a subject that generates some of the most contentious arguments within and outside the Catholic community in America: the role of trade unions.

These tensions were most prominently on display during the extremely difficult conflict between Governor Scott Walker of Wisconsin and assorted public sector unions that attracted much public attention throughout 2011 and 2012. Though Catholics of good will were found on both sides of the dispute, many supporting the unions' position seemed to believe that the Church should *always* stand with unions, whatever the particular merits of their claims or the demands of the common good.

In the Wisconsin case, the issues concerned not simply the limitations on collective bargaining proposed by Governor Walker and passed into law by the legislature. Other factors touching on the wider common good included an out of control state deficit; unsustainable levels of spending on public sector wages, benefits, and pensions; and grave misgivings about particular ways in which public sector unions were collecting union dues and effectively compelling people to join unions when they preferred not to do so. Many Catholics also wondered if they were somehow obliged to support public sector unions whose wages and benefits had reached such proportions that they threatened to bankrupt the state entities which society needed to fulfill those responsibilities for the common good that only governments can undertake.

Since Leo XIII's *Rerum Novarum,* the Catholic Church has always articulated a positive view of trade unions. In that and subsequent encyclicals, the right to form unions has been squarely based upon the right of free association. When, however, one looks at the entirety of Catholic social teaching on unions, we find the Church's view of unions is considerably more nuanced than many realize. Catholics have, for instance, every reason to insist that:

- efforts to force people to join unions against their will are morally unacceptable because they violate the very basis upon which unions themselves are founded;

- American unions as a whole need to put more distance between themselves and politics; and
- unions are as obliged as everyone else to consider the wider implications of their actions for the common good.

To take the first of these points, the principle of free association cuts both ways. *No one* can be compelled to join unions—even as a condition of employment. As observed by the Catholic ethicist and businessman, Robert G. Kennedy, the Church views "the right to work [as] a liberty that must be protected for every worker. That is, the worker has a right to seek and obtain employment—this is not a right to be given a job—that cannot be unreasonably constrained. While labor unions can benefit workers, every worker should be free to forgo membership if he or she chooses." Kennedy adds, for good measure, that Pius XII was "quite explicit about defending the right of workers not to join unions. He once remarked that it would be ironic if labor unions, which were formed in part to protect the freedom of workers from large, anonymous businesses, were themselves to become large, anonymous organizations that smothered the freedom of workers."[34]

Concerning matters such as negotiating wages and working conditions, the Church regards the involvement of unions as entirely legitimate. Such support, however, does not mean the Church endorses every single demand made by unions. Likewise, Catholic social teaching supports the right to strike—but *only* as a last resort and *not* for explicitly political purposes. Catholics should not consequently assume that every strike is necessarily legitimate.

Each of these limitations reflects the fact that unions are not exempt from the demands of the common good. In his 1971 Apostolic Letter *Octogesima Adveniens*, for example, Paul VI specified that unions can fall prey to the temptation to use their strength to impose excessively burdensome conditions on society and the economy. A union that, for instance, used its power to promote its members' interest at the expense of less powerful or less organized members of society—such as taxpayers and consumers—would be undermining the common good and the opportunities for others to flourish. Pope Paul then specified that when union actions or strikes affect public services, there is a point when union actions can cause "inadmissible" social damage. He even added that unions may not use strikes to obtain demands of "a directly political nature."[35]

This concern for the common good helps explain why John Paul II—the great supporter of Poland's Solidarity trade union—was also surprisingly careful in his choice of words about unions. Echoing Paul VI, he affirmed that unions "must take into account the limitations imposed by the general economic situation of the country." In the context of a severe recession, for instance, unions may have to be willing to accept wage freezes or even reductions.

John Paul was also anxious to separate unions from any ideological framework that might imply viewing unions and their demands as part of some type of class struggle.[36] As if that were not enough, the pope spelled out clear limits to unions' involvement in politics. Unions, he insisted, are *not* political parties. They are subsequently *not* to be directly engaged in political activities. Undoubtedly the activities of unions touch on the realm of politics inasmuch as unions, like everyone else, have responsibilities vis-à-vis the common good. But unions, the pope noted, should not have excessively close links to political parties, precisely because this often leads unions to be used for, or even choose, goals that have nothing to do with their primary objectives.[37]

The Church does not even regard the right to bargain collectively as somehow absolute. Collective bargaining is a *means* to the end of promoting the common good and therefore human flourishing. It is not an end in itself. It follows, as Kennedy observes, that:

Civil authorities may legitimately limit or even suppress the status of a union as the agent for workers in contract negotiations (this is not the same thing as suppressing a union) if collective bargaining, in practice, undermines the common good. But if the state does this, it must ensure that other means are in place, such as civil service regulations, that protect workers.[38]

Plainly Catholic social teaching's affirmation of trade unions is far more nuanced than many often imagine. Catholics should certainly be wary of knee-jerk anti-unionism. Nonetheless Catholics are under no obligation to be uncritically supportive of unions. If the damage to the common good is great enough, or if a union has strayed from its primary mission, or if a union is violating the very principles that lie at the root of its own legitimacy, then calling unions to account may well be the most socially just thing to do.

Catholicism vs. Libertarianism

A rather different critique of Catholic supporters of limited government concerns the question of libertarianism. Some Catholics identified as favoring the cause of limited government since the Tea Party's emergence in 2009 have been accused of having more in common with libertarian ideas than Catholic social teaching. A good example was the criticism leveled along these lines at Congressman Paul Ryan throughout 2012.

In October 2012, a group of Catholic thinkers (accurately described by Robert P. George as belonging to the "Catholic Left") issued a statement, entitled "On all of Our Shoulders." While they specified that "We do not write to oppose Ryan's candidacy or to argue there are not legitimate reasons for Catholics to vote for him,"[39] the statement effectively presented Congressman Ryan as, to cite George, "an unreconstructed

Randian radical individualist and, as such, a clear opponent of Catholic social teaching."

The statement itself did not, George added, offer "a careful, nuanced analysis of Ryan's thought in light of that teaching." Instead it amounted to "a set of Democratic Party talking points festooned with quotations from St. Thomas Aquinas and Popes John Paul II and Benedict XVI."[40] Revealingly, the authors of the statement failed to acknowledge that Ryan's position on the premier social justice issue of our time—abortion—was diametrically opposed to that of the rabidly pro-choice Rand.

On the subject of the economy, the legal philosopher Richard Garnett identified the core problem with the statement's assessment of Ryan's economic views:

> The statement, like much of the "Ryan is a Randian!!" business, overstates significantly the extent to which the policies that are being proposed . . . are, in fact, "libertarian" (let alone Randian). If programs and policies are described tendentiously, and contrasted with rival programs that are described idealistically, they will (no surprise) seem less compatible with Christianity.[41]

Libertarianism itself is a complex phenomenon. Self-identified libertarians range from those who celebrate hedonism (and seem rather anxious for others to do so), to those who describe themselves as virtue libertarians. Some people labeled "libertarian" turn out on closer examination not to be libertarians at all but rather conservatives who believe in a free market economy.

Scholars popularly identified as libertarians include figures ranging from the Nobel Prize economists Friedrich Hayek (an agnostic and lapsed Catholic who actually disliked the term "libertarian") and Milton Friedman (a quiet agnostic from a Jewish background), to Ludwig von Mises (another agnostic of Jewish heritage, sometime-critic of aspects of Christianity, and self-described "paelo-liberal" economist with a penchant for reading the Protestant theologian Karl Barth). In all three cases, these scholars' central theological and philosophical views were much removed from orthodox Catholic teaching. That, however, does not necessarily invalidate their significant contributions to the development of economic thought and policy.

Mises, for instance, played a major role in singling out entrepreneurship as *the* variable being ignored by most twentieth-century economists. He and Hayek were also largely responsible for identifying a key problem with central planning: the "knowledge problem" or the assumption that governments and government officials can assimilate all the knowledge needed to successfully plan an economy. Likewise Friedman played a pivotal role in founding the school choice movement—something since embraced by many Catholic bishops, clergy, and laity in America.

Particular libertarian thinkers (most notably Hayek) were also well-aware that some of the most important developments in modern economic thought, including core ideas about the market economy, were to be found in the writings of medieval and early modern Catholic theologians. In his Nobel Prize speech, for instance, Hayek explained the folly of governments trying to determine the price of goods and services by noting that "the Spanish schoolmen of the sixteenth century . . . . emphasized that what they called the *pretium mathematicum*, the mathematical price, depended on so many circumstances that it could never be known to man but was known only to God."[42] Hayek and others additionally understood and lamented the fact that the cause of liberty in continental Europe had been undermined by the deep hostility of many continental liberals toward Christianity in general and Catholicism in particular.[43]

Notwithstanding this background, what might be called the generic libertarian case for freedom, the free economy, and limited government differs sharply from Catholic arguments in favor of similar things. In many respects this reflects the fact that many libertarians adhere to extremely weak normative positions that rarely go beyond ascribing significance to what is often called "self-authorship." In other instances, the differences appear to flow from their disinterest in, or occasional hostility to, arguments that go beyond utility and efficiency.

In *The Great Persuasion*, the historian Angus Burgin illustrates that from the late 1950s onward, efforts within European and American free market circles to make "thick" moral arguments in favor of free markets and liberty were gradually supplanted by "a relentless emphasis on the superior efficiency of laissez-faire" and gradual abandonment of a "language of values."[44] But the practical problem with viewing normative issues as somehow hopelessly subjective is that while many people may grow to accept the market as more efficient than collectivist and Keynesian arrangements, even Friedman eventually recognized that "[w]e are still far from bringing practice into conformity with opinion."[45] Put another way, while many Americans may agree that markets are more economically efficient, they remained unconvinced of the *moral* case for economic liberty and its associated institutions.

What then is the libertarian case for freedom? And how does it differ from the Catholic argument for liberty? The existence of different, even competing schools of libertarian thought makes answering such questions a potentially hazardous exercise. Looking, however, at the philosophical position articulated by Hayek is quite instructive.[46]

Hayek's argument for freedom is not one that views liberty as something necessary for human flourishing in the sense that Catholicism understands such growth. Hayek in fact quickly dismisses what he calls metaphysical approaches to the nature and ends of freedom; he describes as a "sophism" the notion that "that we are free only if we do what in some sense we ought to do."[47] Why this is a "sophism" is never addressed by Hayek.

Instead Hayek identified the minimization of unreasonable state coercion as a key ingredient of his support for free markets and liberty more generally. Coercion, Hayek argued, makes one person the instrument of another's will, not for the first person's sake, but for the coercer's purposes. This position has some resonance in Catholic critiques of unjust coercion. But it didn't constitute Hayek's main angst about compulsion. In his *Constitution of Liberty*, Hayek placed the emphasis of his moral argument upon his conviction that civilizational progress is radically dependent on individual freedom and thus minimizing coercion.

Progress, Hayek maintains, does not normally occur when economic problems are addressed in a collectivist manner. Progress, he says, usually comes when individuals freely act upon their particular knowledge of their specific circumstances, opportunities, and talents while pursuing their own goals. Hence we should place our trust in the independent and sometimes competitive acts of many people, and permit this process to resolve what is worth keeping or discarding. On this basis, Hayek says that his faith in freedom and markets "does not rest on the foreseeable results in particular circumstances but on the belief that it will, on balance, release more forces for the good than for the bad."[48]

This language is revealing. It suggests that Hayek's justification for minimizing coercion has a strong utilitarian component. Distinctly utilitarian phraseology—"general welfare," "the greatest happiness of the greatest number"—appear regularly in his writings.

When considering economic subjects, there is a place for considerations of utility and the *foreseeable* consequences of actions and rules. Aquinas's meditations on property, for example, presume we *can* indeed reasonably foresee what will happen when property is owned collectively. Moreover, as one arch-critic of utilitarianism and consequentialism John Finnis notes, there are many contexts in which we may reasonably calculate, measure, and weigh the consequences and efficiency of alternative choices. An obvious example, Finnis notes, is a market for those things which may legitimately be exchanged and in which a common denominator (i.e., money) allows comparisons of profits, costs, and benefits to occur.

Finnis observes, however, that making utility calculations or consequences assessments the primary points of moral reference is, strictly speaking, irrational because they assume the impossible: that humans can know and weigh all the known and unknown consequences of particular actions or rules.[49]

In later life, Hayek stated, he was "led, by a very painful process, gradually to reject . . . the utilitarian explanation of ethics." Like others before him, Hayek concluded that the utilitarian calculus *was* impossible. For good measure, Hayek added that utilitarianism was intrinsically linked to rationalistic outlooks, defined as "the idea that we have the intellectual power to arrange everything rationally."[50] Utilitarianism thus inclined people to believe that economies can be planned from the top down.

But while utilitarianism's place in Hayek's case for markets diminished over time, his appeals to progress did not. Like most libertarians, Hayek never ceased stating that free markets facilitate progress while collectivism does not.

That Hayek makes a valid point about economic and technological development is hard to dispute. Millions of once-impoverished Chinese and Indians will testify to the economic development fostered by allowing some economic freedom. Yet Hayek has surprisingly little to say about the *substance* of progress. He certainly does not comprehend progress in terms of human flourishing. Hayek even confesses that "in the sense of the cumulative growth of knowledge and power over nature, [progress] is a term that says little about whether the new state will give us more satisfaction than the old." This intellectual conundrum, Hayek thinks, is "probably unanswerable." Yet for Hayek, it is also immaterial. More significant, he claims, is "successful striving for what at each moment seems attainable," or "movement for movement's sake."[51]

These statements beg many central questions, such as: Toward *what* are we journeying? And what are people *becoming* along the way?

Closely associated with their appeals to progress is the increasingly prominent place accorded by some libertarians to social-evolutionary reasoning to bolster their position. Again, this was true of Hayek, especially from the 1950s onward. In many ways an offshoot of evolutionary biology, the basic hypothesis of social-evolutionary defenses of markets is that the process of entrepreneurial innovation and market exchange embodies a type of natural selection process with which humans interfere at their peril.

Economically speaking, there is an element of truth to this view. Markets do facilitate change that gradually renders many industries obsolete. Over time, this creative destruction improves many aspects of everyone's lives, without anyone formally planning it. For all their reservations about modernity, it is hard to imagine even the most arch-traditionalist "crunchy-con" wants to return to a pre-vaccination world or endure the wonders of sixteenth-century dentistry.

The problem with deploying social-evolutionary logic is that it cannot provide a *principled* reason for anything. In strictly social-evolutionist normative settings, we quickly find ourselves trapped in circular reasoning such as: "Change is good. What is the good? The good is change." Arguing for change for change's sake has never been the most coherent of positions.

Moreover if social-evolutionary positions are taken to their logical conclusion, we must conclude that freedom itself is essentially a fiction insofar as human reasoning and choosing are really of no significance. Instead we are left with John Stuart Mill's soft-determinism: our choices—including our economic decisions—might be "free" inasmuch as they might not be coerced, but they are nevertheless essentially predetermined.[52] In such a world, the "free" part of free markets is delimited, if not voided of meaning. Even more importantly, if free markets and economies more generally simply "evolve," then social-evolutionarily inclined libertarians cannot *morally* object to situations in which such evolution seems to indicate increasing government control over the economy. No one can logically assert on social-evolutionary grounds that there is something *intrinsically* wrong with ever-expanding government.

By contrast, the Catholic argument for economic liberty, private property, free trade, and a limited welfare state acknowledges the strictly economic case for such rights, processes, and institutions, but also goes far, far beyond them. It provides, for instance, a *principled* case for the right to economic initiative based on humans' nature as creative initiators of work and the goods of work and creative reason. Catholic critiques of welfare states are not just attentive to their ever-obvious economic costs. They are also squarely grounded on the damage that welfare states can do to people's opportunities for integral human development.

Similarly the Catholic case for free trade is not simply about allowing nations, regions, towns, businesses, and individuals to find their comparative advantage. It also proceeds logically from the natural right of free association, and derives further legitimacy from its capacity to help realize the universal destination of material goods across national boundaries. Finally, entrepreneurship is understood as more than a discovery procedure that allows us to discern and provide new and better goods and services at steadily-declining prices. Catholicism also sees entrepreneurship as derivative of the intrinsic good of work—so much so that even the entrepreneur whose product or service turns out to be unprofitable can still considered fruitful insofar as his choices have allowed him to participate in this moral good.

Building the Free—and Virtuous—Society

All this suggests that there is no particular need for free market Catholics in America or elsewhere to build their case upon libertarian philosophical claims. One doesn't even need to self-identify as a libertarian to be a supporter of limited government and the free economy. The founder of modern conservatism, that great crypto-Catholic Edmund Burke, was no libertarian. Yet few others argued more passionately in favor of free trade and free markets at a time when it was unlikely to win him many friends among the British political class, let alone the general populace of late eighteenth-century Britain.[53] Without hesitation, free market Catholics can say that while someone like Hayek was an important economist and made significant contributions to the cause of liberty, he leaves much to be desired as a philosopher of freedom.

There is, however, another dimension of libertarianism to which limited-government Catholic Americans ought to be aware. In his much-discussed book *Free Market Fairness*, John Tomasi laments the fact that, strictly speaking, the orthodox libertarian does not believe that there is anything "exceptional, or particularly worth venerating, in the traditional moral and constitutional order of America."[54]

This was most certainly *not* the view of popes such as Pius XII, John XXIII, Paul VI, John Paul II, and Benedict XVI. While expressing concerns about aspects of contemporary

American culture, the Catholic Church has regularly stated its appreciation of many aspects of American life—including the character of its founding. As Pope Benedict proclaimed on the south lawn of the White House in the presence of the President of the United States on April 16, 2008:

> From the dawn of the Republic, America's quest for freedom has been guided by the conviction that the principles governing political and social life are intimately linked to a moral order based on the dominion of God the Creator. The framers of this nation's founding documents drew upon this conviction when they proclaimed the "self-evident truth" that all men are created equal and endowed with inalienable rights grounded in the laws of nature and of nature's God. The course of American history demonstrates the difficulties, the struggles, and the great intellectual and moral resolve which were demanded to shape a society which faithfully embodied these noble principles.[55]

These were not the words of someone who regarded America as "just another" country. They reflect recognition that America represents a distinct experiment in ordered liberty quite unlike any other.

It is also an experiment that cannot be defended by Catholics alone. There are many times and occasions when we can—indeed, must—form strategic and often lasting alliances with Eastern Orthodox, Evangelical, Jewish, Mormon, and secular-minded Americans (especially Michael Novak's "smiling secularists") as they seek to roll back the state's undue encroachment upon free economic activity, its efforts to unreasonably constrain religious liberty, and its steady undermining of freedom more generally—not least through the subtle and sometimes not-subtle promotion of hedonistic conceptions of human choice and existence.

Every single day, Catholics work throughout America with people from any number of religious and philosophical traditions in defending goods such as life or preventing incursions upon religious liberty. Cooperation with non-Catholics working to promote and protect key conditions of the common good should in fact be normal rather than unusual. The truths of the natural law that shape so much of the Catholic argument for liberty are not, after all, specifically Catholic truths. They are truths accessible to all human beings by virtue of their possession of the reason upon which the natural law is inscribed.

Those courageous eighteenth-century Catholic Americans who joined with equally brave Anglicans, Presbyterians, Congregationalists, Baptists, Deists, and free thinkers in defending their freedom against unjust impositions did not believe in waging a separate fight for liberty. Given the miniscule numbers of Catholics in America at the time, such an option was never practical. But it wasn't simply a case of embracing the logic of "the enemy of my enemy is my friend." Men like Charles Carroll and his cousins Daniel Carroll (one of only five men to sign both the Articles of Confederation and the Constitution of the United States) and Father John Carroll plainly thought that, whatever their theological and philosophical differences with figures like Jefferson, Franklin, Adams, and Witherspoon, they shared enough common ground with these men to join them in the cause of independence.

The need to work with people with whom free enterprise Catholics may not always be in perfect agreement isn't a reason, however, to refrain from seeking to persuade their coalition partners by word and example of how the Catholic view of human liberty and human flourishing can animate the broader limited government movement and infuse its policy positions with deeper moral argumentation. The question of how this might occur is the subject of our final chapter.

Further Reading

Jean-Yves Calvez S.J., and Jacques Perrin, S.J. *The Church and Social Justice* (London: Burns and Oates, 1961).

Congregation for the Doctrine of the Faith, *Instruction on Certain Aspects of the "Theology of Liberation"* (1984), http://www.vatican.va/roman_curia/congregations/cfaith/documents/rc_con_cfaith_doc_19840806_theology-liberation_en.html.

Ryan Patrick Hanley, *Adam Smith and the Character of Virtue* (Cambridge: CUP, 2009).

Joseph Ratzinger, *Eschatology: Death and Eternal Life* (Regensburg: Pustet, 1977/1988).

Chapter 6

A Patriotic Minority: Catholic, Creative, and American

Liberty will maintain her empire, till a dissoluteness of morals, luxury and venality shall have prepared the degenerate sons of some future age, to prefer their own mean lucre, the bribes, and the smiles of corruption and arbitrary ministers, to patriotism, to glory, and to the public weal.

Charles Carroll of Carrollton, 1766[1]

"Here comes everybody," the Irish author James Joyce once famously said of the Catholic Church. For a long time, this has been a particularly apt description of Catholicism in America. Catholic America is truly a mirror of American society, despite always being a minority in a country whose religious roots are profoundly Protestant.

Today that minority status is not simply about demographics. Once Catholics in America were viewed with distrust because of Protestant suspicion about their links with Rome and antagonism toward what was regarded as papist superstition.

In twenty-first–century America, however, the Catholic experience of being a minority is increasingly associated with the fact that being a faithful Catholic means putting oneself at odds with large segments of public opinion on some of the central moral issues of our time. You need only open the *New York Times* or the *Los Angeles Times* on any given day of the week to know that Catholic teachings that clash with secularist expectations on any number of these questions are criticized—

and more often mocked—with an intensity rarely applied to any other religious group.

A Creative Minority

Being a minority in the United States has not been without its benefits for the Catholic Church. It has helped the Church in America avoid, for instance, any temptation to advocate the throne-and-altar arrangements from which many European Catholics had to disentangle themselves. Catholic Americans also experienced religious liberty as an opportunity for growth and expansion. They were thus able to show the rest of the universal Church that embracing religious liberty did not necessarily mean committing oneself to religious indifferentism, religious relativism, let alone the notion of "freedom from religion." As Benedict XVI once pointed out, "the American Revolution [offered] a model of a modern State that differed from the theoretical model with radical tendencies that had emerged during the second phase of the French Revolution."[2]

Looking ahead, however, Pope Benedict had no doubt that Catholicism's immediate future in America and the West would be life as a "creative minority." The phrase, which Benedict used for several years before being elected pope, comes from the English historian Arnold Toynbee (1889–1975). Toynbee's thesis was that civilizations primarily collapsed because of internal decline rather than external assault. "Civilizations," Toynbee wrote, "die from suicide, not by murder."[3]

Creative minorities, Toynbee held, are those who *proactively* respond to a civilizational crisis and whose response allows that civilization to grow. One example was the Church's reaction to the Roman Empire's collapse in the West in the fifth century AD. The Church reacted to this potentially catastrophic event by preserving the philosophy of Athens, the law of Rome, and the wisdom of Jerusalem, while simultaneously integrating the invading German tribes into a universal religious community. Western civilization was not simply saved—it was vastly enriched.

This was Pope Benedict's vision of the Catholic Church's role in the contemporary West, including the United States. In fact, it is probably the *only* viable strategy. One alternative would be for the Church to ghettoize itself in a cultural and psychological bunker. But while the monastic life has always been a vocation for some Catholics, retreat from the world has never been most Catholics' calling; they are called to live in *and* evangelize the world.

Yet another option is "liberal Catholicism." The past fifty years, however, have provided compelling evidence that this path is a sure recipe for decline. Liberal Catholicism has more or less collapsed throughout the world under the weight of its own incoherence. During his famous *biglietto* speech of 1879 on the occasion of being made a cardinal by Leo XIII, Blessed John Newman identified the core problem with "the spirit of liberalism in religion" (what he called the "great *apostasia*") in the following terms:

> Liberalism in religion is the doctrine that there is no positive truth in religion, but that one creed is as good as another. . . . [it holds that] Revealed religion is not a truth, but a sentiment and a taste; not an objective fact, not miraculous; and it is the right of each individual to make it say just what strikes his fancy.[4]

You will not find the spirit of liberalism in religion expressed in *any* document promulgated at Vatican II, including, as demonstrated in chapter four, *Dignitatis Humanae*. But close inspection soon indicates it lurks just beneath the surface of dissenting Catholics' writings. Whether it is biblical exegesis, moral theology, or ecclesiology, their doubts about Catholicism's truth claims have long been manifest.[5]

The demographic evidence for liberal Catholicism's impending extinction is striking. The average age of members of female religious orders that would appear to have consciously moved in many respects, as one dissenting nun put it, "beyond Jesus," is now over seventy. Liberal Catholicism's replication challenge, however, goes beyond the clergy and those in consecrated life. Many self-described liberal lay Catholics have either raised their children to think and act more or less like liberal Protestants (another fast-disappearing species), or decided that their children should be "free to make up their own minds" about religion.

The latter position is not as neutral as it sounds. The American philosopher and Catholic convert J. Budziszewski points out that "declining to teach [the faith] is itself a way of teaching." It tells children that what their parents think about God is unimportant, and that reflecting adequately about the question and nature of God requires no theological or philosophical formation.[6] No one should be surprised that many raised in such families end up knowing or caring little about Catholicism.

By contrast, a creative minority strategy recognizes that to be an active Catholic in America and Europe today is now, as observed by the Archbishop of Paris, Cardinal André Vingt-Trois, increasingly a *free choice* rather than a matter of social conformity.[7] Practicing Catholics in America will consequently be active believers because they have *chosen* and *want* to live the Church's teaching.

If this trend continues, it will likely result in several developments. One may be an overall decline in numbers of Americans who formally identify as Catholic. Apart from some Catholics from Hispanic backgrounds, most of the old cultural ties that once held many Americans close to the Church are dead. When combined with the abysmal catechesis that was the norm throughout the 1970s, '80s, and '90s, this will likely mean that liberal and nominal

Catholics will continue conforming to the prevailing culture to the point whereby their thinking and habits grow ever more indistinguishable from that of secularists. Another safe prediction is the relentless secularization of many nominally Catholic institutions as their token links with the Church continue to fray. Sadly enough, many will surely use their receipt of state funding as an excuse to further dilute their Catholic identity to the point of meaninglessness.

But here is the good news: if Church history teaches us anything, it is that periods of decline in the Church's life are followed, eventually, by phases of renewal. The corruption, scandals, and heresies which sparked the Reformation were followed by the evangelical energies unleashed by the Council of Trent and Counter Reformation that took Christ's message literally to the ends of the earth. Three hundred years later, the Church's abasement at the hands of Enlightenment *philosophes*, absolutist monarchs, and French revolutionaries was followed by nineteenth-century Catholicism's profound revival—a rejuvenation which produced spiritual giants such as the Little Flower, Thérèse of Lisieux, a saint and Doctor of the Church.

There are already signs of considerable renewal in the Church in America. One is the ongoing growth of a clergy happy to articulate Catholicism's specific truth claims and who do so in an intelligent, joyful way. It is partly a self-selective process. There is no conceivable reason why *anyone* in the West today would become a priest or religious unless they truly believed the Church's teaching and wanted to invite others to see its truth. That's one major reason why it is now extremely hard to find dissenters among seminarians—also growing in numbers in America—and priests below the age of fifty.

But what has all this to do with the particular ideas and emphases brought into the public square by pro-free enterprise and limited-government Catholics in America? How do they fit into this overall picture of renewal?

A Stronger Case for Freedom

Part of the answer was alluded to in chapter five's discussion of the differences between Catholicism and libertarianism's conception of the nature and ends of liberty. At the same time, it reflects even broader disparities between Catholic and what might be called "secularist" understandings of freedom.

As an immigrant to the United States, I can attest that the word "liberty" resonates with Americans in ways quite unlike other peoples. Each year thousands of people continue to migrate to America. For the most part, they don't come because they seek government-provided security or the entitlement society. Rather they yearn for the freedom that enables them to build security for themselves and their families in ways much harder to realize in their native lands.

That doesn't mean that liberty—especially economic and religious freedom—is completely secure in the United States. It *never* is. And freedom is never more in danger than when people start to take it for granted, or even begin to imagine that it is better to give up considerable liberty in return for state-provided economic security.

Part of the problem may be an under-appreciation of why freedom matters, even among many of those who profess their willingness to die to preserve it. Because if the end of freedom is nothing more than the experience of pleasure or the satisfaction of animal desires, then human liberty would not seem to point to anything especially noble about the human person.

Once, however, human flourishing is placed in the picture— which is something that Catholics can most certainly do— then freedom's value is suddenly magnified beyond anything imaginable by those who define it primarily as absence of coercion. Unjust and excessive coercion *are* an affront to human dignity. But the affront is even worse when we realize that it is only through freedom that people can choose the goods that lie at the heart of human flourishing.

The Catholic Church often speaks of this freedom in terms of the realization of the theological virtues—faith, hope, and love—as well as the cardinal virtues—justice, prudence, temperance, and fortitude. To many American ears, such words may sound out of time, reminiscent of the rhetoric of a lost age.

Here, however, we should ask ourselves some questions. What is closer to America's Founders who used the language of republican virtue almost as second nature? Is it the Catholic conception of human flourishing? Or is it those who are indifferent as to whether we use our freedom to drug ourselves into a stupor or create a flourishing business? By infusing the movement for liberty in America with the language and reality of human flourishing, Catholics can bring a renewed sense of moral purpose and coherence to that very large section of American opinion which, in pressing the case for liberty, often seems unable to escape the lexicon of efficiency and effectiveness, supply and demand.

Part of the importance of economic and religious liberty is the way they generally limit the reach of government. They also contribute to the common good in other ways. Economic freedom does, for instance, produce more wealth than collectivist economic systems. Likewise religious liberty is a key component of a peaceful society. But at a more fundamental level these freedoms matter because by limiting the size and powers of government and facilitating wealth creation and civil peace, such liberties provide us with the space to use our creativity, our reason, and our free will to orient ourselves to the truths that alone can make us happy, and to live the virtues that the Founders saw as integral to the life of a society of free citizens.

Here the Catholic concept of dignity may be helpful in clarifying matters. The idea of human dignity, as explained by the English philosopher and Catholic convert Elizabeth Anscombe, expresses two things.[8] The first is our essential equality as human beings *qua* human. There are *no* sub-humans and *no* super-humans. There is only *one* human race to which everyone belongs, whatever our strengths and weakness, advantages and disabilities.

Historically speaking, there was an important "American" contribution to the realization of this truth. The fact that all mankind is one was a central conclusion of figures such as the "defender of the Indians," Bartolomé de Las Casas, O.P., a product of the School of Salamanca and the first bishop of the diocese of Chiapas in Mexico, when he insisted at the famous debate at Valladolid (1550–1551) in Spain that the native peoples of the New World were not infantile beings but rather free people from the standpoint of Christian theology and natural law.

Less well-known is that Las Casas based much of his case squarely upon the papal bull *Sublimus Dei*. Issued by Pope Paul III in 1537, this document stated that the native peoples were just as much rational beings as Europeans. On this basis, Paul III outlined two conclusions. First, the peoples of the Americas were able to know and accept the Catholic Faith. Second, "the aforesaid Indians and all other nations which come to the knowledge of Christians in the future must not be deprived of their liberty and the ownership of their property. Rather, they must use, increase, and enjoy this freedom and ownership freely and lawfully."[9]

The reference to property underscores that this same human dignity also means we are intrinsically superior to all other created things. Plants and animals enjoy a certain worth. Yet they do not share in *human* dignity. And living in accordance with our dignity means using our freedom in ways that express the fact of that dignity: that we are humans graced with reason and free will rather than animals that simply follow their instincts and cannot make truly free choices guided by reason.

Here we must repeat: the necessity of a *free* choice for virtue and the good does *not* mean that our laws and government must assume a position of neutrality about such questions. To say that the state *should* be morally neutral is not at all a neutral position. Whenever you say the word "should," you are in fact committing yourself to some moral end. The Catholic Church has always taught that the state has a role in facilitating virtuous behavior, including the virtue of justice.

At the same time, people still need to make *free* choices for the good. As Benedict stated in *Spe Salvi*, "These decisions can never simply be made for us in advance by others—if that were the case, we would no longer be free."[10] While institutions play a role in shaping our choices, Benedict emphasized that "they cannot and must not marginalize human freedom."[11] After all, he added, any structure that "could irrevocably guarantee a determined—good—state of the world" would mean denying the truth of human liberty. Hence, Benedict concluded, "they would not be good structures at all."[12] "*Integral human development*," Benedict reminded us, "*presupposes the responsible freedom* of the individual and of peoples: no structure can guarantee this development over and above human responsibility."[13] Such a claim would, I suspect, resonate with an American Founder as far from (and as suspicious of) Catholicism as Thomas Jefferson.

The Challenge of Consumerism

Transforming, reshaping, and re-grounding America's conception of the nature of freedom in specific truth claims about the human person is obviously a long-term exercise for Catholic Americans. Nonetheless it has tremendous potential to address problems associated with the market economy that many limited-government advocates struggle to address in a coherent manner. One such issue is what the Church calls the problem of consumerism.

Few Catholic Americans have tried harder than John Courtney Murray to seek to identify analogies between Catholic thought about the political order on the one hand, and the American experiment on the other hand. Yet Murray had no hesitation in arguing in 1940 that

> our American culture, as it exists, is actually the quintessence of all that is decadent of the Western Christian world. It would seem to be erected on the triple denial that has corrupted Western culture at its roots: the denial of metaphysical reality, of the primacy of the spiritual over the material . . . Its most striking characteristic is its profound materialism . . . It has given citizens everything to live for and nothing to die for. And its achievement may be summed up thus: It has gained a continent and lost its own soul.[14]

Though the expression is hardly confined to Catholic social teaching, the Church has a very specific understanding of consumerism. By "consumerism," we do not mean the raw fact that, whatever the economic system, everyone is a consumer of goods and services. Nor, from the Catholic standpoint, is consumerism really about "how much stuff" is created and exchanged in the economy. Instead consumerism primarily concerns the *attitude* we adopt toward material goods, the importance we ascribe to goods that are means to an end (and therefore unfulfilling in themselves), and the problem of thinking our happiness can be realized through using and possessing goods which are limited and finite by nature.

Material things and services can help bring about our participation in the goods that are central to human flourishing. We can, for instance, engage the good of beauty by writing a poem, sketching a Mediterranean scene, or even through commissioning and buying works of art and then placing them in our homes for ourselves and others to reflect upon. It is very easy, however, for people to imagine that possessing things is somehow fulfilling in itself; that I become "more" of a person because I possess more cars, more jewelry, or more whatever.

There is something profoundly irrational about thinking that while some is good, more is always better, or that I somehow become a better quality person by, for instance, wearing better quality clothes. The point is not that I should not dress well. At issue are my reasons for *why* I dress well. The choice to dress well because I do not want to convey an impression of excessive casualness in situations that demand seriousness is very different from the choice to constantly acquire fine clothes because I think that the more beautiful clothes I possess, the better the person I am.

Central to the problem of consumerism is old-fashioned materialism. In *Sollicitudo Rei Socialis* John Paul II suggested that consumerism facilitates "a *radical dissatisfaction*, because one quickly learns . . . that the more one possesses, the more one wants, while deeper aspirations remain unsatisfied and perhaps even stifled."[15] The pope extended this analysis in *Centesimus Annus* when describing consumerism as a form of alienation: "people are ensnared in a web of false and superficial gratifications. . . A person who is concerned solely or primarily with possessing and enjoying, who is no longer able to control his instincts and passion, or to subordinate them by obedience to the truth cannot be free."[16] The behavior of those athletes who acquire great wealth and then pursue what's often called conspicuous consumption is a good example. Yet the "bling" culture can permeate any sector of society which can afford to pay (or decides to steal) for the dubious pleasure of becoming a slave to their disordered passions.

Unfortunately many defenders of free markets have little to nothing to say about consumerism. Sometimes this reflects a very weak or hedonistic concept of human flourishing. On other occasions, they may actually believe in liberation through materialism. But conspicuous consumption is not just bad public relations. It is deeply disfiguring of human character. It undermines human flourishing in the sense that the possession of things becomes central to people's identity and a culture develops in which the only ideal is "more."

What then do free enterprise Catholics have to say about this? First we must offer perspective.

Our legitimate concerns about consumerism and materialism should not cause us to trivialize or romanticize the material privation that business, the free market, and economic growth have helped millions of people to escape. Historically speaking, the age of prosperity is relatively recent. The type of consumerism that manifests itself in market economies partly reflects the fact that such economies *enable* increasing numbers of people to partake of goods and services that were once the preserve of relatively few people. The costs of such things are constantly lowered by competition; the spectrum of products of which more and more people can partake is widening on a regular basis; and the relative availability of cheap credit has brought goods and services within the realm of possibility for millions for whom it would have been previously beyond their means.

These facts don't excuse consumerism. It is worth stressing, however, that it is a problem which often comes with prosperity, and generally speaking, prosperity is to be preferred to poverty. Why otherwise would Catholics bother trying to help people escape poverty?

A second point that Catholics should make is that the market itself is *not* the source of the problem. The temptation to engage in undignified, irrational behavior manifests itself whenever people possessing weak moral compasses become intoxicated with the acquisition of material goods and status symbols. As illustrated by the Austrian-American social philosopher Monsignor Martin Schlag, *Caritas in Veritate* stresses that free markets don't exist in a social vacuum.[17] They are shaped by the cultural configurations in which they exist.

And while culture certainly consists of traditions, customs, and laws that influence human choices, they are ultimately shaped by past and present human choices and actions. "It is man's darkened reason," Benedict stated with reference to the market economy, "that produces [harmful] consequences, not the instrument *per se*." It follows that people rather than markets in themselves are responsible for the harm.[18]

Features of life in a market economy such as aggressive advertising that appeal to our baser instincts certainly exacerbate the problem. But consumerism is essentially an attitude of practical materialism, and practical materialism can easily manifest itself in societies in which there is a severe dearth of sufficient material possessions.

Communist societies were among the most materialist ever seen in history. This was not simply because Marxism is grounded in atheism and materialism. The very fact that command economies were chronically unable to provide sufficient goods and services also contributed to people living in these societies focusing inordinate attention upon acquiring and possessing things.

John Paul II spent much of his life living in precisely such a society. Paradoxically, life in Communist Poland may have helped him understand the nature of the problem of consumerism in market economies. Speaking on this subject, the pope stressed, "[o]f itself an economic system does not possess criteria for correctly distinguishing new and higher forms of satisfying human needs from artificial new needs."[19] The central issue in play with regard to consumerism is people's free choice, and the need to *inform* such choices so that, in John Paul's words, they are shaped by a concern for goods such as truth, beauty, goodness, and communion with others.[20]

Here the Catholic tradition has much to offer. Catholic thinkers have written at length about how human flourishing can be facilitated in conditions of material prosperity. It is not true that the only safe route for Catholics to realize their potential in the modern world is to retreat to a monastery or convent (where, as any monk or nun will tell you, there are all sorts of different temptations) or live in relative isolation from others. Many great writers have laid out in considerable detail how to live the Christian life of detachment from material goods in conditions of economic well-being.

In his timeless *Introduction to the Devout Life*, for example, Saint Francis de Sales provides counsel about how to cultivate the life of prayer and the degree of detachment that helps people to live in the midst of considerable material comfort while not allowing their identity to be consumed by the conditions around them. This seventeenth-century classic was still very much in vogue among the Catholics of Maryland during the lifetime of Charles Carroll of Carrollton,[21] and occupied a prominent place in his father's library.[22] In a different way, the Catholic American businessman Frank Hanna has detailed how wealthy people living in the twenty-first century can engage in a careful inventory of their possessions and the way they use them to ensure they do not fall prey to consumerism and instead use their wealth to further human flourishing and the universal destination of goods.[23]

Though he never used the word, Charles Carroll well understood the folly of consumerism. His father had never ceased to remind him that while one should never be stingy, conspicuous consumption was the road to moral (and sometimes economic) ruin.[24] Much of the Maryland high society in which he lived most of his long life was marred by what Carroll sharply criticized as the vices and frivolousness that flowed from thoughtless spending—including that of his own alcoholic son. Carroll specified, however, that one check on such habits was a conscientious attention to business itself. By this, Carroll meant allocating specific amounts of time to organizing commercial affairs as well as developing work habits which themselves relied upon the cultivation of virtues such as prudence, fortitude, and temperance.

Carroll's underlying attitude toward such matters was not driven by something akin to a Protestant work ethic. His approach flowed from his sense of responsibility to fulfill the expectations of those who have gone before us, to be a benefactor to one's family, and to provide something for forthcoming generations.[25] For Carroll, the life of business amounted to a type of stewardship, and stewardship implies we are the masters of how we use what has been entrusted to us, rather than prisoners of what we own.

Concerning external restraints upon consumerism, many people instinctively look to the state. Law and government can do some things on the margins. Examples might include prosecuting those peddling manifestly fraudulent schemes, or those who prey on the impressionable, or engage in activities that really do reduce humans to the level of objects (such as human trafficking and prostitution). There is, however, always the risk that governments can easily slip into a type of Puritanism (or an environmentalism that verges on pantheism) that sees little good in material well-being, with such policies subsequently degenerating into paternalism, infantilizing free adults.

Subsidiarity surely tells us that the primary responsibility for limiting the temptations associated with the affluence generated by market economies lies with non-state organizations, especially families and churches. Parents are usually better placed than government officials to teach their children how to value material goods, use mass media, and apply their minds critically to what they see and hear so that they can make clear judgments about what they are being told in advertising. The long-term goal is to root free markets in a moral culture that enables us to in live in societies akin to the Florence of the High Middle Ages and the Renaissance; communities in which widespread commerce, banking, and trade went hand in hand with the literature of Dante and the art of Michelangelo.

Recasting the Immigration Debate

Consumerism is one of those moral/cultural questions where limited-government Catholics can show American defenders of free enterprise how to address this issue in ways that take concerns for authentic human flourishing seriously but without unduly compromising the case for free markets. There is, however, another matter that has been far more central to public policy debates over the past twenty years which limited-government Catholics have considerable potential to transform: the immigration debate that divides not just America but also Catholic Americans.

One reason for the Catholic Church's deep interest in the immigration discussion is undoubtedly the many migrants who come to the United States, legally and illegally, from Latin America. Most of these migrants are at least nominally Catholic, as are many other recent migrants to America from countries such as Poland but whose challenges receive far less public attention.

Part of the Church's particular concern with immigration is obviously that of a Christian concern for human anguish. In 2012, Benedict XVI spoke of "the immense poverty and suffering" often associated with migration, and how it often led "to painful and tragic situations." Many migrations, he added, are the result of "economic instability, the lack of essential goods, natural disasters, wars and social unrest." The pope went on to note that "the experience of migration often begins in fear, especially when persecutions and violence are its cause, and in the trauma of having to leave behind family and possessions which had in some way ensured survival."[26]

These are just some of the reasons why Benedict XVI asked Catholics to "open their arms and their hearts to every person, from whatever nation they come."[27] Catholic teaching on immigration goes far beyond exhortations to be generous and merciful. It also articulates a framework for thinking through this issue in a manner consistent with a concern for human liberty, human flourishing, and the common good. And part of this involves affirming that there is a right—albeit a *limited* right—to migrate.

In several papal texts, John Paul II identified several grounds for a right to migrate. One is to save our lives and those of our families from threats such as persecution, famine, and war. Another is the responsibility of people to provide for themselves and their families. Echoing John XXIII, John Paul stated that this sometimes means a person needs to leave their homeland to seek better conditions and opportunities.[28] John Paul also maintained that undue restrictions upon people's capacity to exercise their right of economic initiative are legitimate grounds for people to seek out places where there is greater freedom to actualize that right.[29] To this we could add that the Church has never suggested the right of free association somehow automatically ceases at national borders.

There is, however, a second dimension to Catholic teaching about immigration that results in considerable qualifications being attached to the right to migrate. Catholic social teaching is very cognizant of the challenges that immigration creates for the host country. John Paul noted, for example, that "practicing [migration] indiscriminately may do harm and be detrimental to the common good of the community that receives the migrant."[30] Hence, he insisted, the nation-state has the right to regulate the right to migrate in light of its implications for the common good.[31]

This point has been reiterated on several occasions, including in the *Catechism of the Catholic Church*,[32] as well as by John Paul's successor. In 2006, Pope Benedict indicated that while Catholics should welcome migrants, they should also allow "the Authorities responsible for public life to enforce the relevant laws held to be appropriate for a healthy co-existence."[33] Six years later, Benedict was more explicit. "Every state," he stressed, "has the right to regulate migration and to enact policies dictated by the general requirements of the common good, albeit always in safeguarding respect for the dignity of each human person."[34]

As a collective whole, these statements tell us several things. The first is while there *is* a right to migrate, it is not absolute. The right to life and the right to migrate are not on the same level. The former is the foundation of the latter, not vice-versa. Second, each nation's government has the responsibility to formulate immigration policy so that it serves the common good.

These positions can be cashed out in several ways. A country which lacks skilled workers in particular areas crucial for economic development would be within its rights if it decided to accord a certain priority to people with specific qualifications when formulating immigration policy. The same common good also means that no country is obliged to admit criminals, terrorists, or anyone else who threatens civil peace, the lives and freedoms of its citizens, or who refuses to abide by its legal system. Nor is the federal government under any obligation to admit anyone who wants to migrate to America with the sole or primary intention of obtaining welfare benefits.

But even within such parameters, there remains tremendous scope for American citizens and governments to be generous to those seeking a better life in the United States. At a minimum, recognizing a right to migrate in the sense outlined above would imply the removal of unnecessary restrictions (especially those that flow from bureaucratic procedures rather than specific policies) on people who want to migrate to America because they yearn to partake of the liberty and opportunity which America has accorded millions of other migrants in the past.

Free market Catholics have several contributions to these discussions often missed by others debating immigration issues. In addition to spelling out the principles outlined above, they can help dissuade Americans from thinking about immigrants in Malthusian terms according to which people are viewed primarily as an economic burden rather than potential wealth creators.

The free economy is above all a human-centered economy in which human intellect, insight, creativity, free will, and risk-taking are the driving force. Many migrants to America have shown they *are* willing to take considerable risks. They often leave circumstances which, however unpleasant, they knew how to navigate. They then choose to enter a country in which they often don't even speak the language. Archbishop Gomez of Los Angeles underscored this point about risk-taking when speaking of the several million illegal migrants living in America:

> Most of the men and women who are living in America without proper documentation have traveled hundreds, even thousands, of miles. They have left everything behind, risked their safety and their lives. They have done this, not for their own comfort or selfish interests. They have done this to feed their loved ones. To be good mothers and fathers. To be loving sons and daughters.[35]

In this connection, pro-free enterprise Catholics can underscore immigrants' disproportionate contribution to *entrepreneurially*-generated growth in America. A 2010 study by the Kauffman Foundation on entrepreneurial activity in the United States, for instance, indicated that immigrants to America were more than twice as likely to start businesses each month in 2010 compared to native-born Americans.[36] Such trends justify Archbishop Gomez's hope that the "men and women who are coming to this country will bring a new, youthful entrepreneurial spirit of hard work to our economy."[37]

The same trends indicate that, thus far, America has avoided some of the policy errors associated with immigration in Europe. Today, a majority of immigrants to the EU end up on welfare. There are many reasons for this, but one important cause is that immigrants are frozen out of the workplace by most EU states' extensive labor market regulations—the maintenance and even extension of which is a major priority for European trade unions.[38]

There are, however, troubling exceptions to the picture in America. One prominent example is the state of California. In 2012, Heather MacDonald demonstrated in a long piece on the economic and political effects of California's changing demographics that Hispanics and Hispanic immigrants in California were disproportionately dependent on welfare programs. Comparing Hispanic and non-Hispanic households, she noted:

> U.S.-born Hispanic households in California already use welfare programs (such as cash welfare, food stamps, and housing assistance) at twice the rate of U.S.-born non-Hispanic households, according to an analysis of the March 2011 Current Population Survey by the Center for Immigration Studies. Welfare use by immigrants is higher still. In 2008–09, the fraction of households using some form of welfare was 82 percent for households headed by an illegal immigrant and 61 percent for households headed by a legal immigrant.[39]

Some of this, MacDonald notes, is attributable to higher poverty levels among California Hispanics as well as lower educational levels. But, she added, there are also worrying political and economic factors contributing to this undue reliance of far too many immigrants upon welfare assistance. Their dependence upon the government safety net, MacDonald writes, incentivizes them to support politicians who see welfare programs and extensive redistribution as a way to build up reliable voting constituencies.[40] The long-term problem, she notes, is that the dynamics are all in place for these redistributionist policies to continue and even expand:

> Poor Hispanics don't pay in taxes what they cost in state expenditures. And with rising Latino political power,

California's welfare policies will probably become even more redistributionist . . . at least if Latinos remain poor, their drop-out rates don't improve, and they don't feel they can climb the economic ladder.[41]

Addressing these issues is far from simple. They touch on questions ranging from language issues and economic mobility, to the self-interest of politicians and particular electoral dynamics. But to the extent that the welfare state has become part of the problem, Catholics should affirm that immigration to America *cannot* be about becoming more or less reliant on welfare programs over the long term. Unnecessary or excessive levels of dependence on the state hamper people's ability to realize their potential as human beings. Even less should welfare be used to lure immigrants into becoming tame supporters of those politicians who regard welfare as a means of playing the deeply destructive game of identity politics— something that greatly damages a society's cohesiveness and common good more generally.

Nor should Catholics hesitate to point out that between the 1840s and 1960s, millions of Catholics migrated to the United States from some of Europe's poorest and most economically backward regions. Like many recent Latin American migrants, they often brought little in the way of capital, be it human or monetary. Many had a poor-to-non-existent command of English. In some cases they were barely literate.

And yet millions of them *made it*, as Americans often say, and built better lives for themselves and their children without receiving a single welfare check. To say that Catholic immigrants from Latin American nations (or other economically underdeveloped countries) cannot do the same— or to allow them to slip into various forms of dependency in the interests of political expediency—is insulting to their dignity, dismissive of their creative potential, and damaging to the common good.

At the same time, there are good reasons for Catholics to work toward comprehensively addressing the status of long-term illegal immigrants, especially those who were brought to the United States as children by their parents. These particular individuals did not choose to violate America's laws. They are also likely to possess considerable capital in the form of education, not to mention fluency in English, from which America can economically benefit. Yet they are stuck in a legal limbo for which they are not responsible. Providing them with a path for regularizing their legal status is not only an act of mercy, it also removes a significant barrier to their ability to use their freedom for flourishing.

And this brings us to the third concern which limited-government Catholics can bring to the debate: attention to the very real undermining of rule of law caused by both illegal immigration as well as inconsistent and incoherent immigration policies.

Rule of law is a much-used expression, though often with little specification concerning its meaning. In *Natural Law and Natural Rights*, John Finnis identified the rule of law as meaning the following: (1) rules are prospective rather than retroactive and not impossible to comply with; (2) rules are promulgated, clear, and coherent with respect to each other; (3) rules are sufficiently stable to allow people to be guided by their knowledge of the content of the rules; (4) the making of laws applicable to specific situations is guided by rules that are promulgated, clear, stable, and relatively clear; and (5) those charged with the authority to make and administer rules are accountable for their own compliance with the rules, and administer the law consistently.[42]

Looking at each of these elements, we quickly realize why rule of law is such an essential condition of the common good. Without rule of law, it is impossible to maintain a free society. By definition, absence of rule of law means that the state cannot help but be arbitrary and, as Charles Carroll observed long ago, "A free constitution will not endure discretionary powers."[43] Instead one ends up with a society in which procedural restraints on government power become difficult, if not impossible, to maintain. Though it is very politically incorrect to say so, liberty is often more threatened by an absence of rule of law than by a lack of democracy.

In the context of America's immigration debate, some Catholics have been slow to acknowledge that the *illegality* of illegal immigration *is* a significant problem. Trying to minimize or even deny this by using euphemisms such as "undocumented immigrants" sometimes reflects a reluctance to acknowledge this point. It was not for idle reasons that John Paul II once specified that "illegal immigration should be prevented."[44] A general failure to obey the law (even laws we disagree with) contributes to an overall disrespect for law: something that strikes at the root of the common good.[45]

Any Catholic American who doubts the importance of rule of law need only head south of the Rio Grande. In many of the predominantly Catholic countries of Latin America, what Aquinas called "the rule of men"[46] prevails. Corruption is endemic, nepotism is widespread, courts are often viewed with suspicion, and private property is often highly insecure. In their 2007 *Aparecida* statement, the Catholic bishops of Latin America were brutally direct about just how bad the situation is:

Also alarming is the level of corruption in economies, involving the public and private sector alike, compounded by a notable lack of transparency and accountability to the citizenry.[47]

A major negative factor observable in much of the region is the intensification of corruption in society and the State involving the legislative and executive branches at all levels. It also extends to the judicial system, which in its ruling often sides with the powerful and fosters impunity, thereby jeopardizing the credibility of government institutions and increasing the mistrust of the people. That phenomenon goes hand in hand with a deep contempt for legality.[48]

In economic terms, this translates into less investment, less risk-taking, and less security. The overall result, however, is not only less economic growth. Crumbling or absence of rule of law also impedes people's capacity to live out the possibilities opened up by their freedom.

In more recent years, many American Catholic bishops, most notably Archbishop Gomez, have stated that rule of law *is* most certainly one of the major issues in play in America's immigration debate. America's immigration laws are confused, contradictory, irregularly enforced, and subject to conflicting judicial interpretation and constitutionally-questionable executive orders. These are certainly part of the overall rule of law problem that must be part of America's immigration conversation.

They are not, however, reasons for downplaying the damage caused to the rule of law by (1) the residence of several million people who have broken America's laws to live in the United States and (2) America's difficulties in resolving this situation in a manner consistent with rule of law. After all, one major element that drives many immigrants, legal or otherwise, to come to America is that the simple fact that *the rule of law does not exist in their own countries*. That alone should cause all Americans, Catholic or otherwise, to hesitate before being flippant about the rule of law problems associated with illegal immigration.

Catholic and American, American and Catholic

America is not the only destination of immigrants in the world. Yet it remains by far the country to which most people want to migrate. Part of America's success as a nation of migrants has been its ability to absorb people from a genuine plurality of backgrounds so that they become part of *one* nation. Many Americans are proud of the countries from which they or their forebears came and actively celebrate their heritage. But being American means much more than simply changing one's place of residence. It also means embracing values and institutions that are distinctly American—the *Novus ordo seclorum* as it says on the Great Seal of the United States—and to *love* the patrimony that has been attained and protected for us by previous generations. That is part of the essence of patriotism.

Outside the United States, words such as "patriot" and "patriotism" are not always the most fashionable of terms. Throughout much of Europe, it is often associated with the type of nationalism that helped pit European against European from the late eighteenth century onward. The word has also been used by populist and authoritarian regimes to bolster their support, not least by stigmatizing their opponents as "unpatriotic." Even in a contemporary American context, the term has been used for less-than-honorable purposes such as labeling those who favor free trade as being insufficiently patriotic to "buy American"— as if being patriotic means encouraging American businesses to think they should be sheltered from competition through subsidies and tariffs.

Many wonder whether, in an age of globalization, terms like patriotism still carry meaning or have any resonance. One feature of modern globalization has been the growth and spread of transnational institutions of both a private and public nature, not to mention groups not motivated by love of country but rather by religious or ideological fundamentalism.

The Catholic Church has long regarded international forums, organizations, and institutions as a significant (though not the only) means of peacefully resolving disputes between sovereign states. As recently as Benedict XVI's *Caritas in Veritate*, the Church reiterated its call for the development of a world political authority that would engage in a type of global governance.[49] Part of the Church's point is that in an increasingly globalized and integrated world, it is preferable that relations between states be regulated by international law and international institutions rather than a *realpolitik* balance of power.

Many Americans—including many Catholic Americans— are understandably nervous when they hear such ideas articulated. They immediately wonder whether this means American sovereignty is to be subordinated to something like the United Nations: an organization, they accurately point out, which has consistently adopted and promoted policies, protocols, and conventions that run directly contrary to Catholic teaching on core moral subjects ranging from the dignity of human life from conception to natural death, to the nature of the family.

Many Western European Catholics are often puzzled when American Catholics express concerns about these matters. Their puzzlement, however, should not be surprising. The growth and expansion of pan-European institutions at the expense of national sovereignty has been one way that Europeans have resolved, at least for the moment, their penchant for fighting and killing each other at relatively regular intervals.

The costs for Europeans of adopting this approach have been considerable. They include a profound reduction of economic freedom, the pervasive lack of democratic accountability in many EU institutions, the growth of control and interference from the top down that flies in the face of subsidiarity,[50] and what perhaps Germany's most well-known philosopher, Jürgen Habermas (a self-described methodological atheist), has described as the increasing bureaucratizing of many European societies which increasingly resort to legally-dubious means to paper over internal national and inter-European disagreements.[51]

European Catholics also often fail to acknowledge that the Church has been very careful not to be too specific about what global governance might mean, let alone "a world political authority." It need not imply "one world government."

It could easily amount to a framework of international institutions whose responsibilities remain strictly limited to specific functions. In fact Benedict XVI specified in 2012 that when thinking about such an authority, "one should not envisage a superpower, concentrated in the hands of the few, dominating all peoples and exploiting the weakest among them, but rather that such an authority should be understood primarily as a moral force, a power to influence according to reason, or rather as a participatory authority, limited in competence and by law."[52]

But in the midst of discussions about such matters, Catholics in America can also underscore something often glossed over in our globalized world: that the Catholic Church articulates a very positive view of the nation and the idea of patriotism. This especially matters for Catholic Americans because their patriotism has been questioned at different times throughout American history. Until the 1960s, many Protestant Americans were deeply concerned about possible conflicts between Catholic Americans' political allegiance to the United States and their spiritual obligations to the successor of St. Peter.

Even today, many people are surprised to learn that the Catholic Church, which is by its very name, nature, and vocation international in its outlook, teaches that Catholics have positive responsibilities toward their homelands. In its Decree on the Church's Missionary Activity, *Ad Gentes*, the Second Vatican Council, for instance, reiterated that Catholics

> belong to the nation in which they were born; they have begun to share in its cultural treasures by means of their education; they are joined to its life by manifold social ties; they are cooperating in its progress by their efforts . . . they feel its problems to be their very own, and they are trying to solve them. . . . they must give expression to this newness of life in the social and cultural framework

of their own homeland, according to their own national traditions. They must be acquainted with this culture; they must heal it and preserve it.[53]

Much of this is reiterated by the *Catechism of the Catholic Church* which, among other things, stresses immigrants' obligation "to respect with gratitude the material and spiritual heritage of the country that receives them, to obey its laws and to assist in carrying civic burdens."[54]

In the Latin text of *Ad Gentes*, the word used for homeland is "*patriae*." This harkens back to a long tradition of the Church upholding, uplifting, and purifying the love of the good of one's country. Aquinas even drew an analogy between the virtue of patriotism and that of religion. He described this virtue as *pietas*: an attitude of being dutiful, reverent, and full of gratitude toward our parents and homeland. People, Aquinas maintained, were dependent on their parents for their lives. Yet they also relied upon their *patriae* for their historical and cultural character in a manner analogous to the way we depend on God for our existence and all other things bequeathed to us.[55]

In a similar way, Leo XIII used the idea of patriotism to describe the way by which Catholics should love the Church. "The natural law," he wrote, "enjoins us to love devotedly and to defend the country in which we had birth, and in which we were brought up, so that every good citizen hesitates not to face death for his native land."[56] In such circumstances, Réginald Garrigou-Lagrange suggests, "virtue must be heroic."[57]

One pope who certainly understood patriotism's value was John Paul II. No one could have been prouder of his native Poland's enormous cultural and educational achievements. Yet he seamlessly combined this sincere patriotism with fidelity to the universal Church and avoidance of any narrow parochialism. The Polish pope was much given to reflecting upon the mission for the world that Providence had ascribed his own country—called elsewhere the "Christ of Nations" on account of its suffering throughout the centuries—and drew upon these in an effort to describe the nation's place in Catholic thought. In a book that appeared just two weeks before he died in 2005, John Paul wrote:

> The term "nation" designated a community based in a given territory and distinguished by other nations by its culture. Catholic social doctrine holds that the family and the nation are both natural societies, not the product of mere convention. Therefore in human history, they cannot be replaced by anything else.[58]

Empires and other transnational political and legal entities may come and go. Peoples and nations, however, seem to be a fixed part of human ecology.

But *what* is it that the patriot loves? After observing America, Alexis de Tocqueville concluded there were two kinds of patriotism. One is a feeling that ties people's hearts to the place in which they are born, and is "mingled with a taste of old habits, respect for ancestors, and memories of the past."

The second form of patriotism, however, is quite different. Tocqueville called it "well-considered patriotism." By this, he meant something "more rational." It was especially manifested in Americans who, Tocqueville said, took as much interest in the affairs of their townships, states, and the nation as they did in their own well-being, not least because Americans saw a strong correlation between their own happiness and the nation's well-being.[59] In Catholic terms, this might be translated as understanding there is a connection between the flourishing of individuals and communities, and the common good of the nations in which they live, move, and have their being.

John Paul's reflections on national identity resemble aspects of Tocqueville's observations. But the pope went beyond Tocqueville in some important respects. Patriotism, the pope claimed, involved sentimental attachment to the name of a nation, but also a sense of responsibility for what has been handed to us. At the same time, John Paul added, patriotism extends into the realm of those universal *moral* commitments that are given particular shape and expression in specific cultural settings:

> the native land . . . is in some ways to be identified with patrimony, that is, the totality of good bequeathed to us by our forefathers. . . . Our native land is thus our heritage and it is also the whole patrimony derived from that heritage . . . the land, the territory, but more importantly . . . the values and the spiritual content that go to make up the culture of a given nation.[60]

Once understood in this way, we see that patriotism and nationalism are very different phenomena. Nationalism represents the perversion of patriotism by invoking national interest to rationalize selfish, irrational, or immoral ends. Nonetheless, as Germain Grisez writes:

> such ideological distortions do not negate the truth that, just as individuals have a personal vocation, so nations, like other communities, have a proper mission. The divine gifts found within each nation and its homeland have been given to that people not only for them to exploit and enjoy, but for the use and service of others.[61]

Patriotism is thus the love of the *true* good of one's country. Patriotism cannot therefore be associated with either jingoism or condescension toward other nations. And while patriotism has an emotional component, it does not absolve Americans from using our reason and judgment to discern what is in fact America's *true* good. As part of that good, we are bound to ask what is it that America can offer as its unique gifts to the world.

This sounds rather vague, until we realize most nations have shown at different points of their history that they do have particular gifts to offer the world. In England's case, it could range from the literature of Shakespeare to the *Magna Carta*. Twentieth-century Poland provides us with a model of how to resist totalitarianism in ways that—eventually, and after much suffering—played an indispensable role in the peaceful defeat of an unspeakably evil empire.

What then might be some of the specific willing of the good of the United States that Catholics can bring as patriotic Americans to the public square?

One is to affirm that love of one's homeland does *not* bear primarily upon the government. Catholic teaching insists that patriotism encompasses one's love of that larger community that precedes the state and which governments exist to serve. Patriotism is not about love of the government *per se*.

A second contribution is to affirm something about America noticed by plenty of external observers. Writing for the Supreme Court majority in 1952 in *Zorach et al. v. Clauson et al.*, perhaps the most "civil libertarian" of America's Supreme Court Justices, past and present, William O. Douglas stated something that has long been obvious to many Americans and non-Americans alike:

> We are a religious people whose institutions presuppose a Supreme Being. We guarantee the freedom to worship as one chooses. We make room for as wide a variety of beliefs and creeds as the spiritual needs of man deem necessary. We sponsor an attitude on the part of government that shows no partiality to any one group and that lets each flourish according to the zeal of its adherents and the appeal of its dogma. When the state encourages religious instruction or cooperates with religious authorities by adjusting the schedule of public events to sectarian needs, it follows the best of our traditions. For it then respects the religious nature of our people and accommodates the public service to their

spiritual needs. To hold that it may not would be to find in the Constitution a requirement that the government show a callous indifference to religious groups. That would be preferring those who believe in no religion over those who do believe. Government may not finance religious groups nor undertake religious instruction nor blend secular and sectarian education nor use secular institutions to force one or some religion on any person. But we find no constitutional requirement which makes it necessary for government to be hostile to religion and to throw its weight against efforts to widen the effective scope of religious influence.[62]

The understanding of religious liberty operative here is not precisely the same as that articulated by *Dignitatis Humanae*. But nor is it utterly foreign to the vision of the Second Vatican Council. Douglas plainly believed that religion's honored place in America meant that the government's role vis-à-vis religion should not be one of indifference, let alone antagonism, to religious faith. Even more noticeable is Douglas's affirmation that broadly religious assumptions underlie the American experiment.

It is therefore very much an act of patriotism for Catholic Americans to resist the encroachment of what Douglas called "a callous indifference to religious groups" on the government's part and to protest against the promotion of a preferential option for non-belief. Atheism, agnosticism, secularism, and religious indifferentism are *not* neutral positions. Thus if being patriotic means safeguarding and handing on the particular treasures with which a nation has been bequeathed, then Catholic Americans should *relentlessly* work to prevent the type of unjust discrimination against religious believers that manifests itself in the form of overt or covert privileging via the law and politics of secularist claims and assumptions.

Bridging the Social and the Economic

Limited government and free market Catholics are, as we have seen, uniquely positioned to build bridges between the cases for religious and economic liberty on the basis of principled arguments derived from coherent reflection on the nature of human flourishing. There is, however, another connection which they are well-positioned to develop: that between the free economy and the necessary social fabric that will sustain it in America.

In the first place, the Catholic emphasis upon the human person's inherent dignity provides a powerful bulwark for any society anxious to restrict government power. Though social justice Catholics often argue that respect for human dignity tends to translate into expansionist government, less attention is given to the way in which human dignity functions as an inherent *limit* on government power, including the state's economic power.

Once a society takes the view that some humans are somehow intrinsically worth less than others (because of factors such as their gender, age, or health), or decides that human dignity itself is a mere fiction, the road is open for the state to violate any number of natural rights. It allows, for example, the right to life of the elderly or the severely disabled to be subordinated to the state's desire to maintain functioning welfare systems. Ignoring the claims of human dignity also permits the rights to economic liberty, private property, and free association to be diminished in the interests of promoting grand economic plans presided over by governments that pretend to possess a capacity for knowledge that God alone possesses. The same circumstances open the way for the right of individuals and communities to religious liberty to be overridden in the name of an official or unofficial state ideology.

More broadly, if people are routinely contemptuous of others—and therefore see no *principled* reason not to be dishonest, unjust, selfish, and uncivil to one another—then we are effectively stuck in a Hobbesian world in which people behave themselves either because they fear the state or because the state simply imposes its will upon us, whatever that will might be. Realizing a free economy, let alone a free society, in such conditions is impossible. Many of the social preconditions for the workings of business and free markets would wilt and eventually disappear.

This brings us to another dimension of the integration between the social and economic dimensions of free societies that free market Catholics can emphasize. The successful businesses that drive the economic prosperity generated by markets rely upon significant numbers of people keeping promises, accepting the rule of law, working hard, paying their bills, and repaying their loans. In other words, they are dependent upon a moral culture that encourages certain habits while discouraging and even stigmatizing others.

Government has a role in developing such a moral ecology. The punishment of stealing, for instance, goes far beyond simply trying to keep down transaction costs. It reminds us that theft is wrong in itself. But ultimately, as Charles Carroll observed, "The stability of a free republic must depend on the morality of the people. Immoral citizens will elect immoral representatives; or should they by chance select moral and wise ones and wise laws be enacted, they will be disregarded by a corrupt people."[63]

The Catholic principle of subsidiarity suggests that the *primary* place where such moral formation occurs is surely in families and other non-state and non-economic institutions. Congressman Paul Ryan explained this well in a speech toward the end of the 2012 presidential campaign when he said:

There's a vast middle ground between the government and the individual. Our families and our neighborhoods, the groups we join and our places of worship—this is where we live our lives. They shape our character, give our lives direction, and help make us a self-governing people.[64]

The weakness or even absence of this "middle ground" leaves a vacuum. And such a void makes it almost certain that the government will try to fill it, either by design or necessity. That means more bureaucracy, more taxes to pay for it, and the emergence of a vicious cycle whereby civil society is further crowded out, which creates more space for the state to fill, which leads to more bureaucracy and higher taxes, and even less space for civil society. The cost, however, is not just social. The economic repercussions are considerable. It means more disincentives to create wealth as well as growing shortages of the moral and social capital that businesses need to begin, survive, and grow.

Freedom-loving Catholics should therefore stress the contribution made by the family and civil society to the world of the marketplace. As Robert P. George has emphasized again and again to those who are inclined to think that economic liberty and limiting government power might be enough:

> Business cannot manufacture honest, hard working people to employ. Nor can government create them by law. Businesses and government depend on there being many such people, but they must rely on the family, assisted by religious communities and other institutions of civil society, to produce them.[65]

Taking Truth Seriously

Both reason and Catholic faith tell us that, this side of eternity, there is no such thing as the perfect economic system. Nor is there any system of government that guarantees liberty, justice, and all the goods associated with human flourishing. Nonetheless if people's dignity is to be recognized, and if freedom in the religious, political, and economic realms is to be maintained, then greater understanding is required of the mutual reinforcing effects of free markets, religious liberty, and a moral ecology based upon explicit *truth* claims about the nature of the good.

Some advocates of freedom have shown themselves distinctly ill-at-ease with thinking this way about liberty. Milton Friedman, for instance, reacted to one of John Paul's statements about the reliance of freedom upon truth in the following manner:

> I must confess that one high-minded sentiment, passed off as if it were a self-evident proposition, sent shivers down my back: "*Obedience to the truth* about God and man is the first condition of freedom." Whose "truth"? Decided by whom? Echoes of the Spanish Inquisition?[66]

Friedman was right to stress that much harm has been done in the name of truth. But alongside acknowledging this point, the Catholic response to such arguments should be threefold.

First, the discernment of truth is the very purpose of the human intellect. Indeed, truth *is* the mind's conformity with reality. It is thus as fantastical to imagine people can be "free from" the truth about God, humankind, and reality as it is to imagine that one can have a square circle.

Second, one of the twentieth century's primary lessons is surely that specific truth claims about the human person are essential to a principled defense of human beings against unreasonable state coercion. In the absence of reliable and constant knowledge of what makes us truly human and what is therefore truly inviolable, there is no principled basis for opposing the state's decision to simply do whatever it wills. Instead governments can, among other things, murder the innocent, steal their citizens' property, torture those who protest their policies, and discriminate against those who refuse to bow to fashionable ideologies—all according to the whims of whoever is stronger or willing to be the most ruthless.

Third, in those societies in which people are unable or simply unwilling to achieve the dominion over themselves that comes from freely choosing the virtues that can be universally known through reason, we are likely to find order being imposed from the top down. Moreover, there is no reason to suppose in a society that flatly denies the knowability of more than scientific truth that those in charge will choose to act reasonably and virtuously.

From this standpoint, freedom and truth stand or fall together. And as Benedict XVI pointed out to an American audience in 2008, this insight is shared by Catholicism and important elements that influenced the American Founding.

> In a word, freedom is ever new. It is a challenge held out to each generation, and it must constantly be won over for the cause of good. Few have understood this as clearly as the late Pope John Paul II. In reflecting on the spiritual victory of freedom over totalitarianism in his native Poland and in eastern Europe, he reminded us that history shows, time and again, that "in a world without truth, freedom loses its foundation", and a democracy without values can lose its very soul. Those prophetic words in some sense echo the conviction of President Washington, expressed in his Farewell Address, that religion and morality represent "indispensable supports" of political prosperity.[67]

Catholics, Life, and Liberty

For 500 years, hundreds of thousands of Catholics have taken the risk of uprooting themselves and traveling to the

New World in the hope that they could live out the liberty with which all are endowed by God. This *truth* about human beings—that we are indeed made free—was central to the American Revolution, as were a number of related truths about human beings that flowed from this basic point: that people, for instance, *should* be free rather than serfs; that there *are* limits to government power over the lives and property of those who live under their jurisdiction; that, consistent with the rights of others and the just requirements of public order, people *ought* to be free to live out their liberty, the end of which (at least for the Founders) was virtue and truth rather than vice and error.

Toward the end of his life, Charles Carroll spelled out in no uncertain terms what he considered to be the source of these truths. On August 2, 1826, Carroll wrote that he thanked God "for the blessings which through Jesus Christ our Lord, He has conferred upon my beloved country in her emancipation, and upon myself."[68] For Carroll, these blessings did not proceed from a master clockmaker who wound up His Creation and then let it play itself in a deterministic fashion. Nor had they merely evolved out of nothingness—a position that absurdly assumes something can come from nothing. Rather, they embodied truths fully revealed to us in the God-Man, Jesus Christ.

This did not mean that Carroll believed the blessings of these truths were somehow eternally guaranteed to either America as a whole or its Catholic citizens in particular. As a student of literature and history, Carroll knew that not all experiments in liberty end well. In fact, most do not. Like most of the Founders, Carroll pondered how the Roman Republic had been transformed into an Empire in which its emperors were ascribed godlike status. Along with figures such as Washington, Adams, and Madison, Carroll was appalled by the terrorism and seemingly endless war unleashed by the French Revolution in its pursuit of *liberté, égalité, fraternité.* But Carroll was set apart from his fellow revolutionaries who saw the American Revolution as a reiteration of the freedoms and rights established by England's Glorious Revolution of 1688. For Carroll, one of the lamentable results of the Glorious Revolution, for all its strengths, was that it confirmed his status and that of other Catholics in the British Isles and her colonies as second-class subjects.

This may help to explain why, immediately after penning the words above, Carroll felt compelled to recommend "to the present and future generation the principles of [the Declaration of Independence] as the best earthly inheritance their ancestors could bequeath to them."[69] Plainly he believed the truths embodied in these principles and the freedoms they had helped realize were only as secure as each generation chose to make them. And the importance of securing these liberties, in Carroll's view, went way beyond America. He asked his fellow citizens to "pray that the civil and religious liberties" that the revolutionary generation had secured for America "may be perpetuated to the remotest posterity and extended to the whole family of mankind."[70]

Carroll's insistence that Americans should *pray* for the maintenance and spread of these freedoms is revealing. As a student of the Jesuits, he would have been familiar with the expression often attributed to Saint Ignatius of Loyola: "Pray as if everything depends on God, work as if everything depends on you."

There is no evidence Saint Ignatius actually uttered these words. Nevertheless they come close to summarizing the path ahead for Catholic Americans who favor limited government, the market economy, and a society which takes religious liberty seriously. Work, they must—but not everyone's work is the same. Some will labor within the Church to make their case to their fellow Catholics more inclined to interventionist economic policies as well as those who seem not to grasp what's at stake in the Church's struggle for religious liberty. Others will toil within the broader society as they seek to persuade their fellow Americans that the case for freedom is best explained in terms of the human flourishing that is its end, rather than relying on arguments incapable of distinguishing between beauty and ugliness, creativity and passivity, or truth and error. And some will find themselves operating in the difficult and complicated world of American politics—an environment not always especially amenable to principled arguments and where means are regularly mistaken for ends.

Happiness is certainly the goal of human life. It is the object of human liberty. But in our redeemed yet also fallen world, the realizing of human flourishing is always fragile and somewhat tenuous. It is also easily lost through our errors, the willful misuse of our liberty, and perhaps above all through our apathy if we let that precious inheritance of which Charles Carroll spoke slowly slip away into the twilight world of soft despotism of which Alexis de Tocqueville warned us.

In other words, our efforts are never enough. One heresy which constantly rears its head throughout the Church's history is Pelagianism: the claim that people can realize moral perfection without the help of divine grace. While Catholicism, Eastern Orthodox Christianity, Orthodox Judaism, and the central tradition of natural law philosophy are virtually alone today in formally affirming that humans *do* possess free will, the Church also tells us, especially through the medium of Saint Augustine's writings, that our salvation comes through the unmerited gift of God's grace. It is the grace for which we should pray and which we have the free choice to accept or refuse. But Catholics also believe that grace opens to us the opportunity to continually choose to live out the promises and freedom bequeathed upon us by that grace, or, conversely, to render our new life in Christ "dead" through choices that promote human disintegration.

Like countless others before him, Tocqueville was much influenced by Augustine's thought. Some have interpreted this as helping to explain some of *Democracy in America*'s more gloomy themes.

Yet Augustine was not quite the pessimist that later generations of theologians made him out to be. Augustine was after all a *Catholic*. This meant he had the faith that nothing happens by accident; that people are not the mere playthings of an arbitrary God who cares little for those He has created in His Image. For all his interior personal struggles with Catholic faith, Tocqueville had a similar confidence that societies such as America that valued liberty in the fullest sense of that word were something *intended* by God, though often realized in unexpected ways and through a multitude of uncoordinated, sometimes unintended efforts. In a way, Tocqueville sums it all up in one of my favorite passages from *Democracy in America* with words that express convictions and sentiments that Americans—and Catholics—have long understood:

> Men think that the greatness of the idea of unity lies in means. God sees it in the end. It is for that reason that the idea of greatness leads to a thousand mean actions. To force all men to march in step toward the same goal— that is a human idea. To encourage endless variety of actions but to bring them about so that in a thousand different ways all tend toward the fulfillment of one great design—that is a God-given idea.
>
> The human idea of unity is almost always sterile, but that of God is immensely fruitful. Men think that they prove their greatness by simplifying the means. God's object is simple but His means infinitely various.[71]

Further Reading

Charles Chaput, *Render unto Caesar: Serving the Nation by Living Our Catholic Beliefs in Political Life* (New York: Doubleday, 2008).

Congregation for the Doctrine of the Faith, *Doctrinal Note on Some Aspects of the Participation of Catholics in Political Life*, www.vatican.va/roman_curia/congregations/cfaith/documents/rc_con_cfaith_doc_20021124_politica_en.html.

Frank J. Hanna III, *What Your Money Means: And How to Use it Well* (New York: Crossroad, 2008).

Saint Francis de Sales, *Introduction to the Devout Life* (New York: Doubleday, 1990).

John J. Wright, *National Patriotism in Papal Teaching* (Westminster, MD: Newman Press, 1956).

Acknowledgments

Any book has many fathers and mothers. *Tea Party Catholic* is no exception. So while I am responsible for the thoughts, ideas, and errors contained within, I am very grateful to the many friends and colleagues who helped shape the reflections in this text. Needless to say, only I am responsible for the thoughts articulated within its pages.

When John Zmirak first suggested this topic to me as a book, it immediately struck me as the right subject for our times. His insight was that *now* was the time to restate the Catholic argument for liberty and human flourishing, to illustrate its capacity to inform the American experiment, and to spell out its implications for the debates about the economy, religious freedom, and the role of government that dominate so much of the American public square today. His insights and comments have helped produce a tighter text.

In this regard, this book should not be understood as an effort to reinvigorate what some called in the 1990s the "Catholic moment." It simply attempts to draw out of Catholic teaching a fresh way of thinking about some of the dominant issues confronting Catholics and other Americans, and to illustrate how they can shape broader American discussions, both within and outside the Catholic fold.

Readers will also notice the efforts throughout these pages to link some of this book's ideas to the American Founding: to people, events, and writings about which I had previously known some things but, as I discovered, plainly not enough. In that connection, encountering the life and writings of America's only Catholic Signer of the Declaration of Independence, Charles Carroll of Carrollton, proved to be a revelation and a delight. It still surprises me that, even for many well-informed Catholic Americans, Carroll remains a relatively unknown figure. For Catholics in America who believe in limited government, religious liberty, and a free economy, and who want to ground these things in a robust conception of human flourishing and commitment to the Catholic Faith, Carroll's life and thought should be an indispensable reference point. In this connection, I must thank Charles Carroll Carter for his encouragement concerning this book's modest effort to underscore the importance for Catholicism in America of one of the most illustrious members of his family.

Thanks must be particularly extended to Ryan Anderson, Thomas C. Behr, Edwin Feulner, Father Kevin Flannery, S.J., Frank Hanna III, Ismael Hernandez, Kishore Jayabalan, Robert G. Kennedy, Leonard Liggio, Kathryn Lopez, Father C.J. McCloskey, Michael Matheson Miller, David Milroy, Kris Alan Mauren, Richard Reinsch, Father James Schall, S.J., Father Phillip de Vous, George Weigel, and Andreas Widmer. Over many years, I have discussed several of the themes of this book with these and other Catholic Americans. They will surely recognize some of the fruits of those discussions within these pages.

Then there are the many non-Americans—especially Michael Casey, Archbishop Gintaras Grušas, Father Gregory Jordan, S.J., Bishop Kęstutis Kėvalas, Bishop Jean Laffitte, Santiago Legarre, Elena Leontjeva, Ambassador John McCarthy, Father Anthony Percy, Cardinal George Pell, Alexandre Pesey, Bishop Dominique Rey, Tómas Rodríguez and Carroll Ríos de Rodríguez, Father Alexander Sherbrooke, Manfred Spieker, Monsignor Martin Schlag, Father Raymond de Souza, Cecilia G. de Vázquez Ger, and Christof Zeller-Zellenberg—who follow the life of the Church in the United States very closely and, like many "outsiders," often see things that escape the attention of "insiders."

The intellectual debt that I owe to that band of scholars, otherwise known as the "new natural law school," will be evident to those readers who follow such discussions. The formation which I originally received from John Finnis—who remains for me the model of intellectual rigor and coherence— since reinforced by interactions with, and readings of, Germain Grisez, Joseph Boyle, and Robert P. George continues to shape me. Equally impressive, however, has been their courageous witness inside and outside the Church with regard to the truths about freedom and morality spelled out in what I regard as the most profound of Blessed John Paul II's encyclicals, *Veritatis Splendor*.

There are three other men who must be mentioned here. The first is Michael Novak: a true *parfait gentil knyght*. His contributions to Catholic social thought and the place of Catholics in the broader tradition of freedom in America and the West more generally are difficult to overstate. His courage in making his case about the free economy and the limits of government at a time when neither was in fashion in America as a whole or in the Catholic Church in America more specifically has borne much intellectual and moral fruit. The number of people in his debt is uncountable.

The second is Father Robert Sirico. His work in promoting and above all institutionalizing with Kris Mauren the cause of economic freedom as part of a boarder vision of a free, virtuous, and just society grounded in Christian anthropology has reshaped lives. More important, however, has been his witness as a priest of the Lord Jesus Christ to the truth of the Catholic Faith and his ability to communicate this saving truth to some of the great, but also many, many more of the humble of this world.

Then there is Alejandro Chafuen. One of the few genuinely modest and self-effacing men I know, Alex is one of nature's gentlemen and has devoted much by way of time, energy, and intellect to the cause of freedom. His were among the very first efforts to ground historically the case for limited government and economic freedom within the natural law tradition, specifically that developed by scholastic thinkers of the medieval and early modern periods. Many of us are in his debt.

Thanks must also be extended to Gwendolin Herder of the Crossroad Publishing Company, and her willingness to commit to this project.

Finally, my abiding thanks to my beloved wife, Ingrid, and our beautiful daughter, Madeleine. More than anyone else, they continue to teach me the deeper meaning of life, liberty, and the pursuit of happiness.

S. J. G.
May 2, 2013
Feast Day of Saint Athanasius

Notes

Introduction

1 George Washington, "Letter to the Roman Catholics in the United States of America," in W. B. Allen (ed.) *George Washington: A Collection* (Indianapolis: Liberty Fund, 1988), 189.

2 Cited in Allen Sinclair Will, *Life of Cardinal Gibbons: Archbishop of Baltimore*, Volume 1 (New York: E. P. Dutton and Company, 1922), 309.

3 "Therefore, brothers, we are children not of the slave woman but of the freeborn woman. For freedom Christ set us free; so stand firm and do not submit again to the yoke of slavery." Galatians 4:31–5:1.

4 Archbishop José H. Gomez, "Immigration and the 'Next America': Perspectives from Our History." Address at the Napa Institute, July 28, 2011, http://www.ncregister.com/daily-news/immigration-and-the-next-america-perspectives-from-our-history/

5 Cited in Bernard C. Steiner, *The Life and Correspondence of James McHenry* (Cleveland: The Burrows Brothers, 1907), 475.

6 Cardinal Donald Wuerl, "New Evangelization is the Re-Introduction, the Re-Proposing, of Christ," October 9, 2012, http://www.zenit.org/article-35675?l=english.

7 Ibid.

8 John Paul II, Encyclical Letter *Centesimus Annus* (1991), 42, http://www.vatican.va/holy_father/john_paul_ii/encyclicals/documents/hf_jp-ii_enc_01051991_centesimus-annus_en.html (hereafter *CA*).

9 Second Vatican Council, Decree on the Apostolate of the Laity, *Apostolicam Actuositatem* (1965), 7, http://www.vatican.va/archive/hist_councils/ii_vatican_council/documents/vat-ii_decree_19651118_apostolicam-actuositatem_en.html (hereafter *AA*). Emphasis mine.

10 See George Weigel, *Evangelical Catholicism: Deep Reform in the 21st Century Church* (New York: Basic Books, 2013), 226.

11 Germain Grisez, *The Way of the Lord Jesus*, vol. 2, *Living a Christian Life* (Quincy, IL: Franciscan Press, 1993), 860.

12 See Robert P. George, "Bioethics and public policy," in Luke Gormally (ed.), *Issues for a Catholic Bioethic* (London: Linacre Centre, 1997), 274–99.

13 See "Bishop criticizes USCCB committee's reaction to Ryan budget," *Catholic World News*, June 14, 2012, http://www.catholicculture.org/news/headlines/index.cfm?storyid=14639.

14 The draft, entitled *The Hope of the Gospel in Difficult Times* (2012) may be found at http://www.commonwealmagazine.org/blog/?p=21843.

15 See, for instance, David Gibson, "Catholic bishops fail to agree on statement on the economy," *Religion News Service*, November 13, 2012, http://www.religionnews.com/faith/leaders-and-institutions/catholic-bishops-fail-to-agree-on-statement-on-the-economy.

16 See David Brody, *The Teavangelicals: The Inside Story of How the Evangelicals and Tea Party are Taking Back America* (Grand Rapids, MI: Zondervan, 2012), 18–22.

17 A "thick" philosophical argument or idea is one that goes beyond simply describing something and instead implies moral meaning. The words "virtue" and "vice," for instance, don't just describe a particular way of acting. They also imply there is something specifically morally good about virtue and something particularly lacking in vice. A "thin" philosophical concept, by contrast, is usually primarily descriptive and avoids questions of moral evaluation.

18 See Edwin Cannan, *An Economist's Protest* (London: P. S. King and Son, 1927), vi–vii.

19 See, for example, Angus Burgin, *The Great Persuasion: Reinventing Free Markets since the Depression* (Cambridge: HUP, 2012), 26–29.

20 James Hitchcock, "The Welfare Snare: Christian Conflict with the Liberal State is by Design," *Touchstone Magazine*, 25 (3), 2012, 4.

21 Anarcho-capitalism is a libertarian position that favors eliminating government in favor of emphasizing individual sovereignty and allowing private actors and free markets to fulfill government's traditional responsibilities. The Catholic Church, by contrast, sees government as a *natural* institution that exists to provide laws designed to resolve problems facing a given political community in order to promote the specifically political common good of that community.

22 See, for example, Leo XIII, Encyclical Letter *Quod Apostolici Muneris* (1878), http://www.vatican.va/holy_father/leo_xiii/encyclicals/documents/hf_l-xiii_enc_28121878_quod-apostolici-muneris_en.html.

23 Distributism is an economic and political theory that broadly understands itself as opposed to both socialism and capitalism. It stresses a broad distribution of property ownership, closeness to the land, prefers credit unions to banks, and is opposed to concentrations of ownership, whether it be in the hands of government or private owners. Instead it places heavy emphasis on the local as well as the proliferation of small businesses. There are several schools of distributism, but most have been influenced by Catholic social teaching as well as the writings of Hilaire Belloc and G. K. Chesterton.

24 Though the phrase "Enlightenment" is used to describe a period in European intellectual thought that lasted from the late seventeenth until the late eighteenth century, it was not a monolithic movement. Though there was a common emphasis on the natural sciences and

critical reasoning, there were also important differences between various streams of Enlightenment thought. For example, the late French Enlightenment, associated with figures such as Rousseau and Voltaire, emphasized the need to remove the constraints that inhibited human beings from becoming fully free. Politically, this tended to translate into top down direction of social and economic life by the state in the name of the constructs such as the "General Will," and an intense suspicion of religion (especially Catholicism) as well as those communities that insisted on a certain degree of freedom from the state. By contrast, the Scottish Enlightenment numbered many Christians (including clergy) among its ranks and was not especially hostile to religion (notwithstanding David Hume's skepticism). It also emphasized the benefits of constitutionally limited government, the freeing up of economic activity, as well as the importance of custom and tradition as conveyors of knowledge.

25 Congregation for the Doctrine of the Faith, *Instruction on Christian Freedom and Liberation "Libertatis conscientia"*(1986), 6, http://www. vatican.va/roman_curia/congregations/cfaith/documents/rc_con_cfaith_doc_19860322_freedom-liberation_en.html (hereafter *LC*).

26 Joseph Ratzinger, *Christianity and the Crisis of Cultures* (San Francisco: Ignatius Press, 2006), 34.

27 Ibid., 35.

Chapter 1: Catholic and Free

1 Hugh Nolan (ed.), *Pastoral Letters of the United States Catholic Bishops*, vol. 1, 1792-1940 (Washington, DC: United States Catholic Conference, 1983), 228.

2 See Ronald Hoffman (in collaboration with Sally D. Mason), *Princes of Ireland, Planters of Maryland: A Carroll Saga, 1500–1782* (Chapel Hill, NC: University of North Carolina Press, 2000), 284. During the Revolutionary War, Carroll's fears of a total breakdown of order within the thirteen colonies were such that he told his father that he despaired that "nothing but peace with GB [Great Britain] on tolerably reasonable terms can save us from destruction." Ibid., 314.

3 See Scott McDermott, *Charles Carroll of Carrollton: Faithful Revolutionary* (New York: Scepter Publishers, 2002), 111.

4 Cited in Thomas O'Brien Hanley, S.J., *Charles Carroll of Carrollton: The Making of a Revolutionary Gentleman* (Chicago: Loyola University Press, 1982), 211.

5 Cited in ibid., 137.

6 Cited in Thomas O'Brien Hanley, S.J., *Revolutionary Statesman: Charles Carroll and the War* (Chicago: Loyola University Press, 1983), 149.

7   See also Matt 11:30; John 8:36; Rom 8:1; 1 Cor 7:22.

8   Saint Augustine, *The City of God against the Pagans*, trans. R. W. Dyson (New York: Cambridge University Press, 1998), Book IV, ch. 3.

9   See Sylvain Gouguenheim, *La Réforme Grégorienne* (Paris: Temps Présent, 2010), 22–23.

10   Cicero, *De Officiis* I, trans. Walter Miller (London: G. Putman's Sons, 1913), 70.

11   Cicero, *The Orations of Marcus Tullius Cicero*, Vol. 4, *The Fourteen Orations against Marcus Antonius*, trans. C.D. Yonge (London: G. Bell and Sons, 1913–21), VI, 19.

12   Leo XIII, Encyclical Letter *Libertas Praestantissimum*, (1888), 1, http://www.vatican.va/holy_father/leo_xiii/encyclicals/documents/hf_l-xiii_enc_20061888_libertas_en.html.

13   See Servais Pinckaers, O.P., *The Sources of Christian Ethics*, trans. Sister Mary Thomas Noble (Washington, DC: Catholic University of America Press, 1995), 240–54.

14   See Benedict XVI, "Easter Vigil Homily," April 23, 2011, http://www.vatican.va/holy_father/benedict_xvi/homilies/2011/documents/hf_ben-xvi_hom_20110423_veglia-pasquale_en.html .

15   Parts of this section draw upon Samuel Gregg, *On Ordered Liberty* (Lanham, MD: Lexington Books, 2003), 29–50.

16   Sancti Thomae de Aquino, *Quaestiones disputatae de veritate a quaestione II ad quaestionem IV,* Roberto Busa, S.J. (ed.) (Romae: Textum Leoninum, 1970), q. 8, a. 6c.

17   Réginald Garrigou-Lagrange, O.P., *Reality: A Synthesis of Thomistic Thought*, trans. Patrick Cummins O.S.B. (Ex Fontibus Co., 2012), 12.

18   See Council of Trent, Decree on Justification (1547), Canons 4–8, in Heinrich Denzinger (ed.), *Compendium of Creeds, Definitions, and Declarations on Matters of Faith and Morals*, 43rd ed., Peter Hünermann, Robert Fastiggi and Anne Englund Nash (eds.) (San Francisco: Ignatius Press, 2012), 385.

19   David Hume, *A Treatise on Human Nature*, L. Selby-Bigge (ed.) (Oxford: Oxford University Press, 1738–40/1951), bk. 2, pt. 3, s. III.

20   See Thomas More, *The Complete Works of St. Thomas More*, vol. 13, *A Treatise Upon the Passion*, Garry E. Haupt (ed.), (New Haven, CT: Yale University Press, 1976), 226/14.

21   Thomas More *The English Works of Sir Thomas More*, W.E. Campbell et al., (eds.), vol. 1 (London: Eyre & Spottiswoode, 1931), 495.

22   See Garrigou-Lagrange, *Reality*, 190.

23   Benedict XVI, "Ten Commandments Are Sign of God's Love for Us," Zenit News Agency, September 10, 2012, http://www.zenit.org/article-35488?l=english. Emphasis mine.

24 Second Vatican Council, Pastoral Constitution on the Church in the Modern World, *Gaudium et Spes* (1965), 74. http://www.vatican. va/archive/hist_councils/ii_vatican_council/documents/vat-ii_ const_19651207_gaudium-et-spes_en.html (hereafter *GS*).

25 See Gregg, *On Ordered Liberty*, 29–50.

26 Benedict XVI, Encyclical Letter *Spe Salvi* (2007), 21, http://www. vatican.va/holy_father/benedict_xvi/encyclicals/documents/hf_ben-xvi_enc_20071130_spe-salvi_en.html (Hereafter *SS*).

27 *GS*, 39.

28 Though it was never a monolithic movement (Deists disagreed about the nature of the soul and the afterlife), Deism generally holds that reason, be it in the form of natural theology or philosophy, is sufficient to demonstrate that God exists. It rejects, however, any notion of a Divine Revelation, religious dogmas and doctrines, as well as any religious authority such as the Church. In moral terms, Deists tended to embrace the language of the virtues or a type of "common sense" morality, as one finds in Benjamin Franklin.

29 Blessed John Paul II, "Address to the United States Ambassador to the Holy See, December 16, 1997, http://www.vatican.va/holy_ father/john_paul_ii/speeches/1997/december/documents/hf_jp-ii_spe_19971216_ambassador-usa_en.html.

30 John Courtney Murray, S.J., *We Hold These Truths: Catholic Reflections on the American Proposition* (Garden City, NY: Doubleday Image Books, 1964), 9.

31 Cited in Bradley Birzer, *American Cicero: The Life of Charles Carroll* (Wilmington, DE: ISI Books, 2010), 6.

32 Charles Carroll of Carrolton to Charles Carroll Jr. in Thomas O'Brien Hanley, S.J. (ed.), *The Charles Carroll Papers* (Wilmington, DE: Scholarly Resources, 1972), document 1492.

33 Cited in Jonathan Elliot (ed.), *Debates in the Several State Conventions on the Adoption of the Federal Constitution* (Philadelphia: Lippincott, 1907), Virginia, June 20, 1788.

34 Thomas Jefferson, *Notes on the State of Virginia* 1784, Queries 14 and 19, 146–9, 164–5, in Phillip B. Kurland and Ralph Lerner (eds.), *The Founders' Constitution* (Chicago: University of Chicago Press, 1986), Vol. 1, Ch. 18, Doc. 16.

35 John Adams, "Letter to Zabdiel Adams," June 21, 1776, in Founding. Com, http://www.founding.com/founders_library/pageID.2144/default. asp.

36 See George Washington, "Farewell Address, 1796," University of Virginia, The Papers of George Washington Collection, http:// gwpapers.virginia.edu/documents/farewell/intro.html.

37   See Edward C. Papenfuse, "An Undelivered defense of a Winning Cause: Charles Carroll of Carrollton's 'Remarks on the proposed Federal Constitution,'" *Maryland Historical Magazine* 712 (1976): 246–8.

38   Murray, *We Hold These Truths*, 50.

39   Much of Blackstone's thought relied heavily on the English system of common law, which itself first emerged in medieval Catholic England. See Russell Kirk, *The Roots of American Order*, 4th ed. (Wilmington DE: ISI Books, 2003).

40   Charles-Louis de Secondat, Baron de La Brède et de Montesquieu (1689–1755) was a French political thinker. His most significant intellectual contribution was to produce a modern theory of the separation of powers between the executive, judicial, and legislative branches (which was itself first developed in the medieval period). His 1748 book, *De l'Esprit des Lois* (*The Spirit of the Laws*), was immensely influential upon a whole generation of European and North American intellectuals (including Charles Carroll) and reflects the influence of the idea of subsidiarity. See McDermott, *Charles Carroll of Carrollton*, 40–43.

41   See Donald S. Lutz, "The Relative Influence of European Writers on Late Eighteenth-Century American Political Thought," *American Political Science Review*, Vol. 78 (1983): 185–97.

42   Jacques Maritain, *Reflections on America* (1958), XIX, III, http://maritain.nd.edu/jmc/etext/reflect3.html#XIX.

Chapter 2: An Economy of Liberty

1   Pontifical Council for Justice and Peace, *Compendium of the Social Doctrine of the Church* (2004), 343 (hereafter *Compendium*). http://www.vatican.va/roman_curia/pontifical_councils/justpeace/documents/rc_pc_justpeace_doc_20060526_compendio-dott-soc_en.html.

2   Calvin Coolidge, "Address to the American Society of Newspaper Editors," Washington, DC, January 17, 1925, http://www.presidency.ucsb.edu/ws/?pid=24180.

3   For Carroll's educational background, see Hanley, *Charles Carroll of Carrollton*, 152; and Hoffman, *Princes of Ireland, Planters of Maryland*, 150–6, 167, 169.

4   See Hoffman, *Princes of Ireland, Planters of Maryland*, 148.

5   Cited in McDermott, *Charles Carroll of Carrollton*, 208.

6   For detailed outlines of the business activities of Charles Carroll (the Settler), Charles Carroll of Annapolis, and Charles Carroll of Carrollton, see Hoffman, *Princes of Ireland, Planters of Maryland*, 61–77, 98–123, 218–50, 260–64; and Hanley, *Charles Carroll of*

Carrollton, 174–85. Carroll was opposed to slavery but was worried that his slaves would be unable to sustain themselves after being freed. Eventually he introduced a bill into the Maryland Senate to abolish slavery gradually. The bill failed to gain a majority. See Lewis A. Leonard, *Life of Charles Carroll of Carrollton* (New York: Moffat, Yard and Company, 1918), 218.

7   Coolidge, "Address to the American Society of Newspaper Editors."

8   See Hanley, *Charles Carroll of Carrollton*, 199.

9   See Alexis de Tocqueville, *Journey to America*, trans. George Lawrence (New Haven: Yale University, 1959), 271.

10   Alexis de Tocqueville, *Democracy in America*, J.P. Mayer (ed.), trans. George Lawrence (New York: Harper and Row, 1969), 541.

11   Ibid., 539.

12   John Tomasi, *Free Market Fairness* (Princeton: Princeton University Press, 2012), 294.

13   See M. Bench-Jones *The Catholic Families* (London: Constable, 1992).

14   See H. U. Faulkner, *American Economic History*, 3rd ed. (London: Harper & Brothers, 1935), 286.

15   A. Fanfani, *Catholicism, Protestantism and Capitalism* (Notre Dame: University of Notre Dame Press, 1984), 28–29.

16   This analysis and critique of Weber draws upon Samuel Gregg, "La fin d'un mythe: Max Weber, le capitalisme et l'ordre médiéval," *Journal des Economistes et des Etudes Humaines*, 13, no.2/3 (2003): 185–96.

17   D. Kelly, *The Westminster Confession of Faith* (New York, Summertown Texts, 1992).

18   Raymond de Roover, *Business, Banking, and Economic Thought in Late Medieval and Early Modern Europe* (Chicago, IL: University of Chicago Press, 1974).

19   Robert S. Lopez, *The Commercial Revolution of the Middle Ages, 950–1350* (Cambridge: Cambridge University Press, 1976), vii.

20   See Edwin S. Hunt and James M. Murray, *A History of Business in Medieval Europe 1200–1550*, 6th ed. (Cambridge: Cambridge University Press, 2006).

21   See Alejandro A. Chafuen, *Faith and Liberty: The Economic Thought of the Late Scholastics* (Lanham, MD: Lexington Books, 2003).

22   Jürg Niehans, *A History of Economic Theory: Classic Contributions 1720–1980* (Baltimore, MD: John Hopkins University Press, 1990), 16.

23   Jacques Delacroix, "Religion and Economic Action: The Protestant Ethic, the Rise of Capitalism, and the Abuses of Scholarship," *Journal for the Scientific Study of Religion*, Vol. 34 (199): 126–7.

24   For the theory and practice of absolutism, see H.M. Scott (ed.), *Enlightened Absolutism: Reform and Reformers in Later Eighteenth-Century Europe* (Ann Arbor, MI: University of Michigan Press, 1990).

25 See Rodney Stark, *The Victory of Reason: How Christianity Led to Freedom, Capitalism, and Western Success* (New York: Random House, 2005).

26 See Thomas Aquinas, *Summa Theologiae*, T. Gilby, O.P. (ed)., (London: Blackfriars, 1963), II–II, q. 61 a. 4c; and II–II, q.77 a. 1, a. 4c and ad. 2. (Hereafter *ST*)

27 *GS*, 64.

28 Oswald von Nell-Breuning, S.J., "Socio-Economic Life," in H. Vorgrimler (ed.), *Commentary on the Documents of Vatican II*, Vol. V. (New York: Herder and Herder, 1969), 291.

29 Ibid., 299.

30 Leo XIII, Encyclical Letter *Rerum Novarum* (1891), 5, http://www.vatican.va/holy_father/leo_xiii/encyclicals/documents/hf_l-xiii_enc_15051891_rerum-novarum_en.html.

31 See Samuel Gregg, *Challenging the Modern World: Karol Wojtyła/John Paul II and the Development of Catholic Social Teaching* (Lanham, MD: Lexington Books, 1999), 162–65.

32 John XXIII, Encyclical Letter *Pacem in Terris* (1963), 18, http://www.vatican.va/holy_father/john_xxiii/encyclicals/documents/hf_j-xxiii_enc_11041963_pacem_en.html.

33 John Paul II, Encyclical Letter *Sollicitudo Rei Socialis* (1987), 15, http://www.vatican.va/holy_father/john_paul_ii/encyclicals/documents/hf_jp-ii_enc_30121987_sollicitudo-rei-socialis_en.html (hereafter *SRS*).

34 *CA*, 32.

35 Ibid.

36 Ibid.

37 See *ST*, II–II, q. 49, a. 1, a. 3, a. 4.

38 Anthony G. Percy, *Entrepreneurship in the Catholic Tradition* (Lanham, MD: Lexington Books, 2010), 57.

39 Ibid., 73.

40 Pontifical Council for Justice and Peace, *Vocation of the Business Leader: A Reflection* (Vatican City: Pontifical Council for Justice and Peace, 2012), 35.

41 Ibid., 40.

42 Ibid., 51.

43 Robert G. Kennedy, *The Good that Business Does* (Grand Rapids, MI: Acton Institute, 2006), 58.

44 Pontifical Council for Justice and Peace, *Vocation*, 2.

45 Ibid., 3.

46 Ibid., 51.

47 Ibid., 61.

48 Ibid., 9.

49 Ibid., Appendix.

50   Stephen R. Munzer, *A Theory of Property* (Cambridge: Cambridge University Press, 1990), 15.

51   See Grisez, *Living a Christian Life*, 790.

52   See *ST*, II–II, q. 66, a. 2.

53   John XXIII, Encyclical Letter *Mater et Magistra* (1961), 109, http://www.vatican.va/holy_father/john_xxiii/encyclicals/documents/hf_j-xxiii_enc_15051961_mater_en.html (hereafter *MM*).

54   Ibid.

55   Saint Basil the Great, *Homiliae in illud Lucae "Destruam horrea mea"* no. 2, J.P. Migne (ed.), *Patrologia Graeca*, vol. 31 (Paris: Imprimerie Catholique, 1857), 263.

56   Saint Clement of Alexandria, Homily "What Rich Man will be Saved?" no. 13, *Patrologia Graeca*, vol. 9, 618.

57   See Samuel Gregg, *Banking, Justice and the Common Good* (Grand Rapids, MI: Acton Institute, 2005), 23–38.

58   Pius XI, Encyclical Letter *Quadragesimo Anno* (1931), 51, http://www.vatican.va/holy_father/pius_xi/encyclicals/documents/hf_p-xi_enc_19310515_quadragesimo-anno_en.html.

59   See *ST*, II–II, q. 129, a. 1 and 2; and q. 134, a. 1.

60   Washington, "Farewell Address, 1796."

61   Adam Smith, *The Glasgow Edition of the Works and Correspondence of Adam Smith*, vol. II, *An Inquiry into the Nature and Causes of The Wealth of Nations*, R.H. Campbell and A.S. Skinner (gen. eds.), (Indianapolis, IL: Liberty Fund, 1776/1981), IV, iii. c. 11.

62   Ibid., IV, ii. 12.

63   Ibid., IV, viii. 4.

64   Francisco de Vitoria, O.P., *De Indis*, I, q. 3 a. 1, in *Political Writings*, A. Pagden and A. Lawrence (eds.), (Cambridge: Cambridge University Press, 1991), 278–84.

65   See Hanley, *Charles Carroll of Carrollton*, 213.

66   Ibid.

67   See Hanley, *Revolutionary Statesman*, 34, 91.

68   See Hanley, *Charles Carroll of Carrollton*, 214–6.

69   See Hanley, *Revolutionary Statesman*, 276.

70   Ibid., 34, 43.

71   Charles Carroll of Carrollton, "To Edmund Jennings, May 29, 1766," in Thomas Meagher Field (ed.), *Unpublished Letters of Charles Carroll of Carrollton* (New York: United States Catholic Historical Society, 1902), 116–20.

72   Cited in Hanley, *Revolutionary Statesman*, 337.

73   Ibid., 337.

74   Pius XII, "Radio Message of 1 June 1941," *Acta Apostolicae Sedis* 33 (1941), 195–205.

75 See Paul VI, Encyclical Letter *Populorum Progression* (1967), 56–58, http://www.vatican.va/holy_father/paul_vi/encyclicals/documents/ hf_p-vi_enc_26031967_populorum_en.html.

76 Benedict XVI, Encyclical Letter *Caritas in Veritate* (2009), 42, http:// www.vatican.va/holy_father/benedict_xvi/encyclicals/documents/hf_ ben-xvi_enc_20090629_caritas-in-veritate_en.html (hereafter *CV*).

77 *CA*, 33.

78 Ibid.

79 *CA*, 34.

80 See Benedict XVI, "Address to Participants at an International Congress Organized by the Pontifical Academy for Life," November 7, 2008, http://www.vatican.va/holy_father/benedict_xvi/speeches/2008/ november/documents/hf_ben-xvi_spe_20081107_acdlife_en.html.

81 These principles are neatly summarized in *Compendium*, 302. Note that the Church does not leave this purely to the realm of freedom of contract. At the same time, the economic well-being of the business is noted as part of the equation. http://www.vatican.va/roman_ curia/pontifical_councils/justpeace/documents/rc_pc_justpeace_ doc_20060526_compendio-dott-soc_en.html.

82 Ronald Reagan, "Remarks Announcing America's Economic Bill of Rights," July 3, 1987, http://www.reagan.utexas.edu/archives/ speeches/1987/070387a.htm .

83 Cited in Terry Golway, *Ronald Reagan's America: His Voice, His Dreams and His Vision of Tomorrow* (Naperville, IL: Sourcebooks MediaFusion; Har/Com edition, 2008), 167.

Chapter 3: Solidarity, Subsidarity, and the State

1 Tocqueville, *Democracy in America*, 692.

2 William Beach and Patrick Tyrrell, *2012 Index of Dependence on Government* (Washington, DC: Heritage Foundation, 2012), http://www.heritage.org/research/reports/2012/02/2012-index-of-dependence-on-government.

3 See Robert Rector, "Obama's attack on 'workfare'," *National Review Online*, August 8, 2012, http://www.nationalreview.com/ articles/313350/obama-s-attack-workfare-robert-rector.

4 Patrick Tyrrell and William W. Beach, "U.S. Government Increases National Debt—and Keeps 128 Million People on Government Programs." January 8, 2013, http://www.heritage.org/research/ reports/2013/01/us-government-increases-national-debtand-keeps-128-million-people-on-government-programs.

5   Peter Ferrara, "America's Expanding Welfare Empire," *Forbes*, April 22, 2011, http://blogs.forbes.com/peterferrara/2011/04/22/americas-ever-expanding-welfare-empire/.

6   See, for example, Nathan Glazer and Daniel P. Moynihan, *Beyond the Melting Pot*, 2nd ed. (Boston, MA: MIT Press, 1970); and Charles Murray, *Losing Ground: American Social Policy, 1950–1980* (New York: Basic Books, 1994).

7   John Allen, "Chaput in Philly swims against 'nostalgia and red ink'," *National Catholic Reporter*, September 14, 2012, http://ncronline.org/news/faith-parish/chaput-philly-swims-against-nostalgia-and-red-ink.

8   *GS*, 32.

9   See, for example, John Paul II, Encyclical Letter *Veritatis Splendor* (1993),52,57,http://www.vatican.va/holy_father/john_paul_ii/encyclicals/documents/hf_jp-ii_enc_06081993_veritatis-splendor_en.html (hereafter *VS*), 52, 57.

10   *VS*, 48–49.

11   *SRS*, 38.

12   *SRS*, 45.

13   See "Seven Themes of Catholic Social Teaching," http://www.usccb.org/beliefs-and-teachings/what-we-believe/catholic-social-teaching/seven-themes-of-catholic-social-teaching.cfm.

14   See Thomas Aquinas, *Summa Contra Gentiles* (Notre Dame, IN: University of Notre Dame Press, 1997), III, c. 71, n. 4.

15   *CA*, 48.

16   Ibid.

17   Ibid.

18   *ST*, II–II, q. 48.

19   On this subject, see Samuel Gregg, "Catholicism and the Case for Limited Government," in Philip Booth (ed.), *Catholic Social Teaching and the Market Economy* (London: IEA, 2007), 250–69.

20   See Benedict XVI, Encyclical Letter *Deus Caritas Est* (2005), 28, http://www.vatican.va/holy_father/benedict_xvi/encyclicals/documents/hf_ben-xvi_enc_20051225_deus-caritas-est_en.html (hereafter *DCE*).

21   Ibid.

22   Ibid.

23   Ibid.

24   *CV*, 57.

25   *CV*, 6.

26   Ibid.

27   Rick Santorum, "The Return of Welfare as We Used to Know It," *Wall Street Journal*, 2012, http://online.wsj.com/article/SB10000872396390443404004577579680920159326.html?mod=WSJ_Opinion_LEFTTopOpinion .

28 Francis, "Audience with the Diplomatic Corps Accredited to the Holy See," March 22, 2013, http://www.vatican.va/holy_father/francesco/speeches/2013/march/documents/papa-francesco_20130322_corpo-diplomatico_en.html.

29 See Carl Bunderson, "St. Francis' poverty often misunderstood, priest explains," *Catholic News Agency*, March 24, 2013, http://www.catholicnewsagency.com/news/st-francis-poverty-often-misunderstood-priest-explains/.

30 Augustine Thompson, O.P., *Francis of Assisi: A New Biography* (Ithaca and London: Cornell University Press, 2012), 195.

31 See Bunderson, "St. Francis' poverty often misunderstood, priest explains."

32 Tocqueville, *Democracy in America*, 513.

33 Maritain, *Reflections on America*, XIII.

34 Ibid., IV.

35 This section draws upon Samuel Gregg, "Health, Health Care and Rights: A New Natural Law Perspective," *Notre Dame Journal of Law, Ethics and Public Policy* 25 (2011): 463–79.

36 Germain Grisez, *The Way of the Lord Jesus*, Vol. 3, *Difficult Moral Questions* (Quincy, IL: Franciscan Press, 1997), 417–8.

37 Christopher O. Tollefsen, "Welfare Rights vs. Welfare States," *Public Discourse*, November 21, 2008, http://www.thepublicdiscourse.com/2008/11/110.

38 Ibid.

39 See Department of the Treasury, "The Debt to the Penny and Who Holds It," http://www.treasurydirect.gov/NP/BPDLogin?application=np. This figure is constantly updated.

40 See Congressional Budget Office, *The 2012 Long-Term Budget Outlook*, June 5, 2012, http://www.cbo.gov/publication/43288.

41 Congressional Budget Office, *An Update to the Budget and Economic Outlook: Fiscal Years 2012 to 2022*, August 22, 2012, http://www.cbo.gov/publication/43539.

42 See David Wessel, "The Numbers Inside a Hot-Button Issue," *Wall Street Journal*, August 5, 2012, http://online.wsj.com/article/SB10000872396390444246904577571042249868040.html?mod=WSJ_hpp_LEFTTopStories.

43 Office of Management and Budget, *Fiscal Year 2012: Budget Tables—Budget of the US Government*, 50, http://www.whitehouse.gov/sites/default/files/omb/budget/fy2012/assets/hist.pdf .

44 Ibid., 55.

45 Rodger Charles, S.J., *Christian Social Witness and Teaching: The Catholic Tradition.*, vol. 1, *From Biblical Times to the Late Nineteenth Century* (Leominster: Gracewing, 1998), 95.

46 Quoted in M. Pachant, "St Bernardin de Sienne et l'usure,» *Le Moyen Age*, 69 (1963), 743ff.

47 See also J. T. Noonan, *The Scholastic Analysis of Usury* (Cambridge, MA: Harvard University Press, 1957).

48 Werner Sombart, *The Quintessence of Capitalism*, trans. M. Epstein (New York: Howard Fertig, 1967), 314.

49 Benedict XVI, *Light of the World* (San Francisco: Ignatius Press, 2010), 47.

50 Ibid.

51 Sean Fieler, "Easy Money Is Punishing the Middle Class," *Wall Street Journal*, September 27, 2012, http://online.wsj.com/article/SB1000 08723963904441800045780162002873 41688.html?mod=WSJ_ Opinion_LEADTop.

52 Nicolaum Oresme, *Tractatus de Origine, Natura, Jure et Mutationibus Monetarum* (1355), http://phare.univ-paris1.fr/textes/Oresme/Tractatus. html.

53 See Juan de Mariana, S.J., *De monetae mutatione (1609)*, http://www. acton.org/publications/mandm/mandm_scholia_57.php#frm.

54 Smith, *Wealth of Nations*, I. iv. 4, 10.

55 Cited in Hoffman, *Princes of Ireland, Planters of Maryland*, 325.

56 *Votes and Proceedings of the Senate of the State of Maryland* (Annapolis, 1777–1819), April 9, 1777. After denouncing the law, Carroll engaged in a long argument with his father about how best to mitigate it. His father was extremely aggressive in calling for its immediate repeal, while Charles thought the times called for a more gradual approach. The law itself contributed to rampant inflation in Maryland as well as the wider inflation that gradually took hold of the thirteen colonies throughout the war. Moreover many debtors did in fact, as Carroll and his father had predicted, use the law to avoid paying back the full amount of what they owed their creditors. See Hoffman, *Princes of Ireland, Planters of Maryland*, 318–33. Maryland's legal tender law was eventually repealed in December 1780.

57 See Hanley, *Revolutionary Statesman*, 310.

58 Ibid., 346.

59 Ibid., 225.

60 Ibid., 434.

Chapter 4: The First Freedom

1 "Charles Carroll of Carrollton to Reverend John Sanford," October 9, 1827, *American Catholic Historical Review* 15 (1898), 131.

2 Benedict XVI, "Address to the Bishops of the United States of America on their *ad limina* visit." January 19, 2012, http://www.vatican.va/

holy_father/benedict_xvi/speeches/2012/january/documents/hf_ben-xvi_spe_20120119_bishops-usa_en.html.

3   See Francisco Suárez, S.J., *Selections from three works of Francisco Suárez, S.J.: De legibus, ac Deo legislatore, 1612. Defensio fidei catholicae, et apostolicae adversus anglicanae sectae errores, 1613. De triplici virtute theologica, fide, spe, et charitate, 1621* (Oxford: Clarendon Press, 1944).

4   J. Brodrick, *Robert Bellarmine, 1541–1621* (London: Longmans, 1950), 224.

5   *Maryland Toleration Act*, September 21, 1649. Yale Law School, http://avalon.law.yale.edu/18th_century/maryland_toleration.asp.

6   See Hoffman, *Princes of Ireland, Planters of Maryland*, 142, 274–8

7   James H. Hutson, *Religion and the Founding of the American Republic* (Washington, DC: The University Press of New England, 1998), 15.

8   See Elihu S. Riley, *Correspondence of "First Citizen"—Charles Carroll of Carrollton, and "Antilon"—Daniel Dulany Jr., 1773, With a History of Governor Eden's Administration in Maryland 1760–1776* (Baltimore, 1902), 230–1.

9   Cited in Hanley, *Charles Carroll of Carrollton*, 81.

10 Ibid., 69–70, 81. See also Hoffman, *Princes of Ireland, Planters of Maryland*, 278.

11 Cited in Hanley, *Charles Carroll of Carrollton*, 200.

12 Cited in ibid., 202.

13 See Hanley, *Revolutionary Statesman*, 190.

14 See Hoffman, *Princes of Ireland, Planters of Maryland*, 266–7, 273.

15 Cited in Hanley, *Charles Carroll of Carrollton*, 201.

16 Tocqueville, *Democracy in America*, 295.

17 Cited in George Wilson Pierson, *Tocqueville in America* (Baltimore and London: The John Hopkins University Press, 1938), 298.

18 Joseph Ratzinger and Marcello Pera, *Without Roots: The West, Relativism, Christianity, Islam* (New York: Basic Books, 2006), 109.

19 Ibid.

20 Interview Of The Holy Father Benedict XVI During The Flight To The United States Of America, Tuesday, April 15, 2008, http://www.vatican.va/holy_father/benedict_xvi/speeches/2008/april/documents/hf_ben-xvi_spe_20080415_intervista-usa_en.html.

21 Jacques Maritain, *Man and the State* (Chicago: University of Chicago Press, 1951), 183.

22 See Joseph Ratzinger, *Theological Highlights of Vatican II* (New York: Paulist Press, 1996), 145.

23 Joseph Ratzinger, "Homily at mass *pro eligendo romano pontifice*," (2005), http://www.vatican.va/gpII/documents/homily-pro-eligendo-pontifice_20050418_en.html. Emphasis mine.

24 See John Rawls, *A Theory of Justice* (Harvard: Harvard University Press, 1971), 320.

25 James Klab, "The Church and Social Programs," *Catholic World Report*, October 16, 2012, http://www.catholicworldreport.com/Item/1665/The_Church_and_Social_Programs.aspx.

26 Lord Acton, *Essays on Freedom and Power*, G. Himmelfarb (ed.), (Boston: Crossroad, 1948), 45.

27 See, for instance, Rom 13:1–6; 1 Pet 2:13–17.

28 Joseph Ratzinger, *Values in a Time of Upheaval* (San Francisco: Ignatius Press, 2006), 59.

29 Joseph Ratzinger, *Salt of the Earth* (San Francisco: Ignatius Press, 1996), 240. The preceding two paragraphs draw upon Gregg, "Catholicism and the Case for Limited Government," 250–69.

30 Second Vatican Council, Declaration on Religious Liberty, *Dignitatis Humanae* (1965), 7, http://www.vatican.va/archive/hist_councils/ii_vatican_council/documents/vat-ii_decl_19651207_dignitatis-humanae_en.html (hereafter *DH*).

31 See Robert P. George, *Making Men Moral* (Oxford: Clarendon Press, 1993), 219–29.

32 See Robert P. George, "Religious Liberty and Political Morality," *In Defense of Natural Law* (Oxford: Clarendon Press, 1999), 131–6.

33 See George, *Making Men Moral*, 221.

34 *DH*, 1.

35 Ibid.

36 St. Augustine, *Enchirdion as Latjrentium de De Fide, Spe et Caritate*, Johann Georg Krabinger (ed.), (Oxford: OUP, 1861), Chapter 7.

37 *DH*, 3.

38 See John Finnis, "Secularism's Practical Meaning," in *The Collected Essays of John Finnis*, vol. V, *Religion and Public Reasons* (Oxford: Oxford University Press, 2011), 56.

39 See, for example, John Rawls, "The Idea of Public Reason Revisited," *University of Chicago Law Review*, 64, 1997: 787 n. 57, 798–9.

40 See Finnis, "Secularism's Practical Meaning," 56–58.

41 George Weigel, "All in for the First Amendment," *National Review*, September 10, 2012, 40.

42 See Brian Anderson, "How Catholic Charities Lost its Soul," *City Journal* 10, 1, (2000), http://www.city-journal.org/html/10_1_how_catholic_charities.html.

43 See Second Vatican Council, Declaration on Catholic Education *Gravissimum Educationis* (1965), 6, http://www.vatican.va/archive/hist_councils/ii_vatican_council/documents/vat-ii_decl_19651028_gravissimum-educationis_en.html; and *Code of Canon Law* (1983), Canon 797, http://www.vatican.va/archive/ENG1104/__P2M.HTM.

44 See James Hitchcock, "Liberalism favors rights of individuals over churches," *Crisis Magazine*, 14 December 2012, http://www.crisismagazine.com/2012/Liberalism-favors-rights-of-individuals-over-churches.

45 Benedict XVI, Apostolic Letter issued "Motu Proprio *Intima Ecclesiae Natura*," (2012), Art. 10. § 3, http://www.vatican.va/holy_father/benedict_xvi/motu_proprio/documents/hf_ben-xvi_motu-proprio_20121111_caritas_en.html.

46 Ismael Hernandez, "Tell Pharaoh to Keep his Money," *Crisis Magazine*, July 3, 2012, http://www.crisismagazine.com/2012/tell-pharaoh-to-keep-his-money.

Chapter 5: But What About . . . ?

1 Thomas More, *The Complete Works of St. Thomas More,* Vol. 1, *Poems, Life of Pico, The Last Things*, A. Edwards, K. Rodgers, & C. Miller (eds.) (New Haven, CT: Yale University Press, 1997), 171/1.

2 *CA*, 25.

3 Vernon L. Smith, "The Clinton Housing Bubble," *Wall Street Journal*, December 18, 2007.

4 Smith, *Wealth of Nations*, I. ii. 2.

5 Francis, "Palm Sunday Homily," March 24, 2013, 3, http://www.vatican.va/holy_father/francesco/homilies/2013/documents/papa-francesco_20130324_palme_en.html.

6 See Bernard Mandeville, *The Fable of the Bees: or, Private Vices, Public Benefits* (1704/1715), http://oll.libertyfund.org/index.php?option=com_staticxt&staticfile=show.php%3Ftitle=846&layout=html#chapter_66840.

7 See James R. Otteson, *Adam Smith's Marketplace of Life* (Cambridge: CUP, 2002).

8 *SS*, 37.

9 *CV*, 78.

10 *CA*, 25.

11 *Compendium*, 347.

12 See, for example, ibid., 348.

13 Smith, *Wealth of Nations*, I.10.82.

14 Michael Novak, *Free Persons and the Common Good* (Lanham: Madison Books, 1989), 78.

15 See *ST*, I–II, q. 26, a. 4, and I–II, q. 94, a. 2.

16 Grisez, *Living a Christian Life*, 37.

17 *CV*, 36.

18 *CV*, 34.

19 *CV*, 35.

20   CV, 6.

21   Ibid.

22   Tocqueville, *Democracy in America*, 526.

23   See Base Point Analytics, "Early Payment default: Links to fraud and impact on mortgage lenders and investment banks" (2007), www.basepointanalytics.com/mortgagewhitepapers.shtml.

24   Bishops Conference of England and Wales, *Choosing the Common Good* (Stoke-on-Trent: Alive Publishing, 2010), 10, http://www.cbcew.org.uk/document.doc?id=35.

25   Ibid., 12.

26   See Samuel Gregg, "Moral Failure: Borrowing, Lending and the Financial Crisis," in Philip Booth (ed.), *Verdict on the Crash: Causes and Policy Implications* (London: IEA, 2009), 145–52.

27   On the early development of the notion of social justice in Catholic social thought (as opposed to official teaching), see Thomas C. Behr, "Luigi Taparelli D'Azeglio, S.J. (1793–1862) and the Development of Scholastic Natural-Law Thought as a Science of Society and Politics," *Journal of Markets and Morality* 6, no. 1 (2003): 99–115.

28   The term "social justice" emerged in Catholic social teaching in the 1930s in an effort to restore Aquinas's concept of "legal" or "general justice" to its primary place in the Church's treatment of justice. This achieved two things. First, it reestablished the idea of general justice as the understanding of justice from which all other modes of justice, such as commutative and distributive justice, flow. Second, it directed attention beyond excessively narrow conceptions of commutative and distributive justice when thinking about what justice requires. On this subject, see John Finnis, *Natural Law and Natural Rights* (Oxford: Clarendon Press, 1980), 185, 462; Paul-Dominique Dognin, O.P., "La notion thomiste de justice face aux exigences modernes," *Revue des Sciences Philosophiques et Théologiques* 45 (1961), 601–40; and Samuel Gregg, "What is Social Justice?" *Library of Law and Liberty*, April 1, 2013, http://www.libertylawsite.org/liberty-forum/what-is-social-justice/.

29   *Catechism of the Catholic Church (*hereafter CCC*)*, 1928.

30   CCC, 1928–1948.

31   CCC, 1948.

32   LC, 67.

33   James Schall, S.J., "The Pope and the Poor," *Catholic World Report*, March 18, 2013, http://www.catholicworldreport.com/Item/2095/the_pope_and_the_poor.aspx#.UWLwBDdXot0.

34   Cited in Annamarie Adkins, "Public Employee Unions and the Common Good: Robert Kennedy Discusses Catholic Principles for Navigating an Emerging Conflict," Zenit News Agency, March 6, 2012, http://

www.zenit.org/article-31931?l=english. Kennedy's reference is to Pius XII, "Speech to the A.C.L.I.," March 11, 1945, *Acta Apostolicae Sedis*, vol. 31 (Città del Vaticano: Libreria Editrice Vaticana, 1945), 70.

35 Paul VI, Apostolic Letter *Octogesima Adveniens* (1971), 14, http://www.vatican.va/holy_father/paul_vi/apost_letters/documents/hf_p-vi_apl_19710514_octogesima-adveniens_en.html.

36 John Paul II, Encyclical Letter *Laborem Exercens* (1981), 20, http://www.vatican.va/holy_father/john_paul_ii/encyclicals/documents/hf_jp-ii_enc_14091981_laborem-exercens_en.html (hereafter *LE*).

37 Ibid.

38 Cited in Adkins, "Public Employee Unions and the Common Good."

39 "On all of Our Shoulders: A Catholic Call to Protect the Endangered Common Good," October 9, 2012, http://www.onourshoulders.org/.

40 Robert P. George, "The Catholic Left's Unfair Attack on Paul Ryan," *First Things*, October 12, 2012, http://www.firstthings.com/onthesquare/2012/10/the-catholic-leftrsquos-unfair-attack-on-paul-ryan.

41 Richard Garnett, "The 'On All of Our Shoulders' statement," November 9, 2012, http://mirrorofjustice.blogs.com/mirrorofjustice/garnett_rick/.

42 F. A. Hayek, "The Pretence of Knowledge," Lecture to the memory of Alfred Nobel, December 11, 1974, http://nobelprize.org/nobel_prizes/economics/laureates/1974/hayek-lecture.html.

43 See F. A. Hayek, *The Collected Works of F.A. Hayek*, vol. 4, *The Fortunes of Liberalism*, Peter G. Klein (ed.) (Chicago: Chicago University Press, 1992), 237–48.

44 Burgin, *The Great Persuasion*, 209.

45 Milton Friedman, "The Battle's Half Won," *The Wall Street Journal*, December 9, 2004, A16.

46 Parts of this section draw on Gregg, *On Ordered Liberty*, 21–22.

47 F. A. Hayek, *The Constitution of Liberty* (London: Routledge and Kegan Paul, 1960), 16.

48 Ibid., 41.

49 See Finnis, *Natural Law and Natural Rights*, 111–8.

50 F. A. Hayek, *Knowledge, Evolution and Society* (London: Adam Smith Institute, 1983), 46.

51 Hayek, *Constitution*, 41.

52 See John Stuart Mill, *A System of Logic* (London: Longmans, 1859), bk. 6, chapters 2 and 11.

53 See Edmund Burke, "Thoughts and Details on Scarcity" (1795), in Isaac Kramnick (ed.), *The Portable Edmund Burke* (New York: Penguin Books, 1999), 194–213.

54 Tomasi, *Free Market Fairness*, 271.

55 Benedict XVI, "Welcoming Ceremony Address at the White House," Washington DC, (2008), http://www.vatican.va/holy_father/benedict_xvi/speeches/2008/april/documents/hf_ben-xvi_spe_20080416_welcome-washington_en.html.

Chapter 6: A Patriotic Minority

1 Charles Carroll of Carrollton, "To Mr. Bradshaw, November 21, 1766", in Field, *Unpublished Letters of Charles Carroll of Carrollton*, 96–97.

2 Benedict XVI, "Christmas Address to the Roman Curia," December 22, 2005, http://www.vatican.va/holy_father/benedict_xvi/speeches/2005/december/documents/hf_ben_xvi_spe_20051222_roman-curia_en.html.

3 Arnold Toynbee, *The Study of History*, vol. 4, *The Disintegration of Civilizations* (Oxford: OUP, 1939), 78.

4 "Speech of Cardinal Newman on receiving the Biglietto in Rome," May 12, 1879, http://www.newmanfriendsinternational.org/newman/?p=240.

5 These post-conciliar realities are outlined in detail in James Hitchcock, *History of the Catholic Church: From the Apostolic Age to the Third Millennium* (San Francisco: Ignatius Press, 2012), 494–526.

6 J. Budziszewski, *What We Can't Not Know* (San Francisco: Ignatius Press, 2011), 162.

7 Cardinal André Vingt-Trois, *Une mission de liberté* (Paris: Editions Denoël, 2010).

8 See Elizabeth Anscombe, "The Dignity of the Human Being," in Mary Geach and Luke Gormally (eds.), *Human Life, Action and Ethics: Essays by G.E.M. Anscombe* (Exeter: Imprint Academic, 2005), 67–76.

9 Cited in Bartolomé de Las Casas, *In Defense of the Indians*, 3. ed., trans. Stafford Poole, C.M. (DeKalb, IL: Northern Illinois University Press, 1999), 101.

10 *SS*, 24.

11 Ibid.

12 Ibid.

13 *CV*, 17.

14 John Courtney Murray, S.J., "The Construction of a Christian Culture," (1940), http://woodstock.georgetown.edu/library/Murray/1940A.htm.

15 *SRS*, 28.

16 *CA*, 41.

17 See Martin Schlag, "The Encyclical *Caritas in Veritate*, Christian Tradition and the Modern World," in Martin Schlag and Juan Andrés

Mercado (eds.) *Free Markets and the Culture of the Common Good* (New York: Springer, 2012), 106.

18 *CV*, 36.

19 Ibid.

20 Ibid.

21 See Hanley, *Revolutionary Statesman*, 411.

22 See Hoffman, *Princes of Ireland, Planters of Maryland*, 281.

23 See Frank J. Hanna III, *What Your Money Means and How to Use it Well* (New York: Crossroad, 2008).

24 See Hoffman, *Princes of Ireland, Planters of Maryland*, 151.

25 See Hanley, *Charles Carroll of Carrollton*, 151–3.

26 Benedict XVI, "Message for World Day for Migrants and Refugees," October 29, 2012, http://www.zenit.org/article-35838?l=english.

27 Benedict XVI, "Address to the Pontifical Council for Pastoral Care of Migrants and Itinerant People," May 15, 2006, http://www.vatican.va/holy_father/benedict_xvi/speeches/2006/may/documents/hf_ben-xvi_spe_20060515_pc-migrants_en.html.

28 See *LE*, 23; *MM*, 45.

29 See *SRS*, 15.

30 John Paul II, "Message for World Migration Day (2001), 1, http://www.vatican.va/holy_father/john_paul_ii/messages/migration/documents/hf_jp-ii_mes_20010213_world-migration-day-2001_en.html.

31 John Paul II, "Message for World Migration Day" (1993), 4, http://www.vatican.va/holy_father/john_paul_ii/messages/migration/documents/hf_jp-ii_mes_19930806_world-migration-day-93-94_it.html.

32 See *CCC*, 2241.

33 Benedict XVI, "Address to the Pontifical Council for Pastoral Care of Migrants and Itinerant People," May 15, 2006, http://www.vatican.va/holy_father/benedict_xvi/speeches/2006/may/documents/hf_ben-xvi_spe_20060515_pc-migrants_en.html.

34 Benedict XVI, "Message for World Day for Migrants and Refugees," October 29, 2012, http://www.zenit.org/article-35838?l=english.

35 Gomez, "Immigration and the 'Next America': Perspectives from Our History."

36 See Robert W. Fairle, *Kauffman Index on Entrepreneurial Activity 1996–2010*, Kansas City: Ewing Marion Kauffman Foundation, 2011, http://www.kauffman.org/uploadedFiles/KIEA_2011_report.pdf.

37 Gomez, "Immigration and the 'Next America:' Perspectives From Our History."

38 See Yann Algan et al., "The Economic Situation of First and Second-Generation Immigrants in France, Germany and the United Kingdom," *The Economic Journal*, 129 (2010), F4–F30.

39   Heather Mac Donald, "California's Demographic Revolution," *City Journal*, 22 (1), 2012, http://www.city-journal.org/2012/22_1_california-demographics.html.

40   Ibid.

41   Ibid.

42   See Finnis, *Natural Law*, 270–3.

43   Cited in Hanley, *Charles Carroll of Carrollton*, 253.

44   John Paul II, "Message for World Migration Day" (1995), 2, http://www.vatican.va/holy_father/john_paul_ii/messages/migration/documents/hf_jp-ii_mes_19940810_world-migration-day-1995_it.html.

45   The Church teaches there is a general presumption in favor of Christians obeying the law, even laws that might seem unjust. See Saint Alphonsus de Liguori, *Theologia Moralis*, L. Gaudé (ed.) (Rome: Ex Typographia Vaticana, 1905–12), Vol. 1: 80–81. But when the law is radically unjust because it commands an act excluded by a moral absolute (such as murder) or prohibits an act that people have a strict duty to perform (such as attend Mass on Sundays), people should not comply. See *ST*, II–II, q. 104, a. 4; and Grisez, *Living a Christian Life*, 878–83.

46   Thomas Aquinas, *Sententia Libri Ethicorum*, Vol. 11, n. 10, in Busa (ed.), *Thomae Aquinatis Opera Omnia*.

47   CELAM, *Concluding Document of Aparecida*, May 30, 2007, 70, http://www.celam.org/aparecida/Ingles.pdf.

48   Ibid., 77.

49   *CV*, 67.

50   See Samuel Gregg, *Becoming Europe: Economic Decline, Culture, and How America Can Avoid A European Future* (New York: Encounter Books, 2013), 271.

51   See Jürgen Habermas, *The Crisis of the European Union: A Response* (Cambridge: Polity, 2012).

52   Benedict XVI, "Speech to the Participants in the Plenary Assembly of the Pontifical Council for Justice and Peace," December 3, 2012, http://www.vatican.va/holy_father/benedict_xvi/speeches/2012/december/documents/hf_ben-xvi_spe_20121203_justpeace_it.html.

53   Second Vatican Council, Decree *Ad Gentes* on the Mission Activity of the Church (1965), 21, http://www.vatican.va/archive/hist_councils/ii_vatican_council/documents/vat-ii_decree_19651207_ad-gentes_en.html.

54   *CCC*, 2241.

55   See *ST*, II–II, q. 101, a. 1.

56   Leo XIII, Encyclical Letter *Sapientiae Christianae* (1890), 5, http://www.vatican.va/holy_father/leo_xiii/encyclicals/documents/hf_l-xiii_enc_10011890_sapientiae-christianae_en.html.

57   Garrigou-Lagrange, *Reality*, 12.

58   John Paul II, *Memory and Identity* (New York: Rizzoli, 2005), 77–8.

59   See Tocqueville, *Democracy in America*, 235–7.

60   John Paul II, *Memory and Identity*, 66.

61   Grisez, *Living a Christian Life*, 839.

62   343 U.S. 306 (1952), *Zorach et Al. v. Clauson et al.* No.431. Supreme Court of United States. Argued January 31–February 1, 1952. Decided April 28, 1952. Appeal from the Court of Appeals of New York, 314–5.

63   Cited in Hanley, *Revolutionary Statesman*, 169.

64   "Paul Ryan Delivers Remarks On Upward Mobility And The Economy," October 24, 2012, http://www.mittromney.com/news/press/2012/10/paul-ryan-delivers-remarks-upward-mobility-and-economy.

65   Robert P. George, "Business and Family in a Decent and Dynamic Society," in Samuel Gregg and James Stoner (eds.), *Profit, Prudence and Virtue* (Exeter: Imprint Academic, 2009), 63.

66   Milton Friedman, "Goods in Conflict," in George Weigel (ed.) *A New Worldly Order* (Washington, DC: EPPC, 1992), 77.

67   Benedict XVI, "Welcoming Ceremony Address at the White House," (2008).

68   Cited in Joseph Gurn, *Charles Carroll of Carrollton, 1737–1832* (New York: P. J. Kenedy & Sons, 1932), 242–3.

69   Ibid.

70   Ibid.

71   Tocqueville, *Democracy*, Appendix 1, 734–5.

About the Author

Samuel Gregg is research director at the Acton Institute. He is the author of many books, including his prize-winning *The Commercial Society* (2007), *The Modern Papacy* (2009), and *Becoming Europe* (2013). He lectures regularly in America and Europe on topics encompassing political economy, Catholicism, and morality and the economy. His writing has appeared in academic journals and magazines, including *National Review*, *The American Spectator*, *Foreign Affairs*, and *Crisis Magazine*, as well as newspapers such as the *Wall Street Journal*, *Investors' Business Daily*, and *The New York Post*.

You Might Also Like

George Weigel

Practicing Catholic
Essays Historical, Literary, Sporting, and Elegiac

Paperback, 312 pages, ISBN 978-08245-00221

A papal biographer and one of the leading interpreters of Catholic social teaching in America, George Weigel is also renowned for his insights into historical figures, American culture, and great works of literature. In this collection of his essays, Weigel explores the dynamics of the 1960s, the thoughts of Pope John Paul II, the legacy of John Courtenay Murray, S.J., the religious journey of Evelyn Waugh, and the deeper significance of baseball—among many other topics. Sit back with these polished, provocative essays and prepare to be challenged and informed.

"George Weigel's range and intelligence is wonderful, full of urgency, romance, and wickedly pungent wit. Read and enjoy."—R. R. Reno, editor, *First Things*

"Weigel is one of the great writers of our time, a master of the essay. With sharp and elegant prose, he plumbs the profundities of subjects as diverse as baseball and Vatican II, and he takes the measure of some of the great men of the age. These essays are a joy to read, and they enrich both mind and heart."—Mark Henrie, chief academic officer, Intercollegiate Studies Institute

Support your local bookstore or order directly
from the publisher at www.crossroadpublishing.com

To request a catalog or inquire about
quantity orders, please email
sales@crossroadpublishing.com

The Crossroad Publishing Company

You Might Also Like

Frank Hanna

**What Your Money Means
And How to Use It Well**

Hardcover, 256 pages, ISBN 978-08245-25200

Hanna draws on his own success, the know-how of powerful entrepreneurs, and the timeless wisdom of philosophers of the past to offer simple rules of thumb for managing your money. Insights from Aristotle, Cicero, St. Thomas Aquinas, Ralph Waldo Emerson, Andrew Carnegie, and others illuminate the purpose of wealth and the benefits of philanthropy to the giver, the receiver, and the larger society.

"Frank Hanna is no stranger to financial achievement. His record of support for good causes is extraordinary. But what makes his book unique is its simple clarity, engaging style and practical value for every reader, whether wealthy or of more modest of means. This is a wonderful book of wisdom and encouragement—encouragement to use the resources God gives us for a greater purpose and our own deeper happiness, and not be used or owned by them."—Charles J. Chaput, O.F.M. Cap., Archbishop of Philadelphia

*Support your local bookstore or order directly
from the publisher at www.crossroadpublishing.com*

*To request a catalog or inquire about
quantity orders, please email
sales@crossroadpublishing.com*

The Crossroad Publishing Company

You Might Also Like

Pope Francis (Jorge Mario Cardinal Bergoglio)

Open Mind, Faithful Heart

Hardcover, 384 pages, ISBN 978-08245-19971

These challenging meditations on the Scriptures provide valuable insight into how Pope Francis understands the person of Jesus and the Christian calling. Anticipating his retirement as archbishop of Buenos Aires, Argentina, Cardinal Jorge Mario Bergoglio collected his most probing reflections on the meaning of Christian discipleship. In these profound texts, Cardinal Bergoglio draws on the Gospels and the spiritual exercises of Saint Ignatius of Loyola to explain how all Christians are called to follow Jesus in the struggle to make God's reign a reality on earth.

"An open window into the priestly heart of Pope Francis—a heart formed by a lifelong encounter with the Word of God in the Bible, that two-edged sword that cuts through to the truth about our lives and loves, our loyalties and betrayals, our fears for the world, and our hope for the coming Kingdom."

—George Weigel, author of *Evangelical Catholicism*

Support your local bookstore or order directly
from the publisher at www.CrossroadPublishing.com

To request a catalog or inquire about
quantity orders, please e-mail
sales@CrossroadPublishing.com

The Crossroad Publishing Company